The Western Front

To

Frances Ann–Marie Miles

The Western Front

Landscape, Tourism and Heritage

Stephen Miles

Series Consultant
Nicholas J. Saunders

PEN & SWORD
ARCHAEOLOGY

First published in Great Britain in 2016 by
Pen & Sword Archaeology
an imprint of
Pen & Sword Books Ltd
47 Church Street
Barnsley
South Yorkshire
S70 2AS

ISBN 978 1 47383 376 0

A CIP catalogue record for this book is available from the British
Library

Typeset in Ehrhardt by
Mac Style Ltd, Bridlington, East Yorkshire
Printed and bound by Replika Press Pvt. Ltd.

Pen & Sword Books Ltd incorporates the imprints of Pen & Sword
Archaeology, Atlas, Aviation, Battleground, Discovery, Family
History, History, Maritime, Military, Naval, Politics, Railways, Select,
Transport, True Crime, and Fiction, Frontline Books, Leo Cooper,
Praetorian Press, Seaforth Publishing and Wharncliffe.

For a complete list of Pen & Sword titles please contact
PEN & SWORD BOOKS LIMITED
47 Church Street, Barnsley, South Yorkshire, S70 2AS, England
E-mail: enquiries@pen-and-sword.co.uk
Website: www.pen-and-sword.co.uk

Contents

Acknowledgements

Firstly I would like to thank my editor Professor Nick Saunders at the University of Bristol for his continuing commitment and patience in steering this project to its conclusion. His advice was absolutely indispensable and is greatly appreciated. It was most reassuring to have such an experienced writer and academic as editor for this my first book. At Pen and Sword Books I would like to thank Eloise Hansen and Heather Williams, very able Commissioning Editors, who were consistently helpful and attentive.

Many people have helped me with the research for this book but in particular I would like to thank the following: in Belgium and France Dominiek Dendooven and Piet Chielens, In Flanders Fields Museum, Ypres; Michel Rouger and Lyse Hautecoeur, Musée de la Grande Guerre du Pays de Meaux; Steven Vandenbussche, Timby Vansuyt and Lee Ingelbrecht at the Memorial Museum Passchendaele 1917, Zonnebeke; Alexandre Lefevre, Somme Tourism, Amiens; Avril Williams, owner of the Ocean Villas Bed and Breakfast at Auchonvillers; and David and Julie Thomson, owners of the Number 56 Bed and Breakfast in La Boisselle, who were often my hosts. For the use of images in Belgium I would like to thank François Maekelberg, President of the 1914 St Yves Christmas Truce Committee, and Klaus Verscheure of the Danse La Pluie production company, Sint-Denijs. In the UK I was assisted by Anna Jarvis at the Heritage Lottery Fund and Peter Francis, Media and Marketing Manager, and Ian Small at the Commonwealth War Graves Commission. I would also like to thank Dr Wanda George, Mount Saint Vincent University, Canada and Emeritus Professor Myriam Jansen-Verbeke, Catholic University of Leuven, Belgium for allowing me to use the results of the WHTRN survey.

Abbreviations

APWGBHG – All-Party Parliamentary War Heritage Group (UK)
CWGC – Commonwealth War Graves Commission
HGG – Historial de la Grande Guerre, Péronne
IFFM – In Flanders Fields Museum, Ypres, Belgium
IWGC – Imperial War Graves Commission
MGGM – Musée de la Grande Guerre du Pays de Meaux
UNESCO – United Nations Educational, Scientific and Cultural Organisation
WHS – World Heritage Site
WHTRN – World Heritage Tourism Research Network
WW1 – World War One

A note on terminology

In this book 'the Somme' refers to the area where the British army fought in France from August 1915; the Battle of the Somme (July – November 1916) was fought along a front roughly 18 miles (29 kilometres) long stretching from Gommecourt in the north to Curlu in the south. The terms 'along the Somme' and 'on the Somme' refer to this geographical parcel of land and not the modern French *département* or the river of that name.

Modern Conflict Archaeology

The Series

Modern Conflict Archaeology is a new and interdisciplinary approach to the study of twentieth and twenty-first century conflicts. It focuses on the innumerable ways in which humans interact with, and are changed by the intense material realities of war. These can be traditional wars between nation states, civil wars, religious and ethnic conflicts, terrorism, and even proxy wars where hostilities have not been declared yet nevertheless exist. The material realities can be as small as a machine-gun, as intermediate as a war memorial or an aeroplane, or as large as a whole battle-zone landscape. As well as technologies, they can be more intimately personal – conflict-related photographs and diaries, films, uniforms, the war-maimed and 'the missing'. All are the consequences of conflict, as none would exist without it.

Modern Conflict Archaeology (MCA) is a handy title, but is really shorthand for a more powerful and hybrid agenda. It draws not only on modern scientific archaeology, but on the anthropology of material culture, landscape, and identity, as well as aspects of military and cultural history, geography, and museum, heritage, and tourism studies. All or some of these can inform different aspects of research, but none are overly privileged. The challenge posed by modern conflict demands a coherent, integrated, sensitized yet muscular response in order to capture as many different kinds of information and insight as possible by exploring the 'social lives' of war objects through the changing values and attitudes attached to them over time.

This series originates in this new engagement with modern conflict, and seeks to bring the extraordinary range of latest research to a passionate and informed general readership. The aim is to investigate and understand arguably the most powerful force to have shaped our world during the last century – modern industrialized conflict in its myriad shapes and guises, and in its enduring and volatile legacies.

This Book

What to do with the war dead? How best to honour and remember them? And, how should we deal with the tensions between forgetting and remembering? One answer, as Stephen Miles shows in this path-breaking book on the First World War's Western Front, is to visit them, or at least to journey to the places where monuments and memorials have been erected to their memory, even when they are not present by virtue of still being missing on the battlefields.

In the wake of the Armistice on 11 November 1918, battlefield pilgrimages and tours tapped into the need of the bereaved to visit the graves of, and the places associated with, their loved ones. Beginning in the 1920s, and down to the eve of the Second World War, legions of the desolate tramped across the old Western Front, chafed by grief, battlefield guides in hand, seeking a rendezvous of the spirit with the sons, fathers, brothers, husbands and lovers who had not returned. Never before or since have the dead been visited by so many of the living. But why do visitors still come a century on? What do they see today and where do they see it? How have places and attitudes changed under the pressures of Remembrance, commercialization, and the wars in-between?

In, recent decades, visitor numbers to the Western Front of France and Belgium have increased dramatically at the same time as the First World War has become more than history. Since the late 1990s, archaeologists, anthropologists, cultural historians, and heritage and tourism professionals have increasingly made a claim on what was once the preserve of military historians on the one hand, and battlefield scavengers on the other. Over the past two decades, the 'view from below' – the experiences of ordinary soldiers – has been given a more jagged edge, as the remains of men and *matériel* have emerged from the earth, often captured by television cameras. Sometimes, and in ways inconceivable to past generations, the painstaking study of military records and recovered personal belongings, together with DNA analysis, have identified individuals, reclaiming them from the stone-engraved lists of 'the missing'. Families who had never known, or who had forgotten their First World War connections can now visit the graves of their ancestors for the first time in a hundred years.

At the same time, museums along the old battlefields have increasingly engaged their publics with creative exhibitions charting the contributions of those who were brought from across the world to join the 'Great War for Civilization'. Partnering these exhibitions are others which have explored hitherto under-acknowledged aspects of the war, from Trench Art to postcards, from aerial photography to Remembrance flowers, war art, and the contested reconstruction of devastated towns and cities. This new generation of major museums has responded to the needs and expectations of a changing public just as innumerable privately-run café-museums catered to the charabancs of bereaved relatives which began arriving in the early 1920s.

Yesterday and today the places where battlefield visitors go are framed (some would say corrupted) by commerce just as the conflict itself produced vast profits for war-related industries. Different perspectives create widely varied responses to the modern commercialization of the war, from the multitude of tour companies offering specialist itineraries to war-themed food and drink, and from t-shirts and crockery to the undisputed king of Remembrance icons, the ubiquitous poppy as lapel badge, car sticker, umbrella, and edible chocolate flower. Whether buying such items is simply modern-day tourist behaviour, or perhaps a deeper investment in memory and place is debateable – though both must play their part. What is new, or at least more recent, are several different but connected developments which have accompanied the surge in battlefield tourism. In France and Belgium, there are, to different degrees, legal recognition of and protection for First World War remains as cultural patrimony, codes of ethical practice for tourism, and a revitalised interest in re-enactment of battles by enthusiasts.

Stephen Miles documents, explores, and offers his own thoughts and analysis of this spiders' web of issues that is part history, part anthropology, and part heritage and tourism. Drawing on his own original research and fieldwork, he unravels the strands of emotion and memory, of commercialization and commemoration; he tells how those he spoke to are moved to visit the places of their ancestors, and their feelings at having done so. He asks the difficult questions about the rights and wrongs of such activities, about how such landscapes of death and destruction became heritage, and what exactly does that mean for the old killing fields of the Western Front where so many who fought still lie just centimetres beneath the busy roads and fertile fields, rather than in the regimented rows of official war cemeteries.

This is a timely book, published in the middle of the Centenary of the First World War, and on the cusp of changing attitudes and perceptions to a conflict that has passed beyond living memory. It is perfectly pitched to make us rethink what the war meant during the inter-war years, and what it means today in a world full of violence and danger not just to soldiers, but to ordinary people on city streets. Modern conflicts have moved beyond the battlefield to embrace us all. In this singular way, today's visitors to Western Front cemeteries and memorials carry a sense of anxiety about their own personal safety at home unknown to the original battlefield pilgrims and visitors of the years 1919–1939, when grief at the loss of others was paramount.

By interviewing those whom he encountered during his own sojourns along this war landscape, Miles captures a unique snapshot of today as well as of the past. While family histories propel our desire to visit the battlefields, we are not just visitors to the Great War past, but time travellers to our own past, standing in the places not only where young men in uniform suffered and died, but where countless others have stood in later years trying to comprehend their own loss.

The truth of the matter, as this book reveals, is that the Western Front is not solely a century-old physical destination, but also an imaginary place, where multitudes can stand together in one location yet experience widely different emotions and senses of personal identification and validation. The power of landscape to hold and shape us is arguably nowhere as evident as when we are in ancestral places, tied by history, memory, imagination and blood to our own forebears who died before their time. Landscape is indeed the last witness to the First World War, but there are as many Western Fronts as there are visitors to it.

Nicholas J Saunders, University of Bristol, June 2016

About this Book

This book is written from a British and Commonwealth perspective. I make no apologies for this as broadening the book's focus to include the entire Front with its international roll-call of different nationalities would have been an unwieldy undertaking; it would also have necessitated delving into foreign-language sources for which I am ill-equipped. For this reason I have maintained a specific remit although some readers may find their own nation's involvement in the Western Front underplayed (particularly with regard to contemporary tourism). This is regrettable but is in no small measure due to the gap that currently exists in research into tourists from Commonwealth countries outside of Australia, New Zealand and Canada to the Western Front. I hope this imbalance will be rectified in the future. The only concession to the manner in which the Great War is interpreted and experienced by another nation is my inclusion of the Musée de la Grande Guerre du Pays de Meaux in Chapter 6. At the time of writing this was the newest large museum along the Western Front and it would have been remiss of me to have excluded it just because its primary visitor constituency was French. It is here included as an excellent example of innovative war museology.

I deliberately decided to adopt a broad definition of the word 'tourist' in this book which follows that provided by the United Nations as:

> a traveller taking a trip to a main destination outside his/her usual environment, for less than a year, for any main purpose (business, leisure or other personal purpose) other than to be employed by a resident entity in the country or place visited.[1]

Tourism refers to the activities of these people. I make no distinction between a tourist and a visitor, the latter often excluded from tourism statistics if they are day-trippers. I have avoided this difficulty although inaccuracies are likely to exist as, for example, with the status of visiting locals, government officials and soldiers/cadets both contemporary and historic. Overall I have treated tourists as a homogeneous body regardless of such characteristics as age, gender, educational background or ethnicity. This is because I did not want the discussion to be weighed down by a large number of graphs and tables which might have been needed at every turn to explain differences in tourist engagement with the region.

Prologue: The Menin Gate, Ypres – 17 March 2015

As the evening shadows lengthened the crowds began to move as if drawn by some hidden magnetic force. In large groups and small they walked purposefully along the souvenir-lined Meensestraat towards their destination, the Menin Gate, a classical monolith and global iconic symbol of commemoration. Just like these crowds others had walked this road before, laden with heavy guns, ammunition, personal kit and all manner of military impedimenta, singing cheerfully or walking mute and anxious, in wind, rain and sunshine; on they move in our imaginations, the soldiers of the Great War, along this very road towards the pounding guns and muddy trenches. Many were not to return. I join the moving crowd as we follow them to a monument they would not have known but one which belongs only to them, these ghostly figures from fading pages and sepia photographs. It is a special moment.

The soft light falls on the gate warming its surfaces which soon become golden like the mellow walls of a Cotswold village. The police have already closed the road and the crowds thicken; I stand in line amid a rising murmur of conversation. There are accents from every corner of Britain and beyond and groups of school-children vie for position, lively and boisterous. Young children sit cross-legged on the floor eager not to miss the ceremony; others sit aloft on their parents' shoulders with a grandstand view. Selfies are being taken. In essence this could be any crowd. Grey-blue uniformed RAF personnel take position as an Honour Guard, sharing jokes and snatching photos of each other. In the distance there is the sound of boots marching on the cobbles and a large contingent of Dutch army cadets takes up position at the gate, echoing the sounds of military forebears a century ago. Hands on shoulders they shuffle into position with martial precision then stand rigidly to attention. All four corners of the hall are now blocked off and the crowd is ten deep.

The cavernous structure envelopes these crowds waiting patiently and expectantly. Above us is a massive arched barrel vault with three huge roundels now letting in the crepuscular light. On each façade are entrances leading on to steps above which lie rows of bright red wreaths. Above the cornice is a panel reading, 'To the armies of the British Empire, who stood here from 1914 to 1918 and to those of their dead who have no known grave'. And it is to these individuals that my eye is drawn as I become aware of thousands of inscribed names on every surface of the hall, the stairwells and the galleries of the memorial. Carved beautifully and precisely into 60 Portland limestone panels are 54,394 officers and men from United Kingdom and Commonwealth Forces (except New Zealand and Newfoundland) who fell around Ypres before 16 August 1917. The numbers are staggering – name upon name, row upon row – sons, husbands, fathers, uncles are all recorded here, each and every one a human being without the dignity of a burial or final resting place. Here they are listed by regiment, seniority of rank and alphabetically by surname; on one of the upper panels is Brigadier General Charles Fitzclarence the 'GOC (General Officer Commanding) Menin Gate'. There are familiar sounding names and unusual ones too – Scottish, Irish, Welsh, Indian, South African –Christians, Muslims, Hindus and Sikhs. I check later and discover that my own surname appears 40 times. This is an entire army on a vast vertical parade ground standing to attention with lapidary regimentalism and united in death in a martial sense of comradeship. It is hard to take in.

The Menin Gate is arguably the most concentrated symbolic commemorative space in British culture. A whole nation and its Empire made a stand here on the Western Front and vast numbers made the supreme sacrifice. The classical architecture has been interpreted by some as a monument to victory and when opened in 1927 was derided as a grotesque valedictory symbol of military prowess in a war that had caused immense death and suffering; indeed the poet Siegfried Sassoon referred to the Menin Gate as a 'sepulchre of crime'. But the Imperial War Graves Commission, the memorial's builders, intended the gate to be first and foremost a place for commemoration where those who had lost loved ones could grieve and find solace. At the opening ceremony on 27 July 1927 Lord Plumer said quite poignantly of each one of those named: 'He is not missing; he is here'.

Suddenly the sound of boots marching in step resonates around the hall and four navy blue uniformed buglers line up on the cobbles. It is 8.00 pm. The cacophony of conversation reduces to a low susurrus then is all but extinguished as attention becomes directed towards them. Shrill notes ring out followed by an abrupt pause. At this a Master of Ceremonies from the Last Post Association addresses the crowd over a microphone and after welcoming us requests that no-one applauds at the end or at any time during the ceremony. He then moves on to relate the biography of Lance Corporal Marcus Levinge, a New Zealand soldier killed on 17 March 1917 near Messines, not far from Ypres. The crowd are attentive and focussed on this tragic story given greater meaning as the words resonate around the tens of thousands of inscribed names. At this the buglers sound the Last Post which echoes around the vault and provides a visceral focus for remembering the sheer scale of the sacrifice. Marking the end of the soldier's daily labours and the beginning of the night's rest the Last Post is a final farewell to the fallen at the end of their earthly labours and at the onset of their eternal rest. Every evening at the same time since 1928 (except for the Second World War when the ceremony was moved to London) these notes have rung out, a musical inscription to complement the names so carefully chiselled into these walls. The crowd is transfixed and appear stilled and silent apart from the occasional muffled cough. At this an RAF serviceman moves forward to read the Ode of Remembrance, the central and most poignant part of the ceremony:

> They shall grow not old, as we that are left grow old:
> Age shall not weary them, nor the years condemn.
> At the going down of the sun and in the morning,
> We will remember them.[1]

The crowd repeats the last line in unison, a collective utterance, and a promise to keep the memory of the dead alive. Rows of waiting figures – military and civilian – then move across the road and through the Honour Guard to lay wreaths. Dozens of photographs are being taken. A Dutch soldier then walks into the centre of the road and recites with great clarity and composure the Kohima Epitaph:

> When you go home
> Tell them of us and say
> For your tomorrow
> We gave our today.[2]

The buglers sound the Reveille, used to rouse troops from their slumber at the beginning of the day and to return them to daily life, but also symbolising ultimate resurrection of the fallen on the Day of Judgement. The notes fade away as we all remain immersed in our thoughts; some civilians are standing to attention. There is absolute silence and the atmosphere appears freighted with a deep sense of reverence. It is as if the names are looking down on us and in this moment of silence we have succeeded in reaching out to them, the war dead, imbuing them with renewed life through our public remembrance. There is an uncanny concentration of purpose – the huge crowd along with over 54,000 of the dead; we are all participants. The silence and composure lingers and the ceremony does not seem to have an end; the buglers turn on their heels and march quietly away. Only a man removing a rope barrier signals that the ceremony is over. As people begin to realise this they start to whisper to each other then peel off in small groups towards Ypres. In minutes the hall is empty and cars resume their clattering over the cobbles. It has lasted only 15 minutes but this daily act of homage has re-inscribed the memory of the war dead most powerfully on Western Front visitors.

* * *

The Menin Gate perfectly crystallises the major theme of this book: that there exists a strong interrelationship between tourism, landscape (in this case an urban setting) and heritage. Set within a modern townscape the monument stands as a powerful symbolic presence which is attracting increasing numbers of Western Front tourists. It is moreover a focus for memory, contemplation and performance. Memory of the war draws the public to the site and in the same way their presence dictates the nature of commemoration and its changing forms. But the Menin Gate is also part of the war heritage of the region, where the past speaks directly to the present, and memory of past events is put into sharp focus (Figure 2).

Introduction

See that little stream – we could walk to it in two minutes. It took the British a month to walk to it – a whole empire walking very slowly, dying in front and pushing forward behind. And another empire walked very slowly backward a few inches a day, leaving the dead like a million bloody rugs.

F. Scott Fitzgerald – *Tender is the Night* (1934)

The observations of one of F. Scott Fitzgerald's fictional characters say so much about the intensely poignant nature of the Western Front landscape. Wandering around the recently restored trench lines at the Newfoundland Memorial Park in France six years after the guns lay silent, 'Dick Diver' and his companions, like thousands of other battlefield tourists and pilgrims of the 1920s, capture the emotional resonance of a war landscape most succinctly. In front of them lie parcels of land fought over with a resolute and brutal determination which resulted in enormous loss of life. For these tourists being at the place is important: to see the relatively short distances over which men fought and died brings home the terrible nature of this blood-soaked topography. It is as if the ground is crying out to them. Because in this space, known as the 'Western Front', two Empires did indeed collide, a grinding tectonic *Götterdämmerung*, in four years of attritional warfare. It was a conflict 'not to determine who was right, but who was left'.[1]

This book is all about places, objects and people; it views the Western Front as a rich and dynamic cultural landscape which can be understood in a wide variety of different ways. This is in stark contrast to the way in which the region was approached up until the late twentieth century – as a rather inert backdrop to the dominant historical and tactical narratives of the war. Such a one-dimensional approach is rapidly being challenged by new and exciting developments in the study of the Western Front which is now as likely to attract the attentions of archaeologists, anthropologists and museum, heritage and tourism scholars as professional historians. This book throws into sharp relief the three phenomena of heritage, landscape and tourism and in examining the interrelationships between them attempts to contribute to the rapidly changing world of Western Front study.

Just like 'Dick Diver' tourists continue to visit the Western Front: they too cast their eyes over this rather ordinary-looking landscape and try to imagine what it would have been like to be at these places in the heat of battle, abandoned wounded in 'no-man's-land' or manning the trench lines during periods of relative calm; to be subject to incessant shell-fire, sudden gas attack or the victim of a sniper's bullet. The Western Front has an intense power to arouse empathy within us, even though we will never really be able to comprehend these terrifying experiences. It plays heavily on the imagination and has an extraordinary yet uncomfortable ability to arouse the emotions, most potently. Over the last century so many tourists have experienced this deep sense of pathos and will have engaged with a strange 'magic': indeed the Western Front continues to captivate. And central to this is the landscape, a seemingly mute witness, but one that can reveal so many clues to these momentous events. What follows attempts to unravel the nature of this power of place and the dynamics of the relationship between tourists, the places they visit and the objects that complement these visits.

Chapter 1

The Origins and Nature of the Western Front

The First World War (1914–18), which broke out in the summer of
1914 between the Allies – Britain, France and Russia – on the one
hand and the Central Powers – Germany and the Austro-Hungarian
Empire – on the other, was a tragedy of immense proportions.[1] Like blundering
somnambulists, lurching from one event to the next, 'the nations slithered over
the brink into the boiling cauldron of war without any trace of apprehension
or dismay'.[2] Within days the fault lines in Europe cracked and millions went
to war in 'the last fatal flourishes of the old crowned and cockaded Europe'.[3]
In the following years over 42 million personnel from the Allied (8.9 million
from Britain and her Empire alone) and 22.8 million from the Central Powers
were mobilised.[4] In Britain over 2 million men joined these forces voluntarily,
the largest ever voluntary social movement in the country. It was a war
where, perhaps for the first time, the lethal power of industrialised warfare
was pitted against armies still fossilised in a military mentality more akin to
the Napoleonic era. As the war ground on it gathered a lethal momentum of
its own and became global in reach: troops fought and died under a desert
sun in Mesopotamia, battled disease on the Salonika Front and East Africa,
and fell under Turkish bullets amongst the dry scrub of Gallipoli. But it was
the European theatre of operations, and the Western Front in particular, that
played the most prominent role in the war, and it was here that the Central
Powers eventually buckled leading to the defeat of Germany and her allies in
1918.

What is the Western Front?

On 4 August 1914 Britain declared war on Germany in response to that
country's violation of Belgian neutrality. At just after 0800 hrs German troops
had crossed the frontier into Belgium and old obligations fell into place as

Britain pledged to honour the 1839 Treaty of London guaranteeing Belgian independence and neutrality. In the first few weeks German armies swept through Belgium and into northern France executing a version of what was known as the Schlieffen Plan, a massive sweeping advance like a great door closing around the hinge of Verdun, to envelop Paris and take France out of the war before turning on Russia.[5] Within weeks a British Expeditionary Force (BEF) of 100,000 troops had been dispatched to the Continent to assist the hard pressed Belgian and French forces. The Germans intended to achieve a swift victory and advanced to within 10 miles (15 km) of Paris on 5 September. But this soon stalled as combined Allied forces managed to halt them at the First Battle of the Marne (5–12 September). The famous legend of the Paris taxis used to transport 4,000 troops quickly to the front (for a fortnight's wages per trip) has endured but also speaks of the desperation of the situation.[6] The Germans retreated north-westwards and both sides moved rapidly in a series of outflanking movements – 'the race to the sea' – before coming to a halt on 19 October on the Belgian coast; a front had been formed.

This early stage of the war is marked by rapid movement and an attempt to achieve quick victory using nineteenth-century tactical models. But as both sides faced each other across the newly forming front it became clear that the long held doctrine of 'fire and manoeuvre' would not hold up. On 21 October the British command ordered trenches to be dug and the war of movement transformed into a war of attrition which resulted in a bloody stalemate lasting, with very little gain for either side, until the massive German offensives of Spring 1918.[7] The Western Front had been created and soon extended some 460 miles (760km) from Nieuwport on the North Sea to Pfetterhouse on the Franco-Swiss Border.[8] With serpentine grace the line moved south from the sand dunes of the Belgian coast, through the gentle contours of Flanders to the marshy lowlands of the Somme, and on to the lofty ridge of the Chemins de Dames, until passing through the undulating hill country of the Champagne and Lorraine, and the mountainous Vosges. It passed in front of the towns of Ypres, Lille, Arras, Albert, Soissons, Reims, Verdun, St Mihiel and Nancy **(Figure 1)**.

The geology and idiosyncrasies of this landscape dictated the manner in which the Western Front was fortified and the nature of the warfare which developed there. In the 'race to the sea' the Germans managed to occupy the higher ground and were thus able to build deeper fortifications which caused massive problems for the Allies when they tied to dislodge them through bombardment later in the war; the British, in particular, were cursed with occupying the lower lying ground which in many places was dominated by German positions and frequently prone to flooding. The muddy nature of the trenches is a popular theme in British accounts of the war. It would be wrong to think of the Western Front as a series of trenches alone in strictly linear fashion; in addition to trenches the Front was more correctly a line of strong points, bunkers, forts, fortified villages and saps which often overlapped. What is surprising is the enthusiasm with which British forces adapted to the idea of trenches – which were not a new phenomenon, having been used at least as early as the American Civil War (1861–65). In the South African Wars at the beginning of the twentieth century, the Boer fondness for trenches was thought to demonstrate a distinct lack of breeding – 'real gentlemen would stand and fight'. But the industrialised nature of warfare was now more a matter of lethal blanket artillery barrages and the scything efficiency of ever more accurate machine gun technology which could kill or wound hundreds of advancing soldiers with brutal efficiency. Trenches were defensive and made any decisive military gain difficult and costly and often ephemeral.

Despite the enormous military efforts to break this deadlock (such as the massive 'push' of the Somme Offensive, July–November 1916) the war became one of tactically useless engagements and very few of the 'bite and hold' advances made by the British succeeded in capturing significant amounts of ground for very long periods. The war became one of attrition – what the French called *grignotage,* a 'gnawing' or 'nibbling' – where both sides tried to wear their opponents down in terms of manpower, *matériel* and morale. One British officer described Flanders as 'an oppressive, soul-clogging country'.[9]

In the trenches death could come suddenly and at any time – men were shot, bayoneted, blown up, gassed, buried alive, drowned, electrocuted, run over by vehicles, or kicked to death by animals. There were also the problems of cold, heat, rats, lice and the cloying mud (known as 'Flanders porridge'). Bodies often lay unburied and body parts frequently surrounded men in their everyday lives; a French writer described one area as 'an astonishing charnel house ... like a cemetery with the topsoil taken off'[10] and the poet Wilfred Owen talked of a 'topography of Golgotha'.[11] The casualties on this Front were staggering: over 6 million dead and 14 million wounded from both sides including over 750,000 British and Commonwealth dead. It has been estimated that in one area – the Ypres Salient – between October 1914 and October 1918 there were 7 British casualties for every hour of time between these dates. But what is most chilling are the numbers of bodies that were never recovered – some 300,000 – which makes this a war-scape unlike any other in human history. Add to this the tragedy of wounded men trying to come to terms with the horrors of combat and lives that were fractured, displaced and changed for ever long after the war's end. In 1922, 65,000 shell-shock victims were receiving disability pensions and 9,000 were still hospitalised. As one commentator has said, in human lives the Western Front is 'arguably the most expensive real estate in the world'.[12]

The impact of the Great War on British society

It would be difficult to overemphasise the impact the Great War had upon the nations of Europe in its aftermath; in Britain and the Commonwealth the war directly affected wide sectors of public and private life. It was a trauma that cast a 'long shadow' over Britain and the Commonwealth throughout the twentieth century despite being refashioned in the light of World War Two.[13] What is remarkable about the Great War is that it 'has entirely failed to settle down ... [and has] grown stranger, sadder, more bewildering ... as the decades (soon the centuries) turn ... [It] is a mountain that has grown in our rear view mirror, even as we speed away'.[14] Our understanding and engagement with the Great War has been greatly assisted by the contemporary obsession with memory and the 'memory boom' which has burgeoned since the late 1980s.[15] The Great War is still newsworthy and frequently speaks to present concerns; the unfolding Centenary (2014–18) has shown how we refuse to relinquish our collective and private memory of the war, perhaps made more important by the passing of the 'war generation' in the late 2000s. The third generation still remember and 'paradoxically, as 1914–18 has become more remote in time, it seems closer emotionally'.[16]

In Britain and Commonwealth countries memory of the war has a central place in public and private culture. But the Great War means many things to many people: for some it is a lesson in triumph over oppression and foreign dominance; for others it is a lesson in what can go so terribly wrong in geo-political relations and stands as an enduring message of peace; for others it is entirely personal, relating to fallen ancestors, and represents the triumph over adversity of individual participants, rather than nation states. Beyond this, memory of the war can stimulate keen interest from hobbyists with an attachment to particular regiments, corps, units, battles or phases of combat or weaponry; the Great War has an extraordinary capacity to generate a plethora of different interests, standpoints and contemporary concerns like few other conflicts before or after. It brings like-minded people together in a unique 'community of memory' but, with an ability to delineate opposing views, it also pits them against each other in often bitter controversy.[17] War rages but on the eve of the Centenary several studies showed how ignorant certain sectors of the population were of the First World War. In one survey, for example, one in five respondents thought the invasion of Poland sparked Britain's involvement in the war, with 'Don't Know' as the second most popular answer, and only 13% correctly identifying Belgium as the answer. Only 47% knew that the First World War was sparked by the assassination of Archduke Franz Ferdinand.[18] These wide gaps in knowledge highlight the immense public educational opportunities available. Yet despite these gaps there was a strong feeling that the centenary *ought* to be marked in a significant way.[19] This is a timely conclusion, for tourism and an engagement with heritage and place rely heavily on popular understandings of the war.

In 2014 Britain embarked upon a national commemoration of the Great War with respectful gusto reflected in a vast number of national, regional and local events. Between April 2010 and May 2015 the UK Heritage Lottery Fund (HLF) awarded over £70 million to more than 1,200 First World War Centenary projects; 75% of these were for small community-based projects (under £10,000) reflecting the government's intention to place people and communities at the heart of the nation's commemoration.[20] The Centenary has also been underpinned by much media coverage. With 130 specially commissioned programmes and 2,500 hours of programming the BBC, the public-service broadcaster, plans to provide an unprecedented televisual and radio commemoration of the war.[21]

In the summer of 2014 the dramatic events leading up to the outbreak of war were given a particular prominence: from 27 June BBC Radio 4 transmitted a daily 5-minute programme *1914: Day by Day* relating the events as they unfolded a century before on that day; the actual centenary of Britain's declaration of war against Germany, 4 August, was marked by a televised service of remembrance from the St Symphorian Commonwealth War Graves Commission (CWGC) cemetery near Mons. This service was attended by members of the Royal Family and included music from combined British and German choirs, former enemies now united in peace, and recitations of war accounts by men from both sides. That evening the Lights Out Campaign requested all homes and business in the country to dim their lights between 10.00 and 11.00 pm and place a lighted candle in a window ("A million candles for a million men");[22] this was to commemorate one of the most poignant myths of the war as the deadline for Germany's response to Britain's ultimatum came near. As 11 o'clock approached in 1914 the Foreign Secretary, Sir Edward Grey, looked down into the street from his office at the lamps being lit but remarked, "The lamps are going out all over Europe, we shall not see them lit again in our life-time". In 2014 as the time approached candles in Westminster Abbey were gradually extinguished until only one was left at the Tomb of the Unknown Warrior; at 11.00 pm this too was put out providing a stirring parallel with the darkness that was about to spread across Europe a hundred years before.

Perhaps the most visually stunning act of commemoration to date, and the one which captured the public imagination most forcefully, was the installation of 888,246 red ceramic poppies in the moat of the Tower of London; each represented a British or colonial soldier who died in the Great War and were planted gradually up until Remembrance Day on 11 November 2014 **(Figure 3)**. More than 5 million people are estimated to have seen the installation.[23] Other examples included the Centenary Poppy Campaign providing free poppy seeds for the public and local authorities to plant on their land;[24] the planting of new 'Centenary Woods' by the charity The Woodland Trust;[25] and a Centenary Classic Car Run from Swansea to Mametz Woods in France to commemorate Welsh losses during the Battle of the Somme. The creative theme was developed further in the installation of 5000 ice sculptures at Birmingham's Chamberlain Square in August 2014, each melting figure representing a person who had made a sacrifice in the war. Birmingham also developed its own City Centre Floral Trail to commemorate the Centenary but also as its entry into the Royal Horticultural Society's Britain in Bloom competition; figures along the trail recalled the city's vital contribution to the war and included homing pigeons, a war horse and a pair of stretcher bearers **(Figure 4)**.[26] The beginning of the Centenary in 2014 was, however, more than just a focus for the events of the Great War; the year also marked several events from the Second World War such as the 70th anniversaries of both the D-Day Landings and Victory in Europe (VE) Day. The Centenary seems to be broadening the public's appreciation of past military events and in the words of one journalist – marks 'a century of sacrifice.'[27] The Great War continues to have a strong grip on the British psyche and has the ability to focus national consciousness on wider dimensions of remembrance.[28]

Myths of the Western Front

Although the war raged across several continents and involved enormous global military effort, British and Commonwealth memory privileges the Western Front where the lion's share of international resources and manpower was concentrated. It is also the location for the enormous mortality sustained by units from differing nations who have continued to maintain the sanctity of particular battlefields, both physically and symbolically. For the Canadian nation Vimy Ridge (April 1917) and Passchendaele (Third Ypres) (July–November 1917) are key places and dates; for New Zealand the Somme (1916) and Le Quesnoy (November 1918) are iconic; and for India the Battle of Neuve Chapelle (March 1915) is significant in being the place where the Indian Corps fought its first major action as a single unit. For Australia, Fromelles (1916) and Villers-Bretonneux (April 1918) have become key sites although, like New Zealand, the country's national war mythology is dominated by the losses sustained at Gallipoli (1915–16) in Turkey.

For the British nation popular concepts of the war have focussed on the desolation and destruction of trench warfare which has 'stalked every

generation since the Armistice'.[29] Much of this was generated by popular
memoirs and the 'war poets' who, writing for a salacious public, created a
literary war of desired events. The horror and brutality of the battlefields
became the preferred reading of the past and this has been passed down to
contemporary society through literature, film and TV. For one historian,
because of this, the direct material impacts of the Great War have been
obfuscated and 'history ... distilled into poetry'.[30] This popular perception
has found its consummate expression in the central icon of Britain's
involvement with the war, the Battle of the Somme (July–November 1916).
The national narrative has been dominated by the futility of this battle and
fixated by one year (1916) and one day (1 July – the first day), eclipsing the
importance of the rest of that struggle. The Somme, in the words of the
historian A.J.P. Taylor, '... set a picture by which future generations saw
the First World War: brave helpless soldiers, blundering obstinate generals;
nothing achieved'.[31] But in privileging our own iconic events and sites,
washed in the blood of our own compatriots, do we do a disservice to the
sufferings of others? One of the enduring features of the Great War is the
emphasis on casualties amongst combatants; civilian casualties, although
never as great as in the Second World War, are seldom given the attention
they deserve. Tourism to the Western Front is almost entirely concentrated in
the areas of fiercest combat, rarely in the behind-the-lines areas where much
suffering took place under German military occupation.[32] If the Centenary
achieves anything it should result in a more open engagement and 'fresh
perspectives'.[33] A new understanding of the area's heritage, landscape and
tourism can be instrumental in bringing this about.

Heritage, landscape and tourism

Heritage, landscape and tourism are three of the most significant aspects
of the vast and complex physical and conceptual space known as the
Western Front. I will demonstrate here the peculiar relationship that exists
between the three phenomena; all feed on each other dynamically, if at times
imperceptibly, and contribute significantly towards the overall identity of the
area. The war heritage of the Western Front, expressed in physical remains
like pillboxes, trench lines and a 'commemorative layer' of memorials and

military cemeteries, has become part of the landscape, both urban and rural; as such it is the focus of tourist attention and the setting in which the narrative of war and the human story is expounded. Moreover the presence of much material heritage in the area's war museums is an additional feature of the tourist experience. But what is intriguing about the Western Front is the way tourism itself has added new dimensions to the heritage and landscape of the area; tourism has provided a new impetus to present the Western Front as a 'heritage-scape' and is able to endow the landscape with renewed value as memory of the events cease to fade.

Tourism is a major player in constructing new commemorative landscapes and provides a *raison d'être* for preservation and conservation of war heritage; more prosaically the new visitor centres, museums and other amenities supporting battlefield tourism add further layers to the landscape. This introduces a dominant theme of this book – that the Western Front is a multi-dimensional place, a palimpsest where new layers of meaning are added to and amended in a constant process of negotiation. Like all cultural landscapes the area is subject to a fluidity of meanings in a process played out through a range of interpretations; the heritage, landscape and tourism of the area are key forces in this process.

At this point it would be useful to explore the place of memory in our understanding of the heritage, landscape and tourism of the Western Front. Memory of the Great War is arguably stronger now than it has ever been in British and Commonwealth society and we live in an age where there is an astonishing variety of ways in which memory can be transmitted. The public are now as likely to engage with the memory of the war through popular film as they are by reading an erudite work of history.[34] Memories are, in short, the stories we tell ourselves about something or someone; we have now moved from direct experienced memory conveyed by the war's survivors into an era of historical memory which relies on the stories (written or recorded) others told us about the events. But memory can also reside in objects and the intangible legacy of the events such as music, vocabulary and war 'folklore' (see Chapter 5). Heritage, in all its forms, is thus a key ingredient of memory. Alongside this is the enduring presence of the landscape, where the battles were fought and the dreadful events took place. As the 'last witness' the landscape is an essential aspect of memory but, as I will show, where so much has disappeared it needs interpretation. Tourism relies strongly on the material and symbolic heritage of the war as well as the landscape; it acts alongside and interacts with new 'communities of memory' and, despite its more profane aspects, serves to sustain and perpetuate memory. Memory is a common feature of heritage, landscape and tourism and, in essence, the cement that binds them together.

Landscape: a cultural definition

The word 'landscape' was originally an aesthetic description drawn from painting where it referred to a pleasing view;[35] it developed, however, to signify a unit of human occupation and later the broader visual features of the land. Nowadays it embraces all components, rural and urban, and not just the aesthetic aspects. But a modern understanding of landscape is not solely physical; alongside natural forces landscapes have always been, and continue to be, subject to human agency. Because of this landscapes matter to people and can be interpreted by them in different ways. Landscapes can have strong symbolic and ideological associations, being read like 'texts', and like all documents can be interpreted differently.[36] The Western Front is a first-rate example of this phenomenon and, despite its rather bland and bucolic nature, remains hugely significant and charged with meaning. One commentator has referred to it as 'one of the most important modern instances of the symbolic reordering of landscape brought about by war.'[37] It is not just the physical scars of war which matter (although along the Western Front few of these can now be seen); sites of war have strong emotional resonance and can exist in private and public consciousness far away from the places of conflict themselves. Landscapes also exist in the mind and, it could be said, are what we make them. But their reliance on human imagination and perception does not diminish their reality in those for whom they matter so much; landscapes of the mind are just as 'tangible' as landscapes beneath the feet.

Although I am more concerned here with 'sense of place', those who visit sites of war are strongly influenced by mental constructs and the power of the imagination; these are frequently embedded within the individual psyche before any visit. This affords an area like the Western Front an enhanced level of cultural importance. What is remarkable about the landscape is that the events of war were only a relatively brief intrusion into the long history of what came to be known as the Western Front; the heritage of the extensive medieval cloth trade of Flanders, for example, which so greatly enriched cities like Ypres, is in many ways eclipsed by the First World War despite there being a more visually appealing built medieval legacy such as the (albeit reconstructed) Ypres Cloth Hall.[38]

Interpreting the Western Front from the point of view of the battlefield tourist is, however, to only see it from one perspective. If landscapes have a plurality of meanings then the region will be viewed very differently from a range of human standpoints: by a farmer or landowner opposed to intrusion by tourists onto their land; local residents frustrated by further tourism–induced traffic congestion; governments and local authorities eager to improve infrastructure; or the organisers of commemorative services alarmed by the 'touristification' of *their* events. But, conversely, alternate views might be expressed by those with a subterranean bunker on their land keen to gain some extra income; souvenir shop owners making a living from battlefield tourists; archaeologists aware of the rich repository of the past lying beneath the soil; or a CWGC eager to maintain their mission to open cemeteries to the descendants of those who paid the supreme sacrifice, despite increasing pressure of numbers. The Western Front is indeed a complex place meaning many different things to many different people.

But if the Western Front is freighted with meaning what are the dynamics of this process? It is important to outline this here since what follows is predicated on the concept of 'sense of place', the special qualities which distinguish an area of space from those around it. The area in which the war was fought was effectively little different from any other part of France and Belgium before the war. But the events of 1914–18 imbued this area of land with enduring and sacred qualities, regardless of the fact that after the war much of the evidence of the trauma within the landscape was lost. What transforms space – the location for empty routine and the quotidian – into place is the infusion of meaning. Place is thus a 'meaningful location'[39] and through personal and/or collective significance is given distinction above other areas of space. As Yi-Fu Tuan has commented, 'place is a pause in movement' and 'the pause makes it possible for a locality to become a centre of felt value'.[40]

As we move across a landscape our eyes search for points of interest that draw our attention; so a mountain peak, a prominent tree or a large building are likely to make us pause (although cultural factors will clearly affect what we deem worthy of attention). For those travelling across the Western Front the vista is punctuated by the ubiquitous memorials and cemeteries that populate this landscape and to a lesser extent the more innocuous physical remnants of war like pillboxes. The pause creates a *place* and we are struck by a compulsion to investigate further and to 'visit'; the object provides a marker to signify that something happened there. The builders of the first monumental war memorials were under no illusions as to the importance of this. So where things happened, especially where this involved violent death, is a powerful agent in the creation of 'sense of place'. This meaning is created by human decisions which are a key factor in the creation of heritage tourism attractions (Chapter 5).

Chapter 2

Tourism Begins on the Western Front

T he First World War had an impact on British society like no other previous conflict. It affected every corner of the nation and many would have known someone who had been bereaved or were now caring for the injured.[1] The whole nation had been profoundly touched by the war which left a deep scar on British society which remains with us to this day. As a major arena of the fighting the Western Front in Belgium and northern France became a tragic destination for those who now wished to visit the graves of their loved ones or to see the names of those who were still missing. It also invited attention from those who wanted to see the scenes of the conflict.

But what is remarkable about tourism on the Western Front is that it had started long before the war had ended. People had wanted to visit the Front for a variety of reasons and at Ploegsteert Wood south of Ypres a 'Tourist Line' had been set up behind the front trenches where journalists, politicians and other curious, yet distinguished, visitors could observe the conflict in what by 1915 had become a quiet zone.[2] Moreover there is evidence that groups of civilians had started to arrive on the Western Front and the practice of searching for war souvenirs had already begun; in March 1915 Thomas Cook announced that they would be suspending sightseeing trips to the area until the war was over in the face of French opposition.[3] The first in what was to be a long lineage of *Michelin* guides to the Western Front was published as early as 1917. The guide stated: 'This book appears before the end of the war, but the country over which it leads the reader has long been freed'.[4] With hindsight this can be judged as presumptuous in that the most dangerous moment for the Allies – the German offensive of March 1918 – was yet to come. Nevertheless the book hints at an *anticipation* of tourism to the region:

The wealth of illustration in this work allows the intending tourist to make a preliminary trip in imagination, until such time as circumstances permit his undertaking the journey in reality, beneath the sunny skies of France ...[5]

In addition to this, troops indulged in what would be considered after the war as tourist behaviour.[6] This involved excessive souvenir hunting – indeed the word 'souvenir' was brought into the English language by soldiers returning from the war in 1918.[7] They also visited the graves of family and friends; Edward, the brother of the writer Vera Brittain, visited the grave of her fiancé, Roland Leighton, at Louvencourt whilst serving nearby.[8]

There are strong indications that the growth in tourism after the war was predicted long before the conflict had ended. Death surrounded soldiers on all sides and the loss of comrades was for many a daily occurrence. This infused the battlefields with sacred qualities and the nature of post-war visits to these areas was already being couched in the language of pilgrimage. The hallowed nature of the ground was reflected in the desire for a pilgrimage route across the scarred landscape, a *Via Sacra*, after the war, although this was never realised.[9]

The bereaved and the curious: Pilgrims and Tourists 1918–1939

The cessation of hostilities in November 1918 provided opportunities for travellers to visit the Continent again and numbers soon returned to what they had been in the pre-war era. Between 1921 and 1930 the number of people travelling from Britain to the Continent rose from 559,905 to 1,058,936 before falling away in the late 1920s with the onset of the Great Depression. They increased again the late 1930s reaching a peak of 1,436,727 in 1937.[10]

The British government had prohibited the repatriation of the bodies of those killed in battle as early as 1915 and this policy was continued after the war.[11] As a result families were compelled to travel to the former battlefields to visit the graves of the deceased, to embark on a vain search for the missing or just to see where the conflict had taken place. The Western Front was the most visited area from among those where Britain had sent its forces: it had seen the largest numbers of service personnel and deaths in action. It was also easier to access than places like Italy, Salonika, Gallipoli or Mesopotamia which received very few visitors in the post-war years. Travel companies soon seized on the opportunities made available to cater for this increased interest in visiting the Western Front battlefields; Thomas Cook was the most prominent of these, and by 1919 its profits had exceeded the figure for 1913. In addition, organisations which during the war had helped families visit wounded relatives along the Western Front now turned to providing battlefield tours. These included the Church Army, the Salvation Army and the YMCA. Other voluntary organisations who assisted the bereaved were the St Barnabas Society (named after the patron saint of consolation), the Red Cross and, from the late 1920s, old comrades associations (including the British Legion). In 1920 the Ypres League was founded as a veterans and remembrance organisation and one of its remits was to assist pilgrims visiting the battlefields.[12] Between November 1919 and June 1920 the Church Army took 5,000 bereaved relatives to France and Belgium. Between 1920 and 1923 the Salvation Army accompanied 18,507 people to the 'devastated areas' and the YMCA assisted 60,000 people up until 1923.[13]

A tourist industry had existed in the devastated areas of France and Belgium before the war and this was now reconstructed and expanded to cater for the increase in visitors to the area.[14] This included hotels, restaurants and cafes; all the trappings of pre-war tourism were present and '[o]ne hundred and fifty places in Ypres alone sold beer to tourists'.[15] There was also the provision of guides and guidebook publication. Between 1919 and 1921 more than thirty guidebooks to the battlefields were published in English[16] some written by ex-service personnel.[17] In the seven months up to January 1920 *Michelin* sold 850,000 copies of guidebooks to the area.[18] During the 1920s guidebooks started to be published describing the battlefields and the wider cultural attractions along the Western Front.[19] Travel in the devastated zone also had a moral and educational purpose as guidebooks emphasised the destruction wrought by German forces with much attention being given to before and after images.[20] The desire amongst tourists for souvenirs from the battlefield led to a voracious traffic in scavenged items ('souveneering') as well as the manufacture of mementos. Much of this continued the practice of 'trench art' whereby soldiers, prisoners and civilians had crafted decorative items using the detritus of war, such as engraved artillery shell cases. Much of this was now sold to tourists to the Western Front.[21] The newly formed Imperial War Graves Commission (IWGC) soon became aware of the need to complete the construction of as many cemeteries as possible including the production of cemetery registers and properly co-ordinated maps to cater for visitors.[22] In 1919 60,000 people visited the Western Front.[23]

Although amenities were developing to assist this large number of visitors, the Western Front was still a shattered and desolate place into the early 1920s. In October 1918 Mgr. Tissier, Bishop of Chalons on Somme-Py, described his area as an 'absolute desert, without water, people or vegetation … a land without colour which we shall call the corpse of a *pays*'. A local government report stated that nine months after the Armistice the north-east Marne region was still 'a tabula rasa, a silent desert with fields split open by shells'.[24] Visitors often had to leave their cars far from the cemeteries they wished to visit and walk long strenuous distances across the pock-marked landscape.[25] Travel in the former war zone could also be dangerous with much unexploded ordnance lying around and gangs of deserters still preying on locals and visitors. Captain J. C. Dunn of the Royal Welch Fusiliers describes how in January 1919 he was instructed to arrest a large group of Australian deserters who were holding out on an island in the Somme.[26] But the devastated nature of the landscape was part of the attraction as parts of the old battlefields started to be opened up to tourists; in 1920 Hill 60 near Zillebeke south of Ypres was bought by a British national and a trench museum was built by British veterans. The trenches were closed in the 1950s but the museum survived up until the end of 2006.[27]

Those wanting to visit the battlefields needed the time and money in order to undertake these journeys and for poorer families this could be a burden. The St Barnabas Society calculated that the cost of one of its pilgrimages was £4; at the time the average industrial wage for men and boys was £3 per week.[28] Appeals for government subsidy to help those who were unable to afford these costs fell on deaf ears.

Pilgrimage remained the central motivating factor for visits and several organisations led pilgrimages to the battlefields. Sanctified with the blood of the fallen the Western Front was holy ground which resonated with deeply held meanings. Organised pilgrimages allowed for a collective expression of grief and at least an opportunity for closure in the company of fellow bereaved families. The presence of others at the cemeteries and ceremonies would have provided at least a modicum of comfort for the bereaved knowing that their pain was also shared with others. Just walking over the scarred battlefields brought consolation to some serving to bring them nearer to the experiences of the dead and bringing order to chaos.[29] Many accounts of pilgrimages at this time echo the principal elements of the pilgrimage experience: a rite of passage, movement into and out of a 'liminal zone' and a sense of community. But the religious tone of these pilgrimages is distinct and the commemorative activities constantly compare the sacrifice of young soldiers with that of Christ. The largest organised pilgrimage in the years leading up to the Second World War was the British Legion Western Front pilgrimage of 1928 which attracted 11,000 people (including 6000 ex-servicemen). Visiting many iconic battle sites including Ypres, Vimy Ridge and Beaumont Hamel, the pilgrimage culminated in a memorial service at the Menin Gate on 8 August. This event is important in showing how there continued to be a public appetite for large ceremonies to remember the dead; it also highlights how commemoration could be integrated with issues of national identity and the need to ensure that Britain's contribution to the Allied victory was maintained in public memory.

There were also many private pilgrimages undertaken by individuals and families. One of the most insightful was that conducted by the family of Lieutenant Morris Bickersteth who was killed near Serre on the first day of the Battle of Somme (1 July 1916). His parents, the Revd. Samuel Bickersteth and his wife Ella, along with their sons Julian and Burgon, who had both fought in the war, undertook four pilgrimages to Morris's grave between 1919 and 1931 (**Figure 9**).[30] What these visits demonstrate is the vast gulf that separated the civilian bereaved at home and returned soldiers who had experienced these terrible events. The accounts written by the Bickersteth family reveal how the two sons try to bring some degree of meaning to the war and their parents' loss by explaining the battlefields in detail and the military objectives of the war. The landscape of the war is also afforded a peculiar private meaning as the family seek out places associated with the last chapter of their loved one's life. They visit the farm which housed Morris's Battalion Headquarters and identify the crossroads where Burgon and Morris had parted for the last time. These are fused with a deeply private meaning for the family but would clearly just be unremarkable places for other visitors. The family began to create their own rituals within this personally charged landscape and the places associated with Morris became their 'stations of the cross'.[31] They also voice their disappointment that in later visits the rebuilding of villages interfered with their memories and rituals. The Bickersteth pilgrimage demonstrates how important actually visiting the battlefields was for the bereaved and how necessary it was for some ex-servicemen to return; it also shows how pivotal ritual is in attempting to understand such a profound loss. This must have been the experience of thousands of other families as they sought emotional catharsis in the face of unimaginable grief.

Although most visitors to the Western Front identified themselves as pilgrims there was also much general sightseeing. The Bickersteths took time to visit other battle sites unconnected with their loss and many pilgrims readily mixed reverential with leisure activities. This touristic behaviour attracted the opprobrium of those who viewed the battlefields in a more serious way. One observer noticed how tourists 'came with a rattle and a clatter through the Menin Gate, all packed together in huge char-à-bancs' with their 'raucous voiced guide'.[32] The sentiment is also reflected in Philip Johnstone's poem *High Wood* (January 1918):

> You are requested kindly not to touch
> Or take away the Company's property
> As souvenirs; you'll find we have on sale
> A large variety, all guaranteed.
> As I was saying, all is as it was,
> This is an unknown British officer,
> The tunic having lately rotted off.
> Please follow me – this way … the path, sir, please,
>
> The ground which was secured at great expense
> The Company keeps absolutely untouched,
> And in that dug-out (genuine) we provide
> Refreshments at a reasonable rate.

You are requested not to leave about
Paper, or ginger-beer bottles, or orange peel,
There are waste–paper baskets at the gate.[33]

What the poem also shows is how at such an early stage the practice of souvenir collecting from the battlefields is well established as is the guides' opposition to it – although perhaps for the wrong reasons.

There is every indication that travel to the Western Front declined during the mid-1920s as reflected in the number of bookings taken by pilgrimage organisations and also comments by IWGC staff. This is also mirrored in low attendance figures to the Imperial War Museum in London at this time,[34] the low point being 1926/7. This could be because people felt the landscape of destruction was not as interesting as it had been or because they no longer wanted to be reminded of the pain of war. A related sentiment was whether it was appropriate to visit the battlefields as a 'holiday'.[35] From 1926–1939 we are able to gauge the popularity of travel to the Western Front from the numbers of people signing the visitors' books in memorials and IWGC cemeteries. Although these provide important indicators not all the books survive and there are other caveats. Not all visitors would have signed the books, others would have signed at more than one cemetery or memorial, and it is difficult to determine which signatures were those of British and Commonwealth tourists. In 1926–7 the lowest number of signatures was recorded, 67,787. Between 1927 and 1932 the numbers increased peaking in 1931 when 104,000 signatures were recorded.[36]

A key feature of this increase might have been the 'war books boom' of the late 1920s. Although not the only ingredient of war memory the publication of such titles as Erich Maria Remarque's *All Quiet on the Western Front* (1929) and Robert Graves' *Goodbye to All That* (1929) made an incisive impact into the cultural awareness of the war. In 1932 signatures dropped to 99,000 perhaps owing to the Depression and devaluation of the pound. But as the 1930s unfolded interest in the Western Front increased again. In 1936 6,000 Canadians made a pilgrimage to Vimy Ridge.[37] Accelerating interest might have run in tandem with opinions surrounding world events as the public became obsessed with the gathering geopolitical storm. In just three months in mid-1938 112,000 people visited the cemeteries and memorials in the period coinciding with the Sudeten crisis.[38] A sense of foreboding and visiting the sites of previous carnage in an attempt to promote eleventh-hour peace may have motivated travel to the Western Front in this period. In 1938/39, 157,583 signatures were recorded.[39] But despite this the expected second war could not be avoided and as Britain prepared for further national sacrifice visits to the Western Front declined and soon became impossible.

From decline to Centenary: tourism on the Western Front 1939–2014

With the German invasion of France and Belgium in 1940 the Western Front became part of occupied Europe. Tourism to the area was not to regain its pre-war popularity until the 1960s. The area did receive some rather unexpected attention during the war, however, as German soldiers based in France were taken on tours of the World War One battlefields as examples of places of shame and triumph.[40] In addition in June 1940 Adolf Hitler made two valedictory tours to Flanders and northern France.[41]

But visitors did not come back to visit the Western Front in large numbers after the Second World War as Britain tried to recover from this new conflagration and memories became fixed on more recent events. Post-war economic austerity reordered everyday priorities and anyway travel to the Continent was extremely difficult. By the beginning of the 1950s the British economy had started to recover and there was a dramatic rise in the standard of living for all. Between 1950 and 1965, the economy grew by 3% and average real wages by 40%.[42] Disposable income grew and there was an increase in free time including more days of paid holiday. By the 1960s the average Britain enjoyed a level of prosperity previously enjoyed by only a small part of the population. At the same time opportunities to travel became easier; the first 'package holiday' had been started in 1950 and in 1960 the number of foreign holidays taken rose to 3.5 million. Yet this was not reflected in visits to the Western Front; in 1951 a planned British Legion pilgrimage to Ypres had to be abandoned due to lack of interest.[43] The lowest ebb for visits to the Western Front came in the early 1960s.

This lack of interest is mirrored in a general climate of cultural indifference to the First World War at the time and is reflected in other areas of national life. The example of the Commonwealth War Graves Commission is indicative of this. The Commission had been forced to evacuate its staff from France and Belgium in 1940 but returned after the war to take on the new task of burying the dead from a new conflict. Nevertheless their resources had contracted and in 1957 they employed only 315 gardeners as opposed to 500 in 1938.[44]

The shifting fortunes of tourism along the Western Front cannot be divorced from changes in cultural attitudes to the First World War in British society. Although a direct causal link between cultural opinion and tourist arrivals is difficult to establish, the increase in tourism by the 1970s in the wake of the re-appraisal of the war in the 1960s cannot be ignored. The 1960s were a time of fundamental cultural change as old values were questioned and protest manifested itself in a diverse range of cultural expressions.

There was a renewed interest in the First World War at this time for a number of reasons. Amongst these was the very real geopolitical tension of the 1960s and, as in the late 1930s, the lessons of the Great War were reinterpreted in the light of contemporary events. The 50th anniversary of the outbreak of the First World War in 1964 coincided with a particularly dangerous period of the Cold War as well as the spectre of accelerating conflict in Vietnam. It was also a time of concern that, as veterans started to die off, memory of the war was sliding from a personally communicated narrative to one understood solely through cultural artefacts.[45] It was also reinforced by a re-appropriation of the cynical critique of the conflict which had been common in the late 1920s. Books like Alan Clark's *The Donkeys* (1961) and Joan Littlewood's play *Oh! What a Lovely War* (1963) emphasised the war's futility, waste and slaughter in the characteristic anti-authoritarianism of the time. The BBC TV series *The Great War* (1964) attracted much interest and captured the imagination of families over its 26 episodes.[46] Many had lived with decidedly tight-lipped relatives who remained silent about the war but now had found the programme a safe and convenient talking point for their memories. War poetry became fashionable again in the 1960s as new anthologies appeared and fresh historical accounts were written making use of newly released archives after 1966. One commentator has remarked that 'public awareness of events was potentially deeper and more widespread during the mid-1960s than at any time since the war itself'.[47] The war resurfaced in public consciousness as it was rebranded as 'cultural memory'.

Numbers of visitors started to increase by the end of the decade so that by the early 1970s the Commonwealth War Graves Commission (CWGC)[48] reported around 50,000 signatures per year for the cemeteries of both World Wars in their North West Europe Area.[49] Nevertheless compared to the inter-war years, and what was to come after, tourism to the area remained modest; in the first edition to Martin Middlebrook's seminal *The First Day of the Somme* (1971) the author remarked how there were so few visitors to the Somme at the time of writing.[50] But numbers did increase so that by 1983 there were concerns that the Last Post Ceremony at the Menin Gate in Ypres was becoming too much of a tourist attraction[50] and in 1984 yearly CWGC cemetery visits were at 250,000.[52] One of the key factors in this increase was that by the 1960s veterans were entering retirement which gave them more time to make these journeys. Running in parallel with this were far-reaching economic and social changes; these included greater leisure time and increasing levels of disposable income which rose by nearly 80% between 1971 and 1990.[53]

Despite the increased interest in the war and visits to the places of conflict organised battlefield tourism remained *ad hoc* and the large scale industry we know today remained largely non-existent. By the late 1970s, however, this was to change. In 1977 the Military Book Society asked an ex-soldier and his wife, Tonie and Valmai Holt, to run a battlefield tour for its members; from this was born Major and Mrs Holt's Battlefield Tours, the first dedicated battlefield coach tour company in the UK. This is an important landmark in the history of battlefield tourism to the Western Front because from this time on the coach tour became a pivotal aspect of the touring scene in the area. The Holts developed their own preferred way of presenting the battlefields using a mixture of sound recordings, contemporary material, poetry and letters underpinned by solid research and an intimate knowledge of the ground.[54] This relied heavily on the new penchant for the emotional stories of the Front as historians began to interview veterans now beginning to 'open up' about their experiences (as, for example, in the series of books by Lyn MacDonald[55]). The Holts sold their company in 1993 but their business model has been adapted by many other companies to great success. In tandem with their coach tours the Holts started to publish a large range of guidebooks to the Western Front and still maintain a prominent position in a rapidly expanding Western Front guidebook publishing industry.

By 1991 six major UK-based tour companies and several smaller ones were running around 200 tours to the Western Front[56] and this had increased to 1000 tours by 2004.[57] Figures from the In Flanders Fields Museum (IFFM) at Ypres at the end of the decade reflect the growing importance of coach tours overall with 17.3% of all visitors to the museum comprising coach passengers in 1999.[58] Tour operators began to work with a new market from 1991 when the First World War was embedded into the English school syllabus (Key Stage 3 of the National Curriculum).[59] There has been strong growth in this market ever since, reflected in visitor figures to the IFFM where in 1999 36% of organised groups were school parties.[60] By the late 2000s, 52% of all tour groups and 49% of all school groups to the Westhoek region of Belgium (which includes Ypres) were British.[61] State secondary school visits to the Western Front received a huge boost in 2012 when the British government pledged £5.3 million to pay for two pupils and a teacher from each school to go on a battlefield tour to commemorate the Centenary.[62] In October 2014 there were 46 operators based in the UK offering tours to the Western Front. These ranged from major coach tour, specialist history/cultural to dedicated schools companies. There were nineteen tour companies and nine private guides working out of France and Belgium who aimed their tours at British visitors.[63]

Alongside the growth in tourism to the Western Front there has been a huge increase in the number of museums, visitor centres and 'café-museums' in the region. **Appendix 1** shows how many of these were opened in the 1990s and 2000s in tandem with the increasing importance of tourism. It is difficult to determine whether these were opened in response to demand for heritage attractions from a public eager to engage with the Great War or whether their opening stimulated increased demand. Nevertheless the increase in tourism to these attractions has been enormous; as an example the numbers of visitors at the Franco-Australian Museum in Villers-Bretonneux increased from 45 in 1992 to 3,300 in 2005.[64] By the late 2000s visitor numbers to the larger attractions became industrial in scale: in 2009/10 the *Historial de la Grande Guerre* at Péronne received 73,551 visitors and the Beaumont-Hamel Newfoundland Battlefield and Memorial 106,882.

Between February and November 2010 198,542 visited the IFFM.[65] It is noticeable how several of these attractions have opened or been refurbished in readiness for the beginning of the Centenary in 2014. The IFFM (newly opened 2012) received 294,579 visitors in 2013; this was 37% more than the museum's average annual visitor number and a 57,000 increase on the previous record set in 2009.[66]

In addition to museums, tourists to the Western Front visit CWGC cemeteries and the range of memorials which populate the landscape. However visitor figures for these are notoriously inaccurate or difficult to obtain; in the case of cemeteries this is because not all visitors leave their signatures and visitor books are often removed and destroyed because of lack of storage space. Despite these caveats the CWGC estimate that there were 228,000 visitors at Tyne Cot cemetery in 2006 and the Thiepval Memorial is estimated to have in excess of 200,000 visitors per year.[67] In 2000 the Department of Veteran Affairs Canada reported over a million visits to the Vimy Ridge Memorial per year and 250,000 to the Beaumont-Hamel Newfoundland Battlefield and Memorial.[68]

The explosion in cultural interest in the First World War in the lead up to the Centenary (2014–18) in the UK (described in Chapter 1) has complemented a massive increase in the importance of the Western Front as a tourist destination. This had started even before the official commencement of the Centenary in Europe in July/August 2014 and in the first five months of 2014 there was an increase in 70% of visitors to Flanders compared with same period in 2013. UK visitors made up 37.2% of these and of these 63.5% were school groups.[69] This increase is further reflected in the massive surge in visitor numbers at a selection of ten sites in the Westhoek area of Flanders for the period January to September 2014 (**Appendix 2**). The table shows how compared to the same period a year before visitor numbers increased by 44% at even a relatively small privately-owned attraction like the restored German trench and bunker system at Bayernwald near Wijtschate. At the 'Memorial Museum Passchendaele 1917' at Zonnebeke the increase was a staggering 135%. Visitor numbers for August and September 2014 for these sites were already as busy as the traditional peak month of May and with increases of 114% and 123% respectively were more than in the same months in 2013.[70] Between July 2013 and June 2014 there were 551,000 and

351,000 'World War One tourists' to the Westhoek and Northern France respectively which were 32.9% and 31.6% of total tourist arrivals in these areas.[71]

The Centenary along the old Western Front is being marked by an enormous number of commemorative activities which parallels events taking place in the UK and other Commonwealth countries. These make a pivotal contribution to the rich 'commemorative environment' of the area and are key features in influencing the tourist decision to visit. Examples of some of these will show how the war is being remembered in the places where it was fought.

Between 10 and 13 August 2014 the Western Front Association staged a large commemorative journey and re-enactment to mark the centenary of the deployment of British land and air forces to France at the outbreak of war. This involved the use of period vehicles, aircraft and a horse-drawn wagon and the journey used land, sea and air forms of transport (**Figure 5**). Over thirty members of the Surrey Motorcycle Chapter rode Harley Davidsons to commemorate the Royal Engineers' Despatch Riders of 1914–1918. The journeys culminated in a Service of Remembrance at the Faubourg d'Amiens Cemetery, Arras.[72] Other events have involved a greater level of symbolism to remember the sacrifices of the conflict. On 17 October 2014 the *Lighting Up the Western Front* event took place where a human chain of 8,400 torchbearers illuminated the old Front over 84 km from the beach at Nieuwpoort to Ploegsteert, the torches symbolizing the moment when troops said they could see each other's lights across the front line. As part of the event the names of all 600,000 victims who fell on Belgian soil were projected onto the Albert I monument in Nieuwpoort, the Yser Tower in Diksmuide and the Belfry in Ypres.[73]

A similar event took place on 18 October in France with the *Chaîne de la Mémoire et de la Paix* when 2,014 participants formed a 10km long human chain in the Weppes district near Lille.[74] A further highly symbolic event was the creation of the Flanders Fields Memorial Garden near Buckingham Palace in London. This used 70 sandbags of soil brought from Flanders symbolizing the ground upon which such sacrifice was made and the close connection Flanders has with British culture.[75] Other events have included stages of the 2014 Tour de France travelling along sections of the Western

Front to commemorate the 15 cyclists from the 1914 race (out of 145 competitors) who died in the war.[76]

The centenary is also stimulating the building of new memorials and commemorative plaques along the Western Front (and also in the countries of the combatant nations). A new memorial naming all 579,606 soldiers killed in northern France during the war – the Ring of Memory – was inaugurated by President François Hollande at Notre-Dame-de-Lorette on Armistice Day, 11 November 2014 **(Figure 6)**. Other examples include a memorial to the Christmas Truce of 1914 near Messines inspired by friendship between German and British schools; this was opened in December 2014 near to one of the best known sites of the truce.[77] Also nearby a European football (UEFA) memorial to the Truce has been built at Prowse Point cemetery near Ploegsteert; this is to honour the role football played in the event **(Figure 7)**.[78]

* * *

Tourism has developed along the old Western Front over many decades and has been subject to varying fortunes. In the early 1990s the writer Geoff Dyer stated: 'Every generation since the armistice has believed that it will be the last for whom the Great War has any meaning'.[79] This has clearly not happened with the Centenary demonstrating the overwhelming importance the area still has in stimulating the interest of ever greater numbers of tourists. The Western Front is a landscape open to constant and dynamic change; tourism plays a key role in adding further layers of meaning and in fashioning the way it is interpreted and renegotiated. The following chapters describe and interpret the nature of this phenomenon and the way tourists interact with the different types of cultural landscape represented on the Western Front.

Chapter 3

Tourism and Tourists on the Western Front

lthough the Great War has now slipped from lived experience into historical memory the Western Front has a magnetic draw for tourists from many countries. Tourists move through the landscape as soldiers did in the war although their journeys now have a different purpose and are safer and easier. The Western Front attracts those keen to learn more about the events that took place there or who follow in the footsteps of family members in a continuation of the pilgrimage motive that has always marked the area. Tourists want to understand what happened and why.

The Western Front is an area charged with meaning and for many has a deeply-felt sense of place. But it is also a prominent cultural icon that is constantly being represented by the media and reinforced through a plethora of images, texts and material objects. Nevertheless despite the prominent position the Western Front has in British culture tourists are still interested in visiting the actual terrain; the physical and sensual experience of the sites is more important to tourists than media, literary or artistic representation alone. Travel to the Western Front is not substitutable and tourists still prefer to follow the story in the context of where the events took place.[1] This is because of the power of the landscape itself and the way it is interpreted as a heritage resource.

Tourism is a potent cultural phenomenon with the potential to change participants themselves as well as the human and physical milieu in which they operate; it is rarely a neutral or inert force. This is seen on the Western Front as the character of communities and commemorative practices are subject to an omnipresent tourism. Tourists have become integrated into the increasingly contemporary interest in memory[2] and tourists are the new 'activists' in maintaining interest in memory of past events. Families are central in the cultural understanding of the First World War and in wider society have frequently played an important role as memory makers; this is a powerful feature of the tourist presence along the old Western Front. Battlefield tourism plays an important role in contributing to the socio-cultural, economic and political nature of the region; by so doing it has an interdependent relationship with landscape and heritage. Here I will explore tourism to the Western Front in terms of the development of sites, the participants, and tourist activities and impacts.

How sites become 'sacred'

As an area of profound cultural significance, the Western Front has attracted the attention of tourists who come to 'look upon' the landscape with interest and curiosity. The sociologist John Urry has termed this the 'tourist gaze'[3] – a way of seeing whereby tourists seek the extraordinary and the authentic in their experience in contrast to their home and paid work lives. The 'gaze' differs between individuals and social groups and there is no universal experience true for all tourists at all times; this is because the 'gaze' is 'socially organised' and strongly influenced by 'professionals' who construct and develop ways of 'seeing' for the tourist.

The 'tourist gaze' implies a heavy reliance on the material and visual legacy of the war. In terms of visual appeal battlefield sites are at a disadvantage in that they seldom leave a significant physical legacy which can be used to understand the events themselves. This is in contrast to other heritage sites such as castles, stately homes and religious buildings. A tourist attraction is somewhere where there is something to 'see' and is worthy of the 'gaze'. So in asking why people visit the Western Front one has to consider what people want to come to see and how a site has developed as an attraction.

According to the anthropologist Dean MacCannell a tourist attraction is the product of a unique three-way relationship between a *tourist*, a *sight* and a *marker*.[4] The *marker* is simply a piece of information about a site which gives it distinctiveness and can be expressed through different objects such as memorials or plaques or perhaps a signpost. The Western Front is a rich repository of these and the tourist visit relies heavily on markers to interpret the landscape. Anything has the potential to become a tourist site through this marking process.

MacCannell identifies five stages through which a site progresses in order to become an attraction and these can be applied to the Western Front.[5] First, **naming**, where the site is given a label and identity which sets it apart from others. 'The Western Front' as a homogeneous space distinguishes it from other First World War 'Fronts' and other culturally significant names can be identified within it (e.g. the Somme, Passchendaele, the Ypres Salient).[6] Second, **framing and elevation**, where a place is given as much exposure as possible and, just like a picture in a frame, showcased in an attempt to stimulate the maximum amount of interest. Memorials and interpretation boards are examples of this stage. Third, **enshrinement**, where markers initially placed for reasons of remembrance and honour can become attractions themselves. Examples of this are the grandiose memorials at Thiepval and Vimy Ridge, now important tourist attractions in their own right. This is the frame competing with the picture. Fourth, **mechanical reproduction**, whereby sites are popularised through increasing 'representation' in the public consciousness. Thus the Western Front is the subject of literature, poetry, art, music, photography, film, TV, the Internet and cartoons.[7] Through this process sites are developed as places worthy of attention and mechanical reproduction is 'most responsible for setting the tourist in motion on his journey …'[8] Fifth, **social reproduction**, the 'representation of cultural objects in everyday practice away from the places where they originated'.[9] The Somme entered the English language and national consciousness after the war as shorthand for great waste, suffering and futility and muddy conditions are described as being 'like the Somme' or Passchendaele. This process would have developed in tandem with the area becoming a tourist attraction. As with other battlefields tourists arrive at the Western Front already familiar with its infamous place in British military history; effectively this allows tourists when visiting to celebrate what they already know.[10]

Why do people visit the Western Front?

Determining motivations for tourism is fraught with difficulty because tourists visit for a variety of reasons according to individuals, personal circumstances and nature of destination. The most basic explanation is that it satisfies an unmet psychological need. This can result in motivations which are either *extrinsic* (a socially controlled reward) or *intrinsic* (a self-satisfying goal). With regard to heritage tourism the most distinguishing factor, and the one that marks it out from others, is learning and the willingness to learn.[11] Tourists visiting the Western Front are certainly interested in learning about the conflict but, as I aim to show, this is just one of many reasons.

The Western Front is made up of a number of different historical sites, museums, cemeteries and memorials each with their own stories, audiences and symbolic resonances. It might appear, therefore, as a heterogeneous mix of sites worthy of interest with the potential to provide differing experiences. The motivations of, say, a British tourist from the north of England or an Australian from rural Queensland might on the face of it be different (and this is to overlook the motivations of other nationalities or local visitors beyond the remit of this book). Nevertheless, I have in this book presented the Western Front as a homogeneous area and make no allowance for the possibility that tourists might experience different areas of it in different ways; this could be determined by the alternative ways local organisations interpret it or by the many and varied aspects of the war narrative.

One of the most useful ways to understand tourist motivation is one which recognises psychological (Push) and cultural (Pull) factors.[12] This suggests that a tourist's choice of destination is determined by motives which propel the individual's desire to travel (Push) and, arising from this, those factors of the destination itself (Pull) which influence the decision. It takes into account an individual's predilection for travel based upon person-specific motivations which attempt to address personal needs; on the other hand it incorporates characteristics of the destination itself.

Appendix 3 adapts this model to the Western Front[13] and demonstrates that many of these motivations are particular to the area as a conflict destination. Several of the Push factors relate to family or personal interest in visiting the graves of the dead or names of the missing. This has been greatly assisted by the growth in Family History and the use of the Internet to research the biographies of the fallen; most tourists who come for this purpose will have investigated the backgrounds of their subjects beforehand.[14] Other factors relate to individuals who played a part in the war and the obsession some visitors have with military history. Others have very specialist reasons and investigate a particular battle, corps, regiment or battalion or even type of weapon. More prosaic motivations are the need for social interaction, rest and relaxation, escape or simply to do something different. This can include the desire to meet like-minded people in significant places and the potential to exchange knowledge, ideas and viewpoints; such interaction, in highly productive social environments, has great power in creating or reinforcing personal identities. But what can be just as meaningful are the opportunities for self-development and the accumulation of new knowledge and experiences; this 'cultural competence'[15] can greatly enhance a person's sense of kudos and personal standing amongst others based upon personal knowledge of the place and events.

Factors which 'pull' tourists towards a destination can include something as straightforward as how near the Western Front is to the United Kingdom and the ease of travelling to it. This is relevant to the level of British interest in the Western Front and goes some way to explaining the comparatively fewer visitors from more distant Commonwealth countries. The impact of marketing to promote an attractive destination image coupled with accurate information, quality of tourist amenities and customer service are also key factors. On a basic level tourists need things to see and do when they arrive at a destination; the Western Front's stock of heritage attractions, including museums, visitor centres and guides, are essential in providing this framework. Events such as ceremonies and anniversaries can assist in making a destination more appealing and are often the main reason why a visit is made. Possibly the most important 'resource' on the Western Front is the proximity of cemeteries and memorials which provide a focus for the visit and are a major draw in themselves. Finally there are intangible aspects, such as the way the area has been represented in literature and the media which are important factors in stimulating interest.

A literary landscape

The First World War was a great literary war marked by the '… unparalleled literariness of all ranks who fought … in an atmosphere of public respect for literature unique in modern times'.[16] Citizen armies from both Allied and Central powers wrote about their experience of the conflict in a massive outpouring of prose and poetry which continued for many decades after the Armistice of 1918. It is important to acknowledge this because literature is a crucial aspect of the heritage of the conflict and in colouring public perceptions of the war. War literature is used extensively and powerfully in guided tours of the Western Front with specialist companies running tours dedicated to war poetry. As a central aspect of cultural understanding of the conflict, war poems, for example, are used in marketing, presenting, and interpreting the war.[17]

What war literature describes most dynamically is the nature of the landscape of the Western Front. The muddy, cratered, shell-shattered wasteland is described by a wide range of accounts which play to our imagination and sensory perceptions of what it must have been like to have lived and fought in such conditions. Consider the German position described by Edmund Blunden (1896–1974) as 'an almost obliterated cocoon of trenches in which mud, and death, and life were much the same thing', where deep dugouts 'were cancerous with torn bodies, and to pass an entrance was to gulp poison'.[18] When visiting the Western Front these images are a powerful adjunct to any appreciation of the landscape and provide a particular type of 'gaze' where the war is understood through a combination of interpretation of the terrain and the reading of textual accounts. This is particularly compelling in a contemporary landscape where destruction has been replaced by a bucolic serenity and the whine of trench mortars by the sound of birdsong and the occasional motor vehicle. This contrast between the din of war and quietude was well used by the soldier poets and is used to effect by tour guides to this day. This was brought out most poignantly on a visit I made to the Toronto Road Cemetery in Ploegsteert (known to British soldiers as 'Plug Street') Wood near Ypres with a guided tour. It was spring and lush carpets of violets lay underfoot. During the war Lieutenant Roland Leighton (1895–1915) had cut some of these flowers growing near his dugout in the wood and sent them to his lover in England. The guide paused to read the poem *Vilanelle* which Roland sent home on 25 April 1915.

Violets from Plug Street Wood,
Sweet, I send you oversea.

(and you did not see them grow
Where his mangled body lay
Hiding horrors from the day;
Sweetest, it was better so.)[19]

Leighton was killed on the Somme six months later. War poetry is able to successfully explore the boundaries between the sacred and the profane in a vivid way; and it can bring together the potency of place, emotion and presence like few other literary genres.

But there are many caveats in the way literature, particularly poetry, is used in our understanding of the war. It is often used out of context, telling us more about the individual than the events, and is not 'necessarily representative of wider experiences or reactions'.[20] What the writer had in mind at the time, who it was written for and under what circumstances, are seldom given consideration. What is equally important is the way poetry is read in a contemporary context and used to project contemporary beliefs and values back onto past events. The idea that the war was futile and wasteful was very much the product of a mood-change in British attitudes at the end of the 1920s, fuelled in great part by the 'war-books boom' and the movies.[21] This anti-war sentiment was given a new lease of life when the war was re-discovered in national consciousness in the 1960s.

It is important to remember that during the conflict and into the early 1920s the war was seen as anything but futile and the losses not considered wasteful. The most iconic British anti-war poet, Wilfred Owen, died leading his men in an attack on the Sambre-Oise Canal a few days before the Armistice. Nevertheless his poetry fitted the 'recognisable set of icons' that had emerged by the 1970s that the war was one of 'poets, men shot at dawn, asinine generals, doomed attacks, universal bereavement'.[22] These themes are subject to repetition and reinforcement so that they have now become dominant myths that are difficult to challenge.[23] Much war poetry is now appreciated for its succinctness at communicating primary emotions; this is indispensable for teachers, TV Producers and, it must be said, for tour guides and the stories they tell.

The Western Front: 'dark' tourism?

The Western Front is a place where many hundreds of thousands of mainly young men were killed, maimed, blinded, gassed and traumatized. It is also a place where the remains of hundreds of thousands lie unburied; when visiting the area it is a sobering thought that their remains still lie somewhere beneath this now mainly bucolic landscape. There is a morbid and macabre aspect of any engagement with the Western Front.

The Western Front can be viewed in the context of 'dark tourism' – defined as 'the act of travel and visitation to sites, attractions and exhibitions that have real or recreated death, suffering or the seemingly macabre as a main theme'.[24] It can include visits to sites of executions, massacres, assassinations, cemeteries, mass graves, memorials, prisons, concentration camps and battlefields. There has long been a close link between tourism and death as the activities of spectators at Roman gladiatorial contests and medieval pilgrims visiting the shrines of dead saints attest. Philip Stone has interpreted dark sites as lying on a spectrum between dark and light with a polarisation between sites **of** darker as opposed to sites **associated with** lighter violent death.[25] This would place an attraction like the London Dungeon, for example, on the lightest side of the spectrum and a concentration camp like Auschwitz on the darkest. Dark sites tend to have a stronger educational theme as opposed to lighter sites which have more of an entertainment theme. The Western Front battlefield lies towards the darkest extreme of the spectrum.

Nevertheless, such categorisations explain the concept only from the point of view of the 'dark' tourism industry – those who set up, manage and develop the 'attractions' themselves; it says nothing about what motivates tourists to visit such places. In attempting to understand why tourists visit dark sites researchers have detected a range of motivations. Initially, the visitor is 'motivated by the desire for actual or symbolic encounters with death'.[26] However, closer examination has detected a number of more precise reasons such as 'curiosity, entertainment, empathic identification, compassion, nationalistic motives, pilgrimage, event validation, identity search, education and a sense of social responsibility'.[27] This suggests a number of different forms of dark tourism and different reasons why a person would visit a dark site. It also hints that dark tourism lies at the interface between the supply and demand sides of the phenomenon.

The tourist experience at a dark site like the Western Front is affected by such characteristics as the passage of time (more recent events are considered darker than those further back in time) and the manner in which a site is presented to the public. Sites can be 'lightened' by high levels of tourist infrastructure and entertainment (as with re-enactments and costumed actors).[28] Thus the way a site is marketed and the image it has are important factors in determining whether a tourist has a dark orientation towards it; site designers and managers play an important role in determining the pre-visit perception, ambience, interpretative message and overall tourist experience of a site. Along the Western Front memorials are presented as honouring the dead, often framed by nationalism and not as sites *of* death *per se*. It is unlikely that tourists visit such places because death is 'the main theme'. In considering the Pyramids in Egypt as an example it will be clear that although these are the tombs of the Pharaohs, and by definition dark tourism sites, tourists will not see them as such but as mainstream heritage sites.[29] A pure 'dark motivation' to visit the Western Front is therefore unlikely to exist because 'tourists may implicitly take away meanings of mortality from their visit, rather than explicitly seek to contemplate death and dying as a primary motivation to visit any dark site'.[30] Although framed by death, such sites are experienced by tourists in different ways and many factors are at play in determining the nature of the visit.

Throughout this book we see how the tourist experience on the Western Front is strongly influenced by its commemorative and heritage aspects. It is a complex place salted with historical, cultural and nationalistic resonances and consequently possesses a range of multi-faceted meanings. For this reason dark tourists are likely to be a minority amongst the large number of visitors whose experiences and reflections on the Western Front are characterised by a range of preoccupations including family history, nationalist sentiment, hobbyist interest and a desire to see the places where history was made.[31] The overwhelming message conveyed by the Western Front is one of loss and remembrance expressed by the ubiquitous cemeteries and memorials that dot the landscape. These are stark reminders of the enormous human cost of the conflict and construct an 'emotional geography' of loss which is a dominant theme in any engagement with the area. This suggests that a form of 'grief tourism' is a strong undercurrent in experiencing the landscape.

Remembrance and commemoration often leaves people with a greater sense of empathy, tolerance, humanity, insight and understanding. Much tourism to the Western Front can therefore result in wholesome, uplifting experiences and a greater appreciation of what is good in human nature.

The use of the phrase 'dark tourism', implying a binary opposition between dark and light, sometimes complicates our understanding of the nature of tourism to this area; it implies there is something negative, distasteful and even deviant about visiting the Western Front. The diversity of tourist experiences demonstrates that this is not always the case. Indeed, much tourism to this area is characterised by the deeply profound effect it has on those who go there.

Pilgrimage and tourism

Travel to the Western Front has incorporated a wide range of orientations including a simple desire to visit the sites of war; the need to satisfy the interests of a spouse or companion; happenstance; or simple curiosity. But more serious reasons for visiting have always existed such as the desire to see the grave of a loved one. This is defined as pilgrimage, travel with a deeper purpose. On a more profound level pilgrimage is a spiritually motivated journey or search of great moral significance; the pilgrim attempts to bring about a personal transformation in moving to a sacred place and the journey is an integral part of this. Medieval pilgrimage to saints' shrines was located in a tightly defined spiritual and social culture and although the modern concept retains aspects of this, it has also expanded. Pilgrimage is now used to embrace a number of secular activities such as visits to the homes of deceased rock stars and iconic football grounds.[32] Modern secular pilgrimage is thought to be emblematic of the need for people to seek out meaning and authenticity where traditional religion has failed.

Ostensibly pilgrimage and tourism have much in common as they both involve movement and the extraordinary. Both contrast the ordinary/compulsory work life spent at home with the non-ordinary/voluntary state enjoyed away from home.[33] But pilgrimage is commonly seen as a different form of travel from tourism, many aspects of which are frivolous and lacking in true purpose. What distinguishes pilgrimage from wider forms of tourism is the pilgrim's concentration of purpose and quest for personal or spiritual transformation. Central to this are the dead who '… continue to be significant for the living …'[34] Thus pilgrimage culture has always been concerned with '… tragedy, disruption, death and the images of death, along with the heroes and saintly figures associated with these issues'.[35]

In the same way that medieval pilgrims travelled to the shrines of dead saints, so after the Great War the public returned to visit the graves of the dead (see Chapter 2). This was driven by a sense of duty and moral obligation and, in the case of the bereaved, an attempt to bring closure. Nevertheless this was immensely difficult in that the family would not have attended the funeral, often a peremptory affair conducted under gunfire, and where the body had been lost there was no grave as a focus for this journey. Due to a ban on repatriation of bodies the same government that sent these men overseas while alive refused to bring them home once dead. Relatives were thus forced to undertake pilgrimages by a government which refused to provide them with financial assistance for their journey. Also, veterans travelled to the battlefields as pilgrims to revisit where they had once fought, often gaining for the first time a strategic understanding of the landscape denied them during the war, and to see the graves of their fallen comrades.[36]

After the war the gap widened between the ordinary tourist and the pilgrim which mirrored the war-time divide between battle-zone and home front. It is interesting how this has persisted until the present day with a latent distinction made between those coming with serious intent and those with more leisure-orientated motives.[37] Nevertheless there has always been an overlap between the more serious aspects of pilgrimage and the less purposeful characteristics of tourism. The borders between the two are not distinct and frequently tourists start out as sightseers and adopt a pilgrimage attitude when confronted with profound engagement with places. It is quite common to see tourists adopt the reverent attitude of the pilgrim whilst at the Last Post ceremony at the Menin Gate then return to the bars, gift shops and restaurants of Ypres afterwards. Conversely pilgrimage is not uniformly serious in nature as individuals mix more light-hearted behaviour with the serious business of attending cemeteries and rituals. It may be the two are not as mutually distinct as is made out and that 'a tourist is half a pilgrim, if a pilgrim is half a tourist'.[38]

Battlefield pilgrimage attempts to bring order out of chaos and provides a solid platform for meaning in the face of loss and suffering. It can be highly cathartic experienced through rituals and symbolic commemorative acts like ceremonies, the use of silence, leaving flowers, the blowing of bugles, and the lowering of a flag. It creates tight bonds between participants through common experience and co-operation; this is regardless of differences in social class or background which are suspended in a unique sense of community spirit.[39] The importance of visiting the grave is key and caring for the grave of the deceased is like tending to them as a living person. It can bring a sense of duty done and closure and even for the third generation of descendants is able to elicit strong emotions.[40]

One of the most interesting phenomena of battlefield pilgrimage is when an individual visits a grave or memorial on behalf of another or a community. These 'representative' pilgrims were common in the years immediately after the war when visitors to the old Front pledged to pay their respects at the graves of their neighbours' menfolk.[41] **Appendix 4** outlines the different forms of contemporary representative pilgrimage which can be divided into private and collective remembrance. Much of the former is made up of family members visiting the graves of their relatives on behalf of the wider family and this visit is intensely private (although many rituals used in collective remembrance like readings and silence are present). But private graves are also visited by those with no family connection who are driven by a deep moral duty to keep the memory alive. These 'memory activists' often research the names of men beforehand, perhaps from their local war memorial, and 'pay their respects' at the grave, often laying a wreath.

Illustrating this practice I noticed while on a battlefield tour that every time the group entered a cemetery with the guide, a certain female passenger remained at the entrance looking through the Cemetery Register. This was to find the name of a soldier who had died on the day of the visit or failing that had the same birthday as her. If she could not find a suitable match she went through a series of other checks to identify a name and grave. She would then 'pay her respects' at the grave and pursue further biographical research when she returned home; often she re-visited the same grave on later visits. She rarely paid any attention to the guide. Speaking to her later it was clear that she possessed deep personal convictions and an almost obsessive duty not just to honour members of her family who had died 'but everyone else that fought in the war'. Although on this occasion this unusual approach was undertaken in public view it was an intensely personal practice and one likely to have a more profound effect on her than contributing to any collective honouring of the dead.

Other forms of private pilgrimage relate to the graves or memorials of writers, poets, actors and politicians who often became well-known after the war. These pilgrims could be from organisations or societies interested in these personalities and again are regarded as 'memory activists', keeping alive the memory of their icons.[42] Representative pilgrimage is also expressed collectively as large scale ceremonies of remembrance are staged to commemorate the dead. Dignitaries often play a major role in these ceremonies in a tradition which dates back to the King's Pilgrimage in 1922 when King George V visited the old Western Front dressed as an ordinary soldier. This was to pay homage to all soldiers, a practice repeated by his son the Prince of Wales in 1928 who joined a large British Legion Pilgrimage. On 4 August 2014 the Duke and Duchess of Cambridge and Prince Harry attended a large televised ceremony at the St. Symphorien Military Cemetery near Mons to mark the centenary of the outbreak of the war. This was a form of representative pilgrimage with senior royals attending on behalf of the Queen, the British Head of State. Nevertheless if pilgrimage contains elements of moral responsibility then much battlefield tourism is a form of representative pilgrimage; rituals are couched in the language of collective remembrance and tourists often say they have come to pay their respects to all the fallen, whether related or not.

The battlefield tourism industry still runs pilgrimages to the Western Front, although these are now sometimes called 'Journeys of Remembrance'. The word 'pilgrimage' is well respected providing a perceptual, emotional and marketing differentiation from other types of tours. Tours run by Remembrance Travel illustrate many of the key distinguishing aspects of a modern pilgrimage. As the travel arm of the Royal British Legion, which describes itself as the National Custodian of Remembrance, the company runs tours to many different combat zones and conflicts where the British army fought, not just the First World War. The dichotomy between tourism and pilgrimage is clearly reflected in the comment that their 'Journeys of Remembrance always endeavour to strike a balance between the content of a traditional Battlefield Tour and the purpose of a personal pilgrimage'.[43] Moreover the central importance of ritual in this type of tour is demonstrated by the inclusion of Acts of Remembrance in the itinerary and a Standard Bearer in the tour's Support party.

Ways of visiting and seeing the Western Front

As 'sight-seers' tourists 'view' places or, using John Urry's phrase, 'gaze' upon them in a way that non-tourists would not. The manner in which Western Front tourists 'gaze' on the landscape is markedly different from the way a local farmer, for example, would regard his land. But the tourist 'gaze' presupposes that the visual dominates everything; in fact there has long been a 'privileging of the eye within the history of the Western societies' where social experience is trivialised to serve the tastes of the 'omnivorous visual consumer'.[44] Although Urry later acknowledged that the 'gaze' could also incorporate other senses the key point is that the visual is always the 'organising sense' – in that tourists come to 'look'.[45]

We have already seen how there are different ways of engaging with the Western Front based upon a number of differences in the attitudes and motivations of visitors. Tourists no longer want to be treated as part of a mass movement and demand instead distinction and difference; a tailored and personalised itinerary and service is now a more common feature of tourism than a 'once size fits all' package. Those providing this service aim to construct and facilitate the experience and this is reflected in the way war heritage is presented to the visitor on the Western Front.

Tourists are essentially consumers who are attracted to products through increasingly sophisticated marketing techniques. The 'market' for battlefield tourism along the Western Front is constantly changing as it tries to keep in step with shifting consumer needs and preferences. These can be understood through broad distinguishing factors such as age, gender, social and cultural background and behaviour. Thus there are many ways of seeing the Western Front based upon 'product characteristics' such as the type of accommodation, whether it is group or individual travel, the tour theme, and mode of transport. Apart from touring by private car, coach, bicycle or on foot, it is possible to visit and experience the Western Front by rail, hired car or taxi with private driver, plane, helicopter, horse and carriage, or on a cruise.[46] Further options are hobbyist interest (e.g. VC winners, war poets, archaeology), educational (schools/universities), professional (e.g. military tours or 'Staff Rides'), peace tourism[47] and nationality (e.g. specialized tours for Australian visitors). Tourism to the Western Front is subject to market segmentation just like any other market. To illustrate the dynamics of the tourism experience on the Western Front two 'ways of seeing' are now discussed: the Coach Tour and the Walking Tour.

1. The Coach Tour

The coach tour is now a well-established way of visiting the battlefields offering 'a high level of convenience and a sense of 'secure adventure'.[48] Coach tours are increasing in popularity as the percentage of the older population, for whom coach travel has long been a popular travel mode, increases; between 2009 and 2014, 41% of those who took coach holidays were retired.[49] The nature of coach tour companies offering tours to the Western Front is outlined in **Appendix 5**.[50] This shows how the majority of these organise battlefield as well as other cultural tours with only a minority solely operating World War One tours.

The advantages of a coach tour to the Western Front are affordability (benefiting from economies of scale); the conviviality and social benefits derived from sharing the tour with like-minded people; the ability to tour wide areas without having to navigate and worry about finding sites and amenities; and the advantages of a knowledgeable guide imparting information and insight to large numbers of passengers simultaneously. The disadvantages are that a coach tour is tightly choreographed, follows a pre-planned itinerary, and gives little scope to passengers for individual exploration. On a deeper level the coach tour allows only limited opportunities to engage with the landscape; there are also limits to what can be seen from the confines of a coach window.[51]

Although passengers do alight from the coach to look at sites of interest they have little control over the time taken at these stops and consequently their appreciation of the war landscape can be rather shallow. They sit in a hermetically sealed environment and are a captive audience for the tour guide who can direct their attention.[52] The experience is thus managed and regulated. This might imply that these experiences are homogeneous but there is evidence that tour passengers take away with them a variety of meanings from their trips. Battlefields are considered more 'multi-generative' than other tourist landscapes in that they stimulate interest in a number of different areas.[53] This suggests that, despite the restraints, even within a tour party there is a rich repository of different Western Front 'gazes' rather than one unifying one (as discussed further in Chapter 8).

2. The Walking Tour

The walking Tour is becoming an increasingly popular way of experiencing and understanding the Western Front and a large variety of these are offered, ranging from a few kilometres to trips taking in wider areas lasting an entire day **(Figure 10)**. Most people setting out on foot focus on particular actions or discrete geographical stages of battles and longer walks of more than a day are less common.[54] Those lasting several days include special events like the Albert-Ypres four day Remembrance Walk staged between 7 and 10 November 2014 and the annual ABF Soldiers' Charity Frontline Walk which follows the 100km between the Lochnagar Crater on the Somme and the Menin Gate at Ypres.[55] Many tour companies offer walking tours supported by a coach which can collect participants at the end of stages and provide better scope for walks on both halves of the day. In addition to guided walks many visitors will walk privately using the large number of self-guided leaflets and walking guidebooks that are available.[56]

In a conflict where the landscape played such an intimate role in tactics and the corporeal and sensual experiences of those who fought, walking is a highly effective way of engaging closely with the battlefield. It is to feel the ground under the feet in an embodied manner. Walking utilises all the senses in the way the body moves and provides a unity of understanding of landscape. In its regular kinaesthetic movement it generates particular 'rhythms of thinking' where 'the mind, the body, and the world are aligned'.[57] To walk is to force concentration and to develop a mindfulness of the landscape[58] unlike any other mode of travelling across the old Western Front. The movement of walking is a way of knowing: 'it is thinking as you watch and watching as you think'.[59]

Soldiers moved through a landscape sensing every subtle contour where knowledge of the land's texture could mean the difference between life and death. It was being close to mud, dust and fetid water; it included exposure to the elements, the feeling of wind and rain against the skin, and raw sensations of heat and cold. Walking has a distinct advantage in that we can 'see with the feet' and engage with our senses and much of the above sensations can be experienced; we can also detect subtle changes in topography which would be impossible with the less tactile practice of driving around in a vehicle. But it would be remiss to expect too much of walking; we will never be able to accurately replicate the terrible circumstances of the trenches. The landscape is no longer shattered, blasted and cratered; we can now move across it using good roads, tracks and paths and no matter how muddy our surroundings we are unlikely to drown in the pools of shell-holes. The landscape of the area is best experienced by walking across it but we will never really be able to know its true dangers and horrors. Nevertheless the vast amount of unexploded ordnance does add a perilous dimension to any walk across the old Western Front **(Figure 8)**.[60]

* * *

This discussion has provided examples of the way the Western Front is experienced and understood in different ways. The coach tour is emblematic of a seemingly inert practice where the 'gaze' is directed by experts who predetermine what there is to see. But it also shows how tourists are more than disembodied sightseers absorbing what is presented before them and not contributing to the formation of experience (for more on this see Chapter 8). There is a world beyond the 'gaze' where tourism is dynamic, multidimensional and performative. Tourists are now seen as much more active in co-constructing their experiences through their bodies, their social interactions, imaginings and what they do.[61] Walking is also indicative of this in that it embraces an active and multi-sensual practice where, assisted by the interpretation of a guide, a landscape is read dynamically, critically and emotionally.

The economic impact of tourism

The Great War caused massive destruction and dislocation throughout Belgium and France which had deep and lasting economic, social and cultural effects for the region. But paradoxically the war also brought benefits as tourist interest in the region developed; in the years immediately following the war tourism was a key aspect in assisting the region's recovery and the economic contribution of tourism is today an important feature in local and regional economic development. Overall annual turnover from all tourist activity in both the Westhoek region of Belgian Flanders and northern France is 110 million Euros; that which can be apportioned directly to a person's choice to visit for 'World War One reasons' is 93 million Euros (45 and 48 million Euros respectively).[62] This shows how prominent war tourism is in the total tourism turnover of these areas.

Expenditure differences between visitors staying overnight, those staying outside the region, and day visitors are shown in **Figure 12**. This demonstrates how overnight stay visitors spend more in both regions and this spend is much higher in northern France. This could be because of the more widely spread area over which Great War tourism is experienced in France and the need for longer stays. Also France has a less concentrated supply of accommodation, unlike in the more urban centre of Ypres. Where there is greater supply there is more competition between establishments and thus (all things being equal) prices, and revenue, should be lower. It could also be because of the greater number of day visitors from surrounding areas to Ypres and their correspondingly greater overall relative spend. **Figure 13** shows how British tourists spent a per capita average of 89.32 and 99.4 Euros per trip in northern France and the Westhoek respectively. Most of this is spent on accommodation with more in the Westhoek than northern France; this is in contrast to the greater overall expenditure for all overnight stay visitors to France.

There are many tourists to the old Western Front who do not visit war-related sites; nevertheless the overall economic contribution of 'battlefield tourists' to the area cannot be overemphasised with both regions acknowledging its importance in their tourism development.

* * *

Tourism has a significant and tangible presence on the Western Front making a highly visible contribution to the economic, social and cultural character of the region. It appears in many guises and tourists look upon the region in many different ways. Tourism directs attention to a heritage and remembrance of the war and plays a role in decoding an intensely symbolic landscape. But tourism is not inert in that it is a force capable of imposing new meanings. It utilizes the concept of place but also has a powerful role in place creation. It thus has agency and an ability to add new layers of meaning to an already multifaceted landscape. From a tourist perspective the Western Front is dominated by two main types of landscape: commemorative and heritage.

Chapter 4

A Commemorative Landscape

In 1914 the poet Laurence Binyon (1869–1943) composed what was to become one of the most famous poems of remembrance in the English language. On 21 September *For the Fallen* was published in *The Times* newspaper with the deeply poignant fourth stanza:

> They shall grow not old, as we that are left grow old:
> Age shall not weary them, nor the years condemn.
> At the going down of the sun and in the morning
> We will remember them.[1]

What is remarkable about this poem is that it was written at a very early stage of the war; the battle of movement was still in progress with the stalemate of the trenches and the creation of a western 'front' still in the future. The commemorative culture which followed the war was thus predicted even before casualties had started to mount. It became evident as the war progressed that the whole issue of commemoration was going to pose an enormous challenge to British society. The sheer scale of death was unprecedented in British and Imperial warfare and the fact that Britain had prohibited the repatriation of bodies meant that new forms of commemoration and burial in a war landscape would be needed.[2] What is noteworthy about the First World War is that it was the first war in British military history where ordinary soldiers were given individual graves and all the dead were remembered by name, not just the elite.[3] What made commemoration particularly problematic, however, was the growing number of those whose bodies would never be recovered.[4] This only added to the agony of families wanting to come to terms with their loss in hindering emotional and psychological 'closure'; it also disrupted the conventional religious practice of the time which required a body and a last resting place as a commemorative focus. For nations wanting to glorify those who had died in war without glorifying war itself it also presented further difficulties.

What is a commemorative landscape?

With the end of the First World War human experience transformed into memory aided powerfully by the recollection of those who had participated in this global catastrophe. These memories took on different forms – transmitted orally or through writings, monuments and material objects like souvenirs.[5] It is this last type that concerns us here in that materiality is important in providing a trigger for memory; memorials are designed to do exactly this in that they focus the mind and the emotions on past events often outside the personal memory of the viewer. Indeed places are integral to the whole dynamics of memory. The French historian Pierre Nora has shown how important *lieux de mémoire* ('places of memory') are in a society where traditional repositories of memory (like peasant cultures) are disappearing.[6] They have been artificially constructed to help us recall the past in a world where constructed history has taken the place of true memory. Although *lieux de mémoire* can take other forms such as objects or events (e.g. treaties), places act as potent stimuli and have the potential to foster 'remembrance' in a dynamic way.

I wish to emphasize that it is not just discrete 'sites' that can act as *lieux de mémoire*; the entire landscape in which they reside is a powerful setting for the workings of memory. Landscape remains 'memory's most serviceable reminder'[7] providing successive generations with a rich and emotive context for remembrance. This gives rise to the concept of the Western Front as a 'commemorative landscape': the large number of cemeteries, memorials and war sites are *lieux de mémoire* in their own right but are also embedded in a wider setting of 'battle-scapes' marked by great suffering and loss of life. Interpretation is needed to look beyond a bland rural landscape, to unpeel its layers of meaning, and truly understand the significance of place.[8] The landscape itself can then be understood in its proper commemorative context. In addition because those who fought on the Western Front have now passed away, the landscape has been given a new validity as the last witness to the events of war. The Western Front commemorative landscape continues to serve emotional, intellectual, spiritual, communal and political functions.

If the commemorative nature of the Western Front was predicted by civilians then this was mirrored in the attitude of soldiers who were the first to recognize the meaning of the shattered land in which they lived and died. So many trenches, dug-outs, craters and subtle topographical features became charged with poignant meaning so that 'the battlefields were themselves visceral commemorative monuments which spoke directly to those whose fighting and suffering created them'.[9] But these meanings were transient as fighting moved back and forth over this newly memorialized landscape. Much of this memorialization is immortalized in the writings of soldiers and used to embellish the narratives of modern tourism; nevertheless much remains lost to the contemporary world, held only within the minds of those now dead. This adds an imperceptible and uncanny layer of meaning to the landscape in that whilst moving across it we are tempted to ask what might have happened on the ground where we stand.

The landscape's immutable and numinous qualities bring dark events to the fore and, as with the commemorative environment of Nazi concentration camps, 'memory feels monolithic, unambiguous, and terrible'.[10] When interpreted by place 'stories' the materiality of landscape takes on new meaning and is highly charged; landscape itself, sanctified by sacrifice, has become the memorial. This is reflected in the desire of several individuals to preserve areas of the Western Front in their ruined state after the war in perpetuity as memorials to suffering.[11] Apart from the selling or granting of land by the French and Belgian governments to combatant nations for cemeteries, memorials or remembrance parks,[12] these proposals never materialized.

The Western Front landscape is an arena for individual and collective commemorations. The basis for memory, however, is always social and memory is transmitted through shared experience; this is frequently formed around small groups such as community, family or the workplace.[13] After the war 'social memories' were created to assist people to grieve for, honour and remember the dead.[14] These memories are passed down from one generation to the next through shared experience and are constantly reiterated and rehearsed through commemorative practice; they are also subject to constant reconstruction and re-negotiation. Attending a service of commemoration, laying a wreath at a grave or listening to the accounts of battle at the graves of the fallen are all examples of 'memory activity'. This is undertaken by those who are members of 'communities of commemoration';[15] these could be established groups like the Royal British Legion or Western Front Association or temporary participants on a coach tour who are seldom aware of their role in shaping memory. The Western Front can be seen as a 'stage-setting' for these practices made all the more emotionally engaging by being undertaken at the battlefield sites themselves **(Figure 14)**.

This is not, however, to imply that commemoration along the Western Front is homogenous in nature. Differences in opinion over who should be remembered and how still prevail. There are also great differences in emphasis and tradition between the 50 nations that fought in the area. This is determined by such factors as the level of the nation's participation in the war, interest in public history, the extent to which commemoration is embedded in a nation's public institutions, and how the war contributed to a country's nation building. There is a stronger commemorative culture in British and Commonwealth countries, for example, than in France and the USA.[16]

The Western Front resonates with a rich variety of meanings; it is no longer interpreted as inert and has the ability to stimulate wide reactions and responses. The depth of this phenomenon is made all the more striking by the way the area is defined according to such factors as a person's cultural background, nationality, gender, level of education or age. Furthermore if someone had an ancestor who fought and died on the Front then they are more likely to attach deeper meanings to the area. This reinforces the idea that all landscapes are socially constructed. As one commentator has remarked: 'Before it can ever be the repose for the senses, landscape is the work of the mind. Its scenery is built up as much from strata of memory as from layers of rock'.[17] It would not be an exaggeration to say that landscape is wholly and entirely a human creation. Human agency had been involved in the development of the Western Front long before the ravages of war laid down a new and dense cultural layer; and further strata continue to be added not least of which is the region's commemorative aspect which is still subject to augmentation and shifting interpretations. The two most enduring visual expressions of the human construction of commemoration are cemeteries and memorials.

Cemeteries: the 'silent cities'

Journeying across the Western Front today the smooth contours of a bucolic landscape are punctuated by hundreds of neat structures, bright white against the seasonal backdrop of russet brown or fresh verdant green. With their pale colours and geometric uniformity these cemeteries, the 'silent cities'[18] of the war's dead, stand out glaringly against the natural colours of their setting. Their stark intensity, particularly in the rarified light of winter, enhances them in a way that is profoundly visual but also deeply compelling and symbolic. If the creation of 'place' involves a 'pause in movement'[19] then the cemeteries of the Western Front provide a singularly important example of where the eye is drawn onwards then arrested in its scanning of the landscape. But these are places imposed on a pastoral tranquility, which at first sight don't immediately blend in. This is no less true of those cemeteries which lie in the region's urban centers or hidden deep in forests. There is something incongruous about these structures; they shouldn't be here and this is what makes an encounter with them so deeply affective. They stand as a blunt reminder that this is a place of death, suffering and sacrifice. As such cemeteries are a tangible component of the region's 'emotional geography' of commemoration.

Today 725,559 British and Commonwealth dead from the First World War are buried in 2,316 military and around 2,000 civilian cemeteries in France and Belgium.[20] As the war progressed the Sisyphean task of recovering the remains of the fallen and recording burials (many of which were *ad hoc* and conducted under fire) was undertaken by a succession of units until the Imperial War Graves Commission (IWGC) was established in May 1917 under the leadership of Major-General Fabian Ware.[21] The IWGC worked tirelessly to provide a dignified resting place for those killed in as respectful a manner possible. By the end of the war over 150,000 scattered graves were known to exist over France and Belgium and a decision was made to move many of these remains to 'concentration cemeteries'. These often already existed particularly around first aid posts (Advanced Dressing or Casualty

Clearing Stations) and hospitals. Concentration cemeteries benefited from the economies of scale and provided a standard form of design recognizable to all. There was also the prescient awareness that because of the ban on repatriation large numbers of relatives would soon want to visit the graves of their loved ones. Concentration cemeteries make graves easier to find and provide an opportunity for an appropriate aesthetic and commemorative environment to be created for the bereaved. In December 1915 the French government gave Britain control over the future upkeep of its war graves in 'perpetuity of sepulture'.[22] By the end of 1921, 132 cemeteries in France and Belgium were complete.[23]

The design of the cemeteries, and thus the nature of the commemorative landscape that exists to this day, was decided upon at an early stage by the fledgling IWGC. A robust belief in uniformity underpinned all their operations; headstones were to be made of the same white-grey Portland limestone and indicate the name, rank, unit, date of death and age of the casualty along with a national emblem or regimental badge inscribed above an appropriate religious symbol. No details of the circumstances of death were allowed – perhaps for lack of space or to avoid courting controversy. The family of the casualty were allowed to add a personal dedication (66 letters maximum) and although they had to pay three and a half pence per letter the fee was later considered voluntary.[24] No concessions were given to rank and Generals lie next to Privates in the cemeteries of the Western Front.

The idea of consistency was also applied to the architectural design of the cemetery. All were encompassed by a low hedge or wall symbolizing protection and the shielding of the dead from the chaotic profanity of the surrounding 'battle-scape'. The wall also marks delineation, separating the 'community of the fallen' from those outside. A Cemetery Register book is contained within a metal cupboard which emphasizes the deference the IWGC gave to visitors from the inception of the cemeteries. Cemeteries with more than 40 burials have a Cross of Sacrifice, designed to imitate Celtic crosses found in many medieval churches, and the superlative symbol of self-sacrifice. Embedded in this structure is a bronze longsword, mirroring the shape of the cross, with its blade pointing downwards. Cemeteries with more than 1000 burials have a Stone of Remembrance upon which is inscribed "*Their Name Liveth for Evermore*".[25] The latter, unlike the Cross of Sacrifice, provides no particular religious symbolism commemorating those from all faiths or none. These architectural features have today become an integral part of the wider landscapes in which they are located.

Perhaps the most impressive aspect of the cemeteries is the preeminent place afforded horticulture in their design and construction. As early as July 1915 the importance of natural beauty in the way the cemeteries were landscaped was being acknowledged and gardening was introduced to make the cemeteries 'less miserable and unsightly'.[26] There was also a strong desire to depart from the rather depressing connotations of the word 'cemetery'[27] and to win civilians over to the controversial policy forbidding repatriation of bodies.[28] The idea was that plants should be chosen to give cemeteries the appearance and ambience of an English country garden; this would be symbolic of the land the dead had left behind and instantly comforting to the bereaved visiting the graves. It would also provide a harmonious natural environment useful in reflection and healing in that plants 'symbolize hope and regeneration'.[29] For both the living and the dead horticulture symbolizes the peace, emotional warmth and comfort of the homeland; such beautification is also the absolute antithesis of the ugliness of battle. To this day visiting a CWGC cemetery is an aesthetically pleasing experience sympathetic to the changes in the seasons and highly symbolic of the home country.[30] The IWGC cemeteries of the Western Front thus contain much that is culturally symbolic and stand in contrast aesthetically to their French and German counterparts.

Although considerable thought and effort went into the planning and design of the cemeteries they were plagued by controversy from the beginning. When visiting CWGC cemeteries today the level of angst involved in the creation of these poignant places is forgotten amongst their beauty and serenity. The policy of no repatriation of remains caused much added grief to relatives, many of whom attempted to defy the authorities by conducting their own exhumations.[31] This also raised painful questions about who owned the bodies of dead soldiers after they had enlisted. In addition the IWGC had been given total control over what was to be allowed into their cemeteries and decided to forbid the erection of permanent private memorials within their confines.[32] Partly this was to avoid a profusion of elaborate monuments and the inevitable contrast between well-off and poor this would generate. Consequently today the only private 'memorials' to the dead within the cemeteries are semi-permanent votive offerings comprising wreaths, wooden crosses, flags or photographs. The underlying rationale behind this decision was that although individuals had made worthy sacrifices, the collective 'community of sacrifice' was an altogether higher cause; the place for the individual memorial was at home.[33]

The cemeteries of the Western Front helped construct a tightly defined sacred landscape where, in the years immediately after the end of hostilities, certain memories were privileged over others. Death was couched in heroic terms, as reflected in symbolism and text, which suppressed any suggestion of mutiny, cowardice, non-sacrificial behaviour or war atrocities. Memory is framed in uniformity and symmetry marked by line upon line of headstones drawing the eye onward or names layered neatly and perfectly on the faces of the walls. The standardization of memory speaks of oneness in death, of simplicity and dignity, but also a martial sense of togetherness and comradeship.

War cemeteries are important locations for the perpetuation of memory amongst visitors, most of whom will be tourists, and visiting cemeteries is a common feature of any tour of the area.[34] Cemeteries are places where memory is recalled or rehearsed through expected and culturally defined forms of behaviour such as ritual performance.[35] They are also places where collective memory is dis-assembled into individual soldier biographies through the 'reading' of headstones. On the face of it the headstone says little about the experiences of war; but it can act as a highly effective 'memory trigger' or portal into an individual's circumstances in life and death. There is something deeply moving in passing these lines of names when one realizes that they were all human beings. But the encounter is given added significance when we are made aware of the men's biographies. These are often characterized by acts of bravery stimulating comparative responses ('what would it have been like for me if I was in that situation?') or perhaps knowledge of the particular circumstances of men's lives before the war. Memory is enriched when we understand the war on a personal level; that it was fought by very ordinary people from ordinary backgrounds.

Tourists choose which cemeteries to visit for many different reasons. Nationality plays a key role as with the war cemeteries belonging to Australia at Villers-Bretonneux, Canada at Vimy Ridge and South African at Delville Wood near Longueval. The involvement of family in the war is also important and tourists will visit those cemeteries where their ancestors lie or are commemorated.[36] Some cemeteries have iconic status for other reasons: Tyne Cot in Belgium is the largest CWGC cemetery in the world with 11,956 burials and the sheer number of headstones there is emblematic of the enormous mortality of the conflict. Others are visited as the last resting place of the youngest, oldest, first or last to be killed, VC winners, famous personalities, or where there is contention surrounding the identity of a burial.[37] The proximity of cemeteries to well-known battle sites is another important factor. What binds these elements together is the interest shown by a tourist industry keen to exploit the engaging narratives and sense of place such sites possess; tour coaches inevitably stop at noteworthy and accessible sites with many cemeteries having few visitors except from those willing to make the effort, often on foot, or who have a very special reason for finding them.

One consistent factor unites CWGC cemeteries: whether visited by the many or the few they are all immaculately cared for with an untiring level of devotion still active after nearly a century **(Figure 15)**.[38] This is a pattern sharply at odds with the commemorative nature of civilian cemeteries which represent the end of familial responsibility, generational attention and adherence to maintenance. As civilian cemeteries age so memory fades and atrophies towards possible de-consecration and decommissioning. With CWGC cemeteries this life-cycle is reversed as painstaking care and maintenance ensures graves do not deteriorate and names are not forgotten amongst the undergrowth. In addition new graves are rarely created and neither do the interred reflect the wide range of ages present in a civilian cemetery.[39] In contrast to the civilian cemetery – where the largest amount of visitation occurs in the period immediately following the burial and then tails-off – visits to graves on the Western Front are increasing by those who refuse to forget even a century after interment. The commemorative landscape is thus unique in providing a solid platform for remembrance, secure in its cultural identity, and strongly defined by tourism.

Memorials: the material expression of memory

If war cemeteries stand out so prominently along the Western Front then they are complemented by the hundreds of memorials dotting the landscape of various sizes and designs. As with the grim task of interment, the pressing need to erect memorials to the fallen in a newly sanctified setting produced an enormous challenge to the victorious nations. This was particularly the case with the highly sensitive problem of 'the missing' and how to provide an appropriate material focus for grief for those families who, it was now becoming evident, would never have a body to bury.

It was decided that every missing soldier of Britain's imperial forces would receive a permanent memorial. There were some who wanted the entire destroyed zone of the Western Front preserved as a memorial to the carnage; influential voices in the British establishment were suggesting that the town of Ypres, in rubble at the end of the war, should not be rebuilt but purchased from the Belgians and left as an eternal memorial to the conflagration. In January 1919 Winston Churchill asserted that 'a more sacred place for the British race does not exist in the world'.[40] These grand schemes, so implausible to our contemporary sensibilities, were eventually scrapped and the British settled for permission to build large scale memorials in Ypres and other places. The Commonwealth nations had plans to commemorate their losses in their own way. In addition to this Ex–Service organizations started to raise funds to build their own divisional, regimental or battalion memorials and individual families planned to build memorials to their menfolk who did not return from the Western Front.[41] Architecturally and commemoratively cemeteries can also be categorized as memorials and headstones are essentially small memorials in themselves. Memorials have been built ever since the end of the conflict and particularly since the 1970s; as the examples in Chapter 2 attest the Centenary has seen a growth in new memorials which have added to the region's rich commemorative landscape.

War memorialization is the public, material expression of loss in battle and is one focus for memory. Such memorials allow for a concentration of attention in order to honour an event or individual and are an arena for ritual and performance. They are an attempt 'by the living to create or reclaim some authentic sense of community with the dead'[42] and this was given a greater meaning after 1918 with the problem of the 'missing'. British memorials on the Western Front were 'designed and built on authentic feelings of pride and sorrow' to ensure the sacrifices of war were not forgotten by future generations.[43] Although the larger memorials of the Western Front were state sponsored with a determined public understanding of commemoration they also allowed for private meanings and expressions of grief. It is telling that the Latin root for 'monument' is 'something that reminds us';[44] this not only refers to the large nationalistic narratives of victory and sacrifice for 'king and country' but also the private memories of loved ones. A common feature of all memorials is that they hold not a singular message but are open to a range of differing interpretations which can change over time. The memorials of the Western Front rely strongly on artistic or pictorial images (iconography), prominent textual inscription (epigraphy) and a rich symbolic resonance to achieve their aim of providing meaning in the face of tragic loss.

The response from the governments who had led their populations into the maelstrom of world war was to build a number of enormous memorials at key places along the old front; this was to perpetuate the memory of the war and provide a focus for families to mourn the 'missing'. There are now 526,816 names listed on memorials to the missing but with no known graves.[45] The principal memorials to the missing on the Western Front are (number of names recorded in brackets): the Memorial to the Missing of the Somme at Thiepval (72,193); the Menin Gate Memorial to the Missing at Ypres (54,394); the Messines Ridge (New Zealand) Memorial (828); and the Tyne Cot Memorial to the Missing (34,949).[46]

Perhaps the most well-known of these, and the one that dominates the Picardy landscape so conspicuously, is the Thiepval Memorial (**Figure 16**). Designed by Sir Edwin Lutyens this monolithic structure was built between 1928 and 1932 and is actually an Anglo–French memorial, the arch symbolizing the alliance between the two nations in combatting Germany in the Somme area. Built on a ridge at the site of some of the fiercest fighting, its red brick and limestone walls can be seen from most parts of the territory fought over so savagely in the Battle of the Somme (1916).[47] It is thus designed to be a highly visible and enduring symbol of national loss. As with the Menin Gate the Thiepval Memorial is not religious and employs much classical imagery; it appears to be grandiose and triumphalist drawing the eye upwards in symbolic adoration rather than downwards in respectful veneration.[48] But a deeper appreciation has led some to interpret it as the very opposite: an expression of civilized optimism against the brutal totalitarian ideas of war.[49] It holds strong interest for modern tourism and is a compelling part of any itinerary of the region (a visitor centre was added in 2004). Nevertheless there is some debate as to whether it is a useful location to understand the battles which raged around it;[50] tourists might be drawn to its gigantic size and symbolic prominence rather than as a key site in interpreting the historical and tactical aspects of the landscape.

But therein lies its power. Approaching the huge piers one is struck by the true magnitude of the structure, not necessarily because of its size, but because of the vast quantities of names that appear on every panel. It is this uniformity and symmetry, an emotional nomenclature, which is so resonantly symbolic with those who visit the Front; line upon line of headstones drawing the eye onward or names layered perfectly on memorials. Row upon row, name upon name, there is a grim taxonomy about these walls, that someone has collected, arranged and categorized the dead meticulously in a vast roll of honour **(Figure 17)**. The lapidary care with which the names have been carved so neatly speaks symbolically as a text more powerfully than the spoken word which disappears into the ether as soon as it is uttered.

Inscribed words, in their material permanence, are there to stay. Like headstones, the martial order of names by regiment and rank keeps alive the security of comradeship that was these men's last emotional fellowship on earth; it also maintains their sense of family, not their kinship, but the newly acquired 'band of brothers' who they now lie alongside if not in body then in name. Because it is the *name* and its association with memory, particularly of the missing, that acts so powerfully here.[51] Names give us identity and individuality; they are part of our persona and mark out our distinctive nature from those around us. It is hugely significant that when a war landscape returns to cultivation, the detritus of combat mostly disappears, and memory fades, then it is the name that endures.

This is again brought out starkly with the intensely moving reading of the names and ages of the dead by British schoolchildren at the Tyne Cot Cemetery Visitor Centre near Ypres. This recording is played continually in the background as visitors view the exhibition containing many artifacts and highly moving letters 'from the front'. It is a form of incantation, mirroring religious funerary rituals, which aids the deceased on their journey to the spirit world and binds the community closer together through common participation.[52] At Tyne Cot it is given added significance in that all these names were real people now buried only metres away. The Western Front is, in essence, an emotional geography defined most potently by the name.

A contemporary criticism of war memorialization is the way it sanitizes war; memorials never speak of the underlying social inequalities in armies or the sheer grotesque indignity of violent death. Whilst choosing a text for the Great Stone in CWGC cemeteries the suggested 'They Lie in Peace' was shelved in fear of some disgruntled veteran changing 'Peace' to 'Pieces'.[53] These clinically designed landscapes of grief came under increased scrutiny at the start of the Centenary in Britain when there was a call for a more gritty approach to commemorating the war. Commenting on the Tower of London's tribute to the war when ceramic poppies, one for every death among allied forces, were placed in the moat, one journalist commented that 'an adequate work of art about the war has to show its horror, not sweeping the grisly facts under a red carpet of artificial flowers'.[54]

Anglo-Saxon memorialization of the war on the Western Front is neat, aestheticized and culturally acceptable. There is no comparison with the French realism in dealing with human remains as at the Douaumont Ossuary near Verdun where the bones of the dead are clearly visible through windows at the base of the structure. Ours is a typically safe approach to commemoration and this has governed the way we have helped construct a commemorative landscape. Nevertheless when interpreting the Western Front one cannot escape from the uncomfortable, perhaps heretical, thought that there is much hidden guilt in these state-funded memorials, their makers 'seeking absolution through accountancy',[55] and shying away from any sense of realism entirely.

Memorials provoke a range of different responses in their viewers depending on various factors. A memorial to French losses in the war will clearly mean more to a French national than someone from another nationality; this is determined largely by culturally specific factors including language, iconography and symbolism. One of the most intriguing questions about memorials is whether they have any meaning apart from what humans bestow upon them? Do memorials have a unified message which exists outside of human interpretation or are they subject solely to the different ways that they are 'read'? This leads to the tricky metaphysical question: would it be a memorial if no-one visited it? The memorials built after the war utilized an array of symbolism that was particular to the time in which it was understood; it is doubtful now if we are truly able to 'read' these memorials in the way they were intended when constructed. Nevertheless if memorials have no meaning for the viewer then paradoxically this can be interpreted as a 'meaning' in itself. It is because memorials are so open to differing interpretations over time and between groups and individuals that the assertion is made here that they are only understood through a human lens; war memorials, like the landscapes in which they reside, are entirely socially constructed.

Ceremonies, rituals and performances

Places are a vitally important aspect of preserving and shaping communal memory. But allied to this is society's need for ritual performance in maintaining continuity with the past and ensuring it is not forgotten. Rituals are a key component in the formulation of communal memory and their importance is greatly enhanced when past events are marked by trauma and suffering, as in war. Through ritualized ceremonies the 'community of grief' is brought together in a unity of purpose which can also have strong nationalistic overtones.

Both private and public ceremonies are a constant presence along the Western Front. Today these take place during private visits to graves and at places connected to individual deaths, actions of regiments or particular battles. But the most prominent regular ceremony is the sounding of the Last Post at the Menin Gate in Ypres (as we have seen).[56] This ceremony is a powerful commemorative event, and has become a major draw for visitors, due to its use of the three essential strands of repetition: calendrical (the event is held every night at the same time); verbal (the same formula is used in the performance); and gestural (e.g. the playing of the Last Post).[57] Repetition is an important and necessary part of any ritual as it reinforces memory. During these ceremonies the memorial space temporarily becomes sacred subject to the culturally sanctioned behaviour of those who share it. This gives it a hallowed nature. Although there are no overt religious overtones to a ceremony like the Menin Gate the rubric does borrow many aspects of religious ritual: an expectation of silence; the use of performative utterances ('At the going down of the sun and in the morning, we will remember them'); sacral acts (the lowering of flags); and public gestures (bowing of heads as a mark of respect). Silence is a powerful aspect of commemoration serving to concentrate thoughts and emotions on the magnitude of loss. It is 'an active carrier of memory'[58] and 'the ultimate response to enormity ... outwith [outside of] language and beyond human expression'.[59] Where language cannot convey grief then silence can. During silence there is an intensity of feeling and perception; the names on the panels of the Menin Gate attain greater meaning as participants express their mute solidarity with them.

Ceremonies have no pre-ordained script and attendees will have been made familiar with the elements of the ritual from their own cultural background. They will have been 'habituated' to the culturally specific phrases, music, gestures and behavioural expectations which are grounded in Western Christian military tradition but also have civilian elements. Nevertheless these expectations are increasingly challenged by behavioural practices brought to ceremonies by the public like applause which is now actively discouraged at the Menin Gate ceremony.[60] Like all ceremonies commemorative events have their custodians, the committees who organise the events; these are 'memory gatekeepers' powerful in crafting a particular form of memory and disallowing those interpretations which conflict with the dominant 'narrative'.[61] At the Menin Gate, the Last Post Association determines the nature and content of the ceremony and those wanting to recite a poem or lay a wreath need to ask their permission.

Anniversaries provide an importance focus for commemoration. Every year since 1919 Armistice Day[62] has been held on November 11 and provides a special concentration and enhancement of memory for those who died in all wars, not just the Great War. Nevertheless, cardinal numbers in 10s or 100s capture our imagination far more than others and a centenary, for example, provides a once in a lifetime opportunity to commemorate the past.[63] The First World War Centenary will magnify the memory of the various anniversaries on the Western Front accompanied by ceremonies which will perpetuate memory in highly public ways.

It is important to recognize that ceremonies are performances: the set ritual ordained by the organizers is 'acted-out' but the participation and co-operation of the attendees is also a performance. It is a two-way process; participants are not a passive audience but active in their engagement with commemoration. Memory is perpetuated and new memories are created by human agency and this requires a commitment from attendees as well as organizers.

The politics of a commemorative landscape

The creation of cemeteries and memorials by the British government via the CWGC and various memorial committees demonstrates the central place taken by the state in the war's commemoration. Memorials were built to help the bereaved come to terms with their loss, but the overriding commemorative ethos in the years immediately after the war was that a great national victory had been achieved. The dominant elite decided what was to be built, where, and how. In tandem with this a set of official narratives was established which allowed no space for the idea that the carnage had been wasteful or futile. Prominent among these was the need to highlight the sacrifice of the nation and provide a material and ceremonial focus for the idea of an 'imagined community' united in grief.[64] But such top-down narratives frequently marginalize or repress alternatives and silence individual memories; they try to organise private grief around state sanctioned narratives and places.[65] The diverse range of individual and group memories of war, however, provided a strong undercurrent beneath the official narrative (as evidenced by the furore over the repatriation ban) and a variety of memories continued to be recalled after the war.

One of the most controversial of these was any attempt to link the sacrifices of the war to a peace message. Peace was not a central part of British commemoration because the country considered the war lawful and the fallen to have died officially for a noble cause. A peace message would diminish this and the CWGC consistently opposed any 'political recuperation' of commemoration.[66] This is in spite of the remark made by King George V while visiting the Flanders cemeteries in 1922:

> I have many times asked myself whether there can be more potent advocates of peace upon earth through the years to come, than this massed multitude of silent witnesses to the desolation of war.[67]

Memorials to peace are not a prominent part of the Western Front landscape. An exception to this is the Island of Ireland Peace Park near Messines, built by An All-Ireland Journey of Reconciliation Trust, and opened in 1998. This is a memorial to both Irish Republican and Loyalist soldiers who fought together in the war. The lack of a visible peace message is despite a recent poll in the UK where 87% of the public wanted a centenary focused on peace[68] and the presence of peace memorials in the UK.[69] Additionally Ypres has been recognised as a 'City of Peace' and seat of the *Mayors for Peace* international organization.[70] A peace message is central to the Government of Flanders Great War Centenary commemorations to spread 'awareness of themes such as tolerance, intercultural dialogue, and international understanding'.[71] 'Peace Tourism' is integral to this although some doubt has been expressed as to whether this will attract tourists in the same way as a narrative of war is able to do.[72]

State-sponsored commemoration upholds certain privileged narratives and in doing so suppresses or ignores others; it is important for us to acknowledge, therefore, that to remember is also to forget.[73] To build a memorial is to forget as the commemorative attention is drawn towards a particular interpretation at the expense of others. It raises questions about who 'owns' memory and what 'sites of memory' are worthy of preservation and commemoration.[74] The Western Front is a political landscape, but also one of amnesia.

* * *

In 1920, as the first of the great 'silent cities' were being completed, Winston Churchill exclaimed in a House of Commons debate: '... there is no reason at all why, in periods as remote from our own as we ourselves are from the Tudors, the graveyards in France of this Great War shall not remain an abiding and supreme memorial to the efforts and the glory of the British Army, and the sacrifices made in the great cause'.[75] This was a bold statement and predicted that commemoration was immutable and enduring. Nevertheless in 1995 the historian Jay Winter was to predict the 'trajectory of decomposition' of war memorials which by then had already 'become artifacts of a vanished age'.[76] But the landscape has not been devoid of meaning over the last two decades; meanings have changed as the fighting generation has disappeared and their descendants attach new meanings to this 'commemorative-scape'. These are meanings that Churchill might not now recognize, formed by contemporary concerns and the renewed impetus to 'keep alive' a memory within a landscape fashioned for commemoration in the raw aftermath of loss. The Western Front continues as a *mise en scène* for an active contemporary commemorative culture, solemnizing and sustaining the names of those who Binyon, in his *For the Fallen*, never wanted the years to condemn.

Chapter 5

A Heritage Landscape

Heritage is what we have inherited from our past. It is not what happened in the past – that is history – but what has survived from the past. It is also what we in the present decide to make of it and is important in modern society because it provides identity, significance and meaning. Although backward looking, the true nature of heritage is in the here and now. Essentially, '… heritage is no longer about the past but draws on the power of the past to produce the present and shape the future'.[1] Heritage is the past infused with present purpose; it is largely determined by the values and needs of the time especially since it involves a process of selection of what actually is valued as heritage. Consequently heritage is highly political and open to argument. It also privileges a past which we hold in affection as a better time than our own, one of simplicity and virtue, not vice.

This is, of course, far from the truth but just like commemoration we prefer a sanitised view of the past ignoring its gritty realities and contingencies. In a world subject to constant change we reach for security and a secure anchor in the past; because what has gone before has already happened it cannot be altered and this provides an attractive refuge for our minds and imaginations. Heritage allows tourists to 'mourn worlds known to be irrevocably lost – yet more vividly felt, more lucid, more real than the murky and ambiguous present.'[2] Much interest in the Great War reflects this harking back to a more pure era and a nostalgia for an 'age of innocence' where old values persisted; but with the tumult of war, courage, honour and virtue were replaced with cynicism and veiled disillusionment.[3] Heritage, as the present day use of the past, is an important component of British national understanding and appreciation of the war.

What is a heritage landscape?

The Great War is understood in a number of different ways but it is the landscape that provides the most intimate and instructive 'textbook' for interpretation. No amount of reading or watching TV documentaries can substitute for the experience of visiting the places of battle. The Western Front is many things to many people; as such it takes on the common features of all landscapes in that they have myriad meanings (polysemic) and speak to people in different ways. A farmer in modern Flanders, for example, will have a different relationship with the land from a tourist, valuing it as an agro-economic resource rather than a place to be visited for personal or national memory. Local planning authorities in the region will view the landscape as a resource to be exploited for other purposes – perhaps for renewable energy or road construction – with a particular economic development agenda. These different perspectives will inevitably lead to conflict. But to the modern countries whose populations fought there, the Western Front is sacred ground and highly symbolic of the extremes of human experience.[4] Commemoration is one way of appreciating this landscape, another layer in the palimpsest; but another is the wealth of material heritage that lies above and below the surface.

The war heritage of the Western Front can be regarded as either tangible or intangible. Applied to the modern Front *tangible* heritage is the inherited material remains, such as cemeteries, memorials, buildings, dugouts, bunkers and the detritus of war such as pieces of shrapnel and ordnance. Moreover *tangible* can be further divided into *movable* (like museum artefacts and paintings) and *immoveable* heritage (such as buildings and memorials). *Intangible* heritage includes festivals, stories, music, oral testimony, vocabulary and ceremonial practices. This chapter will focus on the tangible although it is acknowledged that many forms of intangible heritage are connected with the landscape; additionally, representation of the Western Front through such media as art, photography, film and maps is a vast subject in itself and is not discussed here.

Whilst the tangible places and objects of war exist as material evidence of the conflict they have no value in *themselves* and 'nor do they carry a freight of innate meaning'.[5] Just as landscapes are socially constructed so places and objects are given value and meaning – and thus defined as 'heritage' – by the cultural attention they receive and the activities that are undertaken around them. Tourism is one of these activities. The austere concrete German pillboxes near the New Zealand Memorial at Messines **(Figure 18)**, for example, have been identified as heritage worthy of preservation. They have stories, and are described and explained in books, guidebooks, leaflets and by tour guides in the narrative surrounding the Battle of Messines (June 1917). Their heritage is significant for New Zealand in that they mark a key point in the opening of the battle when their forces attacked these strongpoints. These features have been 'valorised' and protected because they are part of someone's heritage. Thus 'heritage is heritage *because* it is subject to the management and preservation/conservation process, not because it simply *is*'.[6] This suggests that all heritage is *intangible* in that it becomes heritage only when given value by others. It is noteworthy how the material heritage of the Western Front has experienced different levels of importance reaching an all-time nadir in the 1950s (when tourism was also at a low point) before gaining in importance as those who fought in the war gradually passed on and new forms of memory were being sought (Chapter 2). An additional consideration regarding the importance of heritage relates to its economic value; as visiting the scenes of the war increases in popularity so then does the need to revive, preserve and maintain its heritage 'resources'.[7] Prosaically, much heritage is valorised due to its inherent and shifting economic value in a cultural heritage tourism industry.

The material heritage of the Western Front was created through one of the largest episodes of belligerent construction in modern history. Despite the poet Siegfried Sassoon's belief that 'the war was mainly a matter of holes and ditches'[8] trenches were only part of a massive system of defences that spanned the 460-mile Front; accompanying them was a complicated series of fortifications, blockhouses, redoubts, dug-outs, fortified villages and tunnels that required immense and ongoing constructional effort. This was building on a Pharaonic scale, using numerous labour battalions and ordinary soldiers undertaking unpopular fatigue duties; one writer has commented, rather mischievously, that war is the 'continuation of labour by other means'.[9] Because the Germans started to dig-in first they chose the higher ground and were able to build elaborate subterranean defences which served them well. Most British efforts to shell them from their positions, as in the prelude to the Battle of the Somme (1916), were ineffective. This also meant that British defences were relegated to lower-lying and strategically disadvantageous areas; British trenches in waterlogged depressions created the myth of cloying gelatinous mud. The trench systems, however, are what have always been central to British cultural memory of the Western Front.[10] The Allies had 12,000 miles (19,000 km) of trenches (half British) and the Central Powers a further 13,000 miles (21,000 km) (the total enough to circle the earth);[11] in France alone there were 330 million cubic metres (432 million cubic yards) of trenches.[12] For those serving in the forward areas trench life became emblematic of the war experience even though war embraced other tactical dimensions and geographical arenas.[13]

But where are the trenches, fortifications and structures of the war along the modern Western Front? An awareness of this massive effort and the sheer scale of building work leaves the modern visitor rather disappointed; travelling through the region now there are relatively few traces of this enormous endeavour. Much was destroyed during the war and subject to regular recycling (salvaging) of material, a practice which continued in earnest immediately after the Armistice. In both Belgium and France great efforts were made to restore the land to its former economic and communal condition after the war: farmers filled in trenches and buried dug-outs and other subterranean features; weapons and ordnance was removed or buried (much to the delight of modern archaeologists); fortifications dismantled or blown up; woodland replanted; and towns and villages rebuilt.[14] In this process much war *matériel* and building debris was re-used. This process has continued to this day and much of the material legacy of the war has suffered from ploughing and movement of soil, neglect, decay, recycling, 'souveneering' and uncontrolled destruction in the face of progress. Consequently the Western Front is a denuded landscape; for the modern visitor it is relatively unprepossessing, requiring much decoding and interpretation.

Nevertheless a war heritage does exist, if often indistinct and fading, in both urban and rural areas. **Appendix 6** provides a categorisation of Western Front tangible heritage. The inclusion of commemorative sites demonstrates how there is an overlap between heritage and commemorative landscapes and cemeteries and memorials are just as much 'heritage' as they are spaces of remembrance even though this was not the intention when they were built. The war construction mentioned above generated its own built heritage and what survives is now of vital importance to our understanding of the conflict. Buildings caught up in the fighting also have a hugely important modern resonance particularly those which were damaged; the medieval Cloth Hall (*Lakenhal*) in Ypres, for example, was virtually destroyed but painstakingly restored to its pre-war appearance between 1933 and 1967. Despite using some of the original stonework in the reconstruction the Cloth Hall is really a facsimile of the original, a restorative approach adopted with other buildings (e.g. the Albert Basilica). Some villages were so completely destroyed that they were re-built entirely (e.g. Passchendaele) but in other cases villages were left in their ruined state as stark civic *memento mori*.[15] These approaches raise interesting questions about authenticity which I will turn to later.

Other significant objects include wayside calvaries which formed part of battle folklore – places were often referred to as 'Crucifix Corner'.[16] The Western Front contains many important places: some attained iconic significance during the war (as with Talbot House in Poperinghe where British troops enjoyed a quiet respite behind the lines[17]); others were associated with famous people well known in British society before, during, or after the war; and others were connected with events. The area also contains memorial landscapes protected to honour the sacrifices of those who fought in them like the Newfoundland Battlefield and Memorial on the Somme owned by the Government of Canada.[18] Other iconic 'battle-scapes' include the Sunken Lane near Beaumont-Hamel immortalised in the film-footage of Geoffrey Malins.[19] A more conceptual form of heritage is flowers which have cultural significance because of the events of the war; the poppy is as much part of British and Commonwealth heritage as the Menin Gate or Tyne Cot Cemetery.[20] Finally, artefacts, in both public and private collections, are included here in that they are an integral part of the war's heritage and often have deeply held personal value and meanings.

Selective heritage

Heritage by its very nature is selective, determined as much by what someone else deems worthy of value as by the opportunities that present themselves to 'mark' heritage. Places that are iconic in a nation's collective consciousness will maintain a prominent cultural position but this does not necessarily mean they will be accessible to a public desiring to visit them. One of the reasons the Western Front was enshrined within the British national narrative so firmly was because it was relatively easy to visit (for those who could afford it) and this remains an important factor today; this is unlike other areas where British and Commonwealth forces fought such as Gallipoli, Italy, and the Middle East.

On a more local level many of the heritage sites on the modern Western Front are popular due to their accessibility to tourists: the Lochnagar crater near La Boisselle, caused by an enormous mine explosion under German lines on 1 July 1916, is a notable example being near to the large town of Albert and major road links **(Figure 19)**. Other large craters caused by mine explosions like *Spanbroekmolen* (the Pool of Peace) and those around what the British called 'Factory Farm' near Ploegsteert Wood[21] in Belgium were no less significant in the war but get a fraction of the visitors that come to Lochnagar due to their relative remoteness. Furthermore many bunkers and other war-related sites lie on private land;[22] others require special permission and are not so widely known (perhaps deliberately to maintain their exclusive 'aura' and economic value); and others still may be in dense woodland or marshy ground.

The heritage that we experience is thus a selection of what has survived and what has been considered worthy of protection, preservation and development. From a heritage perspective these *lieux de mémoire* should be seen as representing a much larger material heritage but one that is nevertheless given special value. Instrumental in this is the power of tourism; however this is a complex two-way process with tourism endowing places with significance while at the same time places being created to attract tourists. The surviving heritage of the war on the Western Front is, moreover, largely governed by national identities: the Somme and the Ypres Salient are immensely important in British and Commonwealth culture but the area north of Ypres is more so for Belgium,[23] as is Verdun for France.

Heritage is not only determined by what is given value but also by what period of time is considered worthy of preservation. Despite our insatiable appetite for the past it is impossible to preserve it all and 'the sheer pastness of the past precludes its total reconstruction'.[24] A judgement has to made about what is to be privileged; warfare provides particular challenges for this as battles or actions lasting only short periods of time become folklore, while others disappear almost completely. A prime example of this is the Newfoundland Battlefield and Memorial on the Somme, where a nationally important landscape is maintained as it was thought to have been at a particular moment in time. On the first day of the Battle of the Somme, 1 July 1916 –between 0915 hrs and 0945 hrs – the Royal Newfoundland Regiment attacked down a slope exposed to withering fire from German machine guns; it was a tragic and costly failure resulting in 90 per cent casualties. In memory of this event a 40-acre (16.5-hectare) tract of land was purchased after the war by the Newfoundland Government from 250 farmers and the Park opened in 1925.[25] But this preserved land commemorates only a 30-minute action in a 50-month war and ignores traces of later battles fought over the area as well as its importance to soldiers who occupied it before 1 July (notably the South Wales Borderers and Border Regiment). It is also another example of the way Allied combatant nations privileged the Battle of the Somme above other actions during the war.

Personal heritage: a family, a field and a bunker

Interest in family involvement in the war is a key aspect of private heritage and fuels much of the tourist attention in the Western Front. As second generations move to the third, there is a keen public appetite to commemorate their forebears.[26] But alongside this families want to visit the places where their relatives fought and died, and a first-hand engagement with the landscape is a form of commemoration in itself. I gained a close appreciation of how much the battle landscape meant to the personal heritage of one family when I joined them in search of a place connected with the war story of a relative.

In 2010 I was staying at a Bed and Breakfast near Ypres owned by a battlefield guide. Also there was a man in his 60s, with his wife and son, who had come to trace events in the story of the man's late father, an infantryman in a British regiment. This was their first visit to the Western Front, full of keen anticipation and the excitement of discovery, and the trip was really a pilgrimage. The family had undertaken a lot of research before leaving home and facsimiles of the father's war records and Regimental diaries lay on the dining table. The soldier had been wounded near Polygon Wood, to the north of the Menin Road, in an early phase of the Third Battle of Ypres (26 September – 3 October 1917). The details of the attack were well known to this family, the man having described his experiences to them, and the story was supported by the documents. Amongst these were telegrams to the man's mother informing her that he was missing, while others from the Red Cross said he was alive and in a prisoner of war camp; another document was a bill to the family for his Red Cross parcel. The battlefield guide had also undertaken some research and knew where the place was. They allowed me to join them.

The next day we arrived at a ploughed field just off the Menin Road and pored over battlefield maps. The soldier said he had been ordered to advance towards a wood and there in front of us lay Polygon Wood which had been dominated by strong German positions. As we stood there the soldier's son completed the story: on moving forwards machine gun bullets had traversed the line and his father was hit several times across the groin and brought down. He lay there for some time, badly wounded, before a German patrol spotted him and took him away. He was taken to a nearby German Field Dressing Station and, in the words of his son, was lucky he hadn't been taken in by the British or 'I wouldn't be here to tell you this'. The Germans treated him and he was then evacuated as a prisoner of war being re-united with his family at the end of the conflict. His grandson remarked that the injuries had affected his grandfather for the rest of his life.

We stood there in the sunshine in what was a poignant and emotional moment for the family. A story so long recounted was now made complete by at last standing where it had happened. On hearing about the man's medical care the guide pointed out a house nearby under which lay a German bunker used as a first aid post called Cryer Farm. The soldier had said that the Germans hadn't taken him far and we realised that this might be the place. The descent into this dark and damp subterranean shelter provided a new dimension to the story and an overwhelming sense of connection with their father and grandfather; could this have been the place where his life was saved? Of course there was never any certainty; but the sense of place was intense and poignant.

The family were deeply and profoundly moved and their emotions revealed the importance of place in private family heritage. For them the landscape had provided a powerful link with their family history; places of only historic interest to others were for them charged with intense meaning. This family were fortunate to be armed with accurate documentary and oral evidence; not all investigations are like this. Nevertheless the Western Front has been saturated by thousands of such stories and continues to affect descendants long after the events have passed into history; the landscape is a richly woven tapestry of emotional encounters as families discover new connections with their ancestors. As an outsider I, too, could not avoid being affected by this experience; because travelling along the Western Front is also to be a witness to other people's engagement with the area and to gain an insight into their feelings and emotions.

Orphaned heritage

The experience of Britain and Commonwealth countries on the Western Front left an indelible mark on their national consciousness which remains to this day. The area has become an integral part of an 'imagined community' of the nation where people consider themselves to be part of a group even though they do not have face-to-face communication with each other.[27] This is particularly relevant for Australia and New Zealand where the Great War has always been interpreted in the political context of the forging of nationhood. The Western Front is engraved so deeply on national consciousness precisely because it was bought dearly with the nation's blood; the fact that the dead lay buried 'in a corner of a foreign field' gives the area greater validity. Alongside national pride in the area reside the many private memories of the war and of ancestors who fought it; the Western Front resonates with national and private heritage and provides identity for both.

Such ideas were being expressed even during the war as one soldier described the land as 'part of Britain, to be defended'.[28] This was clearly expressed in the way British soldiers began naming features and trenches in their own language and by places familiar to them at home. Trench maps of the region are saturated with familiar sounding names like Owl Trench, Mud Corner and Railway Hollow and many of these were later used for CWGC cemeteries.[29] Then there are the places and street names, so soothingly familiar to our ears but to those who fought provoking even stronger memories resonant of home: The Strand, Piccadilly Circus, Haymarket, Marlborough Trench and Fleet Street. These rarely appear on local maps of the area but are included in guidebooks and remain common parlance amongst guides. However, English names of CWGC cemeteries and memorials do appear on signposts to aid modern tourists in their navigation around the area. In addition to this was the manner in which British soldiers humorously changed the names of places they found difficult to pronounce: Ypres or Ieper became 'Wipers'; Etaples 'Eatables' or 'Eat-apples'; Delville Wood 'Devil's Wood'; Auchonvillers 'Ocean Villas'; and Foncquevillers 'Funky Villas'.[30]

This use of nomenclature to culturally refashion a landscape shows how endearing homeland and language was to British soldiers in the trenches; but it also reflects the way the landscape was entering the national psyche and becoming part of the heritage of the nation. Indeed today there is a palpable 'sense of British appropriation and ownership'[31] of the Western Front. This is expressed through tourism particularly to Ypres which remains Britain's 'Great War town'. It is also demonstrated at British government level by the All Party Parliamentary War Graves and Battlefields Heritage Group who seek to promote and conserve war heritage including that of the Great War along the Western Front.[32] But it is perhaps best exemplified by an inscription at one trench, now a cemetery, on the Somme which says, 'The Devonshires held this trench; the Devonshires hold it still'.

This gives rise to the idea of 'orphaned' heritage where what is perceived to be heritage valued by one population is located on the sovereign territory of another.[33] War, and the aftermath of war, is a common reason for this. The 'owning country' can have a variety of responses ranging from being co-operative to completely disinterested, destructive, or not enacting any form of protective legislation for this heritage which they might not see as 'theirs'. 'Orphaned' heritage can also create tensions between those wanting to visit sensitive war-related heritage and the population of the host nation.[34] Although much built heritage was destroyed after the war along the Western Front the principal reasons for its disappearance were economic (returning urban and rural landscapes to their pre-war situation and productivity). At the same time land was being gifted by the French and Belgian nations to form cemeteries and permission granted to Allied nations to build memorials on their soil. In other cases land was sold to other nations as commemorative space (as at the Newfoundland Memorial Park) and in time several ex-patriots from Britain moved to the area to set up hotels and, more recently, tour-guiding businesses. But apart from these measures the war heritage of ex-combatant countries on the Western Front is owned by another sovereign state. What is advantageous to the host nation, however, is that because foreign nationals are interested in this heritage there are opportunities to develop a tourism industry around it. Because of tourism it is unwise to destroy or neglect this heritage; sites are more likely to be preserved when they are of interest to 'non-local stakeholders'[35] who are particularly vociferous in their opposition to developments which threaten 'their' own heritage.

One of the key questions arising from the value attached to heritage is 'whose heritage is it'? If lying on foreign soil is it the heritage of the owning nation or those who attach the greatest value to it? In the case of built heritage is it the heritage of those who constructed it? There are many examples where these questions are topical along the Western Front today. Several strongpoints were put in place by both sides (more building was undertaken by the Germans) but are less important to those who built and defended them than those who later captured them; the loss of life in securing such strongpoints gives them special significance. The New Zealand Memorial site, mentioned above, shows how a structure built by one nation (Germany) can be re-appropriated by another (New Zealand) on another's soil (Belgium).

The way territory changed hands so frequently complicates the modern heritage of the region considerably. An example of this is the pillboxes at Hill 60 near Ypres which were originally German but later taken over and modified by Australian forces. A further example is the Butte de Warlencourt, an ancient burial mound some 20 metres high, near Pozières. Because of its height above the surrounding land this feature attracted the attention of British attacks and was only taken when its German occupiers withdrew in 1917. It changed hands many times, actually being used as a memorial while fighting continued, and is now owned by the British Western Front Association **(Figure 20)**.[36] Sometimes the heritage of one nation is dramatically incorporated into that of another: at Tyne Cot Cemetery German blockhouses, captured by Australian units, are now architecturally grafted into the commemorative landscape, one of them forming the base for the Cross of Sacrifice. These examples demonstrate how some places can be 'valorised' by different interest groups and this is what provokes so many arguments and disputes concerning heritage. With war heritage the victors who take possession of the ground after conflict are normally in a position to attach their own meaning to sites and this was clearly the case after the Great War. In the ignominy of defeat little value was attached to Western Front material heritage by Germany apart from a temporary revaluation by the Nazis during the Second World War (see Chapter 2).

The value the Western Front has for the British is emphasised by numerous examples of sites being bought by British nationals as a means of preservation in perpetuity. In 1978 the Briton Richard Dunning bought the Lochnagar Crater near La Boisselle on the Somme **(Figure 19)** from the local landowner. At around 300ft (91m) in diameter and 70ft (21m) deep this enormous hole in the Picardy landscape was caused by a massive mine explosion under German lines at 0728 hrs on 1 July 1916, the first day of the Battle of the Somme. The largest of the mine craters along the Front, it is thought to have been the largest man-made explosion up to that point. Scores of Germans were killed and the site, in addition to being an important part of British war heritage, is also a war grave. By the 1970s the crater was being used as a rubbish tip and for motocross, and the fear was that the crater would be filled in, a fate which had befallen its sister mine nearby, known as the Y Sap. Although owned by a British national Lochnagar is preserved as a memorial to all who died in the conflict.[37] Other examples have included land bought for preservation but also to provide educational interpretation: in 2003 the Northern Ireland-based Somme Association bought Thiepval Wood and have conducted a series of war-orientated archaeological investigations within it **(Figure 21)**.[38]

The purchase of the Lochnagar Crater demonstrates how afraid we are that our heritage will be lost, particularly if it is 'orphaned'. Situated on another nation's sovereign territory, tangible heritage can be subject to unsympathetic legislation, lack of resources for preservation, or the fickle attitudes of landowners. Nevertheless the belief that Western Front heritage is the preserve of only one nation is to misunderstand the nature of the conflict; over 50 nations sent troops to fight in the area and the Front was never manned by soldiers from any one nation for the entire duration of the war. Different nations, groups and even individuals therefore have the potential to lay claim to this heritage. It is perhaps more appropriate to view the heritage of the area as belonging to a plurality of interests and valued as 'supranational or transnational'.[39] Both Belgian and French governments are currently negotiating for the Western Front to be designated a World Heritage Site to recognise the heritage of a range of people from around the world who fought in the area – a process which itself is much contested.

Reconstruction and exactitude: issues of authenticity

Much of the built heritage of the Western Front which has survived or later has been recovered is left untouched; shrapnel sprayed walls, shell-damaged bunkers or pocked marked cratered landscapes are graphic reminders of conflict. On a raw level these places need little explanation and speak powerfully of the destructive force of modern industrialised warfare. Just as ruins stimulate the viewer to imagine what a building would have been like, so the evidence of destruction can help to recreate the chaotic circumstances of war. But just as ruined buildings from the past are reconstructed or rebuilt in their previous image, so the heritage of the Western Front is subject to transformation to satisfy contemporary expectations. We want to experience the past as it was, to make it more comprehensible, but also to validate it. The past is frequently inadequate for our needs, lacking sufficient evidence or realism for modern requirements; we want more than what has been left behind. So we often add to our past, augmenting and refashioning it into what we think it should be.[40] A modern heritage industry demands this but also infuses new vitality into moribund places and objects; by reconstructing the past we also give it a second life.[41]

The Western Front has many examples of trench systems, bunkers and entire landscapes that have been preserved or re-created. One of the problems with the physical legacy of the conflict is that because of post-war reconstruction, trench systems and fortifications in open farmland were vigorously removed and ploughed over; much of what is left today is in woodland or areas that would otherwise have been unsuitable for crops. Often the sole evidence we have for old trench lines is the change in colour of the soil across the landscape visible only at certain times of the year, and, most notably, from the air.[42]

Reconstructions are a good way of presenting trenches to a public who are familiar with this type of warfare. At the Memorial Museum Passchendaele 1917 in Zonnebeke a series of reconstructed trenches has been built outside the museum giving the visitor a flavour of trench construction. The 'Trench Experience' has used archaeological, photographic and documentary evidence to reconstruct a series of German and British trenches and shelters with accompanying interpretation panels. The trenches were constructed in a form of 'experimental archaeology' using the same methods of construction employed during the war and often with materials salvaged from excavations of these structures; a German Heinrich Wooden Shelter (1916–17), for example, has been built using the original corrugated steel plates within which are shell fragment impact scars **(Figure 22)**. Another example is at Bayernwald (Bavarian Wood) at Wijtschate near Ypres which has a 300-metre line of restored trench and four German bunkers. It also includes a restoration of 300,000 woven wickerwork branches used to line the trenches (see back cover image).[43]

The underground war is another aspect that has been reconstructed and opened to the public. As the war progressed the area around Zonnebeke near Ypres was so heavily shelled that by the end of 1917 any above-ground protection had been removed; this prompted the British to construct numerous deep subterranean dugouts. Closed up after the war these features have now been given renewed life as they attract interest from archaeologists. In 1983 the underground Bremen Redoubt was excavated at a nearby brickworks and this was open to the public until 1998. Another was discovered under Zonnebeke church and another – the Beecham Dugout – uncovered in the grounds of a local farmhouse.[44] These are important because the subterranean war has captured the imagination of the British public and others. But there are clear problems in opening up such features to the public: the danger of collapse and flooding raises serious questions of health and safety and the need to invest heavily to convert these features for public use would inevitably make any such enterprises economically unviable. For this reason the Memorial Museum Passchendaele 1917 has opened a 'Dugout Experience'. Built seven metres down into the floors of the château (rebuilt 1924) housing the museum this is a reconstruction of a deep dug-out comprising sleeping accommodation, latrines, communication and dressing posts, and headquarters.

After the war, preservation of entire battle landscapes was undertaken to provide a focus for memory and to maintain the 'sacred' landscape in perpetuity. The Canadian Government led the way with the purchase of eight memorial sites (three in Belgium and five in France) reflecting the idea that the war landscape is a poignant memorial in itself. Nevertheless any attempt to preserve the events of battle is likely to court controversy. The privileging of one event of the war at the Newfoundland Memorial Park has been mentioned but the remodelling of this landscape has created other controversies.[45] The Park has been subjected to two major modifications (1922 and 1960) to create a national memorial and preserve a landscape as it would have been on 1 July 1916. This has included the planting of trees – even though there would have been none during the war- and the introduction of species indigenous to eastern Canada. Most controversially in the 1960s some trenches were re-excavated and rebuilt to provide a better appreciation of the site. This introduced factual errors, however, with misleading and inaccurate signage. Amongst these was the incorrect marking of the main trench line and starting point for the Newfoundlanders' fatal assault. As Paul Gough has shown, visitors to the site have been critical of the way memory has been 'reassigned and controlled' to 'lend authority to a particular reading of space'.[46] This is important for Western Front visitors who often have a fetishistic attitude to accurate places, dates, times, and military deployments and actions. To compromise these details is to drain the experience of meaning and introduce a sense of artifice and lack of reality. *Exactitude* is crucial for some. But in defence of those seeking to preserve battle landscapes the traces of the past can be so imperceptible that 'only contrivance secures their recognition'.[47]

This leads to important questions concerning authenticity. Does it matter if our understanding of the war is mediated through reconstructions or sites that have been manipulated? If sites are 'sanitised' – devoid of the reality of war – is our engagement with the First World War diminished? Is it possible to understand war without experiencing mortal danger, illness, hunger, cold or seeing and smelling death? In tourism 'authenticity connotes traditional culture and origin, a sense of the genuine, the real or the unique.'[48] Indeed tourists could be those who seek out authenticity as a counterbalance to a world which is becoming increasingly inauthentic.[49] On one level authenticity refers to whether something is genuine based upon absolute and objective criteria; so if a museum object is claimed to be of a particular date and is later found not to be, then it is inauthentic. There is therefore an *Objective* definition of authenticity.[50] But the problem with this definition is that all heritage is in a state of constant flux so there is no absolute point of reference. Something initially considered 'inauthentic' can with the passage of time be considered 'authentic' and vice versa: for example, a late nineteenth-century mock medieval castle would not have been considered objectively authentic when built but is now an authentic example of built heritage. This suggests that values and interpretations change and that there is human agency in bestowing authenticity on objects.

In the museum context objects can be imbued with authenticity by the imprimatur of 'curatorial authority' as they are separated from others, showcased and endowed with aura.[51] This is *Constructive* Authenticity where authenticity is what others project onto an object or activity through a form of simulated reality. This is manifest in 'the copy' where, because reality is in some way unpalatable, untidy or incomplete, we make full-scale authentic copies of it which are often superior to the original.[52] It is also present in the phenomenon of 'staged authenticity',[53] a particularly strong feature of performances for tourists where the staged folk dance is more 'real' than the original ever was. Thus reconstructed heritage like the Ypres Cloth Hall are 'authentic copies', imbued with authenticity by those who build and manage them. Nevertheless authenticity can also be understood on a level detached from the materiality of objects or sites. Authenticity might not be something 'out there' but something which lies within and related more to the experience than the genuineness of an object or site. This *Existential* authenticity depends on the context and the individual's interaction with others at the site; in this case tourism, in bringing people together, provides a fertile environment for an authentic experience regardless of whether a reconstructed dug-out, for example, is built faithfully to a genuine wartime design or not.

Nevertheless despite the negative comments made about the Newfoundland Memorial Park, tourist complaints about lack of authenticity are relatively rare; it would seem that visitors to the Western Front are not bothered whether sites are truly 'authentic' or not. Reconstructions provide some idea of what the war would have been like and if they achieve an educational purpose then they have succeeded. To properly portray war would have to involve socially unacceptable and distasteful representations so *Objective* authenticity will always remain an unattainable concept. The experience of visitors to the rather bland landscape of the Western Front is in any way less reliant on the accuracy of its material legacy than on it associations; despite a quest for exactitude people engage with the area emotionally and imaginatively.[54] It's less what they have come to see than what they have come to understand, and if they achieve this then authenticity is not important. But the preserved or reconstructed heritage of the area is important because it adds a whole new layer to the cultural landscape of the Western Front. Heritage is constantly changing and the irony is that reconstructed heritage, seen as inauthentic, eventually becomes an authentic heritage, when somebody acknowledges it as such.

Below the ground: digs, bodies and artefacts

Up until the 1990s the Western Front was understood almost totally through the prism of military history. There had been very little systematic investigation of the war landscape as an archaeological resource and the terrain remained an abstract backdrop to historical and tactical accounts. What lay beneath the ground was less important than what happened upon it. Since then military historians have had to share their domain with new and dynamic ways of interpreting this landscape. Because there was so much defensive digging into and damage to the terrain the Western Front is a vast archaeological site with immense possibilities. Great War archaeology is able to connect deeply with the public imagination because it focuses on events which have left their mark on the descendants of the conflict to this day. There is something intensely personal about the ground where millions fought and died, and the space left by the 'missing' only adds to this poignancy. This type of archaeology has the power to shock and enthral; but it can also open up new academic understandings about the war and the way it was fought.

Most archaeology deals with sites whose character has changed over millennia or centuries; the archaeology of the Great War, however, investigates sites that can be dated to days or even hours. Indeed when unearthing the chalk upcast from large mine detonations on the Western Front archaeologists are able to date a soil layer to a precise minute.[55] It would be possible to conduct the archaeology of a single day – perhaps the first day of the Battle of the Somme – on the Western Front, a very rare undertaking for an archaeologist. There is also a potent human dimension where excavations are likely to uncover the remains of the missing which is less common in other forms of archaeology. The discovery of the body of a soldier is to gain a moving insight into a person's violent death and their last moments. Furthermore the visual impact of uncovered skeletons is to provide a different way of remembering the war as opposed to the sanitised nature of military cemeteries.[56] But archaeology is most effective when supported by detailed documentary evidence in the form of military records; private letters, diaries, memoirs and eyewitness accounts; and oral testimonies. Then the war is brought to life in a powerful way.

The remains of military hardware like weapons, ordnance, helmets and tools are commonly found in excavations in the area as well as trench structures and remains of concrete fortifications. These can augment or confirm our understanding of the nature of warfare at the time. Nevertheless, the intensely personal nature of the conflict is brought out strongly with the discovery of private objects which 'adds ... highly emotive texture to the everyday life of soldiers'.[57] Between 1992 and 2000 The Diggers, an amateur archaeological group, uncovered 155 bodies of soldiers from the Boezinge site near Ypres, most of whom had remained unburied between trench lines. A range of personal items accompanied these bodies like toothbrushes, pocket knives, pencils, mirrors and purses containing coins. On one body a miniature white porcelain crucifix was discovered reflecting an intimate connection with religious belief.[58]

Excavations at Serre on the Somme by No–Man's–Land, another excavation group, recovered the bodies of three soldiers – one British and two German – in 2003. Found with one of the Germans was a ceramic pot lid, thought to have contained leather polish, and imprinted with the legend of a department store in Stuttgart. The man also had a jar, perhaps for hair cream, and a nail cleaning/manicure set; this demonstrated the remarkable effort made by men in the trenches to maintain their personal appearance, even amongst the dirt of trench life. The second German soldier had a watch, harmonica, knife, razor and, unusually, a shard of prehistoric flint. The latter suggests he may have been an intensely curious collector or amateur archaeologist, just like the modern enthusiasts who rediscovered his remains.[59] These examples allow the personalities of the men to break through the brutal inhumanity of violent death and the loneliness of abandonment without proper burial. In discovering these quotidian items, so long lost under the earth, we relate to the dead as human beings; the discovery of military hardware or impedimenta alone cannot provide this personal relationship.

What is particularly poignant about the discovery of human remains is the chance to identify individuals and establish contact with their descendants. This is achieved through a combination of artifactual and documentary evidence strengthened by the testimony of family histories. Personal items, identification tags, regimental badges and uniform patterns can be used to establish identity although this is often impossible to confirm conclusively. However a whole new dimension to Great War archaeology has been introduced with the use of DNA profiling; this can be used to match samples from the dead with those from descendants. The technique was used to profile the remains of 250 bodies discovered at Fromelles in northern France in 2009 which were subsequently reburied in a new CWGC cemetery nearby.[60]

What is unusual about Great War archaeology is the way it has departed from traditional archaeological field techniques to embrace anthropological and ethnographic investigational methods. In 'excavating' the emotional and personal aspects of people's lives archaeologists are just as likely to visit car boot sales, militaria fairs, private collections or trawl the Internet as they are to be 'in the field'. This is because so many of the material objects of war are not 'in the ground'. In tracing the 'social life' of objects investigators also interview the descendants of those who knew these items of material culture. The recovery of the Great War objects adds a new and exciting dynamic to objects which have achieved a revived level of importance as the people who used them pass away. These objects are given a 'second life' as new meanings are attached to them;[61] pivotal to this is the identity recovered objects possess in a contemporary heritage tourism industry. The material remains of the Great War form a key part of the tourist engagement with the narrative and are an important complement to the social interpretation of the landscape.

There is a clear interrelationship between battlefield tourism and Great War archaeology: tourist interest in archaeological investigation is predetermined by several TV documentaries and news items concerned with excavating the Western Front; on the other hand archaeology needs public interest to attract funding from the media and grant-awarding bodies. Archaeological discoveries keep interest in the war topical and even directly stimulate tourism. In the late 1990s excavations started at the British-owned 'Ocean Villas' Bed and Breakfast and Tea Room at Auchonvillers on the Somme.[62] This was to investigate the building's cellar, a shelter and first aid post during the war, and associated communication trenches **(Figure 23)**. After these features had been properly examined the trench was consolidated and reconstructed allowing for public access. The site is important in highlighting a behind-the-lines experience rather than the more frequently emphasised front line combat environment. It has also provided a useful interpretative addition to Ocean Villas and artefacts discovered in the excavations were put on display. The Ocean Villas Project is an excellent example of where archaeology can work to stimulate tourism and war remembrance with no overt academic agenda. The presence of a war-related archaeological site adds a new dimension to this business and the owner recently opened a museum and field study centre. In her own words: 'it's not just a B & B – it's a place to learn about the First World War'.[63]

Tourists are also curious onlookers at archaeological sites; First World War 'rescue' excavations in advance of the A19 road development near Ypres in 2003 attracted enormous public attention. During the excavations the remains of a British soldier were uncovered prompting spontaneous acts of commemoration from visitors and the actual discovery site soon became covered with poppies and wooden crosses.[64] This introduces a further and fascinating anthropological layer onto what the Western Front means to tourists with new commemorative and behavioural practices. Indeed the very act of excavation is a commemorative practice in itself energised by an interested public who create new *lieux de mémoire* at archaeological sites.

* * *

Heritage has the power to valorise the past and infuse it with new vigour. But it does this through filters of selectivity and presents a past that is, for a contemporary audience, palatable. Alongside commemoration, heritage adds new and significant layers of meaning to the landscape of the Western Front; this is a phenomenon that continues to evolve as new sites are discovered or developed and old ones given a new lease of life. What is particularly significant about this process of change is the agency of tourism which is creating a new 'stratigraphic layer' of visitor centres, museums, reconstructions and itineraries. With the demise of those who fought in the Great War new understandings are being formed and heritage is at the vanguard of a new way of communicating the memory of the war.

Chapter 6

Museums and Interpretation

The landscape of the Western Front is charged with emotional, spiritual and nationalistic importance and has deep personal and collective significance. It is, however, unprepossessing and limited in its ability to tell its own story. Interpretation is required to strip away the landscape's varied layers of meaning and provide an understanding of its civilian and military dimensions. Interpretation is a decoding process since without explanation the topography remains mute for those seeking to see where the events of war took place. The landscape is the war's last witness but it needs interpretation to reveal its 'invisible heart and soul'.[1]

Interpretation is 'a process ... by which visitors see, learn, experience, and are inspired firsthand'.[2] In order to emphasise the level of impact and magnitude of suffering engendered by the Great War commentators often present an impressive array of facts and figures. But true interpretation goes beyond the transmission of statistics and is more precisely:

> an educational activity which aims to reveal meanings and relationships through the use of original objects, by firsthand experience, and by illustrative media ... [It should reveal] a larger truth which lies behind any statement of fact [and] capitalize ... curiosity for the enrichment of the human mind and spirit.[3]

Interpretation is not just instruction but provocation; effective interpretation explores emotion and empathy and prompts audiences to ask deep questions. The hardships of the past provide a fertile context for such involvement and war is a particularly rich subject for revealing larger truths. This is because it involves an exploration of the extremes of human experience including suffering and loss as well as more appealing human qualities like courage, endurance and sacrifice. It does, however, face the challenge of how to represent violence and death in an acceptable manner.

Interpretation uses a wide range of communicative methods to 'incarnate the facts'[4] – to bring to life otherwise bland details of events and stories from the past. This can include innovative and interactive technology (including multi-media), multi-sensorial engagement, human agency (guides, *animateurs*), re-enactment and Living History. In today's world, where the last combatants of the war have passed away, new repositories of memory are being created to complement those stored in texts and the landscape. The wide variety of interpretation available plays a key role in fashioning this memory and transmitting it to new generations. Interpretation plays a major and growing role in education and is employed for and enjoyed by the large number of school groups who visit the Western Front every year.

Along the Western Front the history and material legacy of the war is presented to the public in museums through different kinds of heritage interpretation. Alongside museums are interpretation boards and trails; guides; self-guided vehicle, cycling and walking routes; re-enactment events; and new interactive media which provide wider opportunities for audiences to understand the Western Front and engage with the 'larger truth'. The visitor to the Western Front has a considerable amount of choice in gaining an understanding of the conflict; this is provided through a selection of museums and visitor centres blending almost seamlessly into a landscape of war-themed pubs, cafes, restaurants, shops and businesses which make up this 'heritage-scape'.

Western Front museums: people and objects

A museum is an institution that 'acquires, conserves, researches, communicates and exhibits ... tangible and intangible heritage ... for the purposes of education, study and enjoyment'.[5] Alongside their curatorial roles museums have an important contribution to make to society in organising knowledge and educating the public. There are a wide range of museums along the Western Front which, although with differing objectives, succeed in furthering an understanding of the conflict. But they do this differently ranging from the large purpose-built institution utilising cutting-edge technology right down to the small collection in a café or restaurant. Although the latter are not normally recognised as museums they play an important role in interpreting the conflict and are therefore discussed here. Western Front museums do not just privilege the tangible in the way they present the Great War; a considerable amount of attention is also given to the war's intangible heritage. The playing of audio-recordings of soldiers' marching songs and modern renditions of this music, for example, is just as valid a form of representation as a display of uniforms, weapons and other war impedimenta.[6]

'Memorial museums' are normally set up to interpret a specific event like persecution, dispossession or violence towards a specific group of people. These types of museum are built around an event not a collection because the legacy of oppression or genocide is often object-poor due to the attempted removal of all identifying traces by the perpetrator.[7] Although memory is a strong underlying element of Western Front museums they differ from 'memorial museums' in being spectacularly object-rich with a surfeit of items to make up any collection; this is due to the scale of industrial manufacture of war *matériel* so much of which still exists or is being re-discovered. What gives objects real power, however, is their associations with people and events. This adds a dynamic social dimension to the interpretation of the past, with the overriding theme of many Western Front museums being concerned with the way the war was experienced in its many forms by people who we now feel able to empathise with.

Alongside its terrifying destructive capacity, war is also creative, and the Great War has left us a rich material legacy of objects that have value for those who manufactured, used or inherited them.[8] Objects have social lives of their own and an object once given no value can often be revalued as a 'memory-object' important in understanding the past. Museums play a key role in revaluing objects and reconfiguring new meanings for them. A biography of a fictional example would be a spent artillery shell-case discarded by the crew of a gun battery during the war, collected from the battlefield by a local family and turned, through artistic endeavour, into a beautifully engraved piece of trench art. This is then sold as a battlefield souvenir to a British family after the war while visiting the grave of a relative. It is given pride of place in the family home before eventually losing its emotional associations as it is passed on to a new generation who fail to maintain these connections. Having lain forgotten in an attic or garage for decades, it is finally given or sold to a museum – an act which imbues it with renewed significance as it is displayed to a newly-receptive public.

In this process, which must have happened for real countless times, the object, one of millions manufactured to inflict death and destruction, is aestheticised and given a new identity as art, and is also revalued as a precious family memento. Having lost value it regains it through the decisions of museum professionals who showcase the object, and thereby indicate that it has importance and an 'aura'. By treating it as special, and of greater value than the many other Great War shell-cases that exist, a level of 'curatorial authority' has given the object a second or even third life.[9] This example shows that museum objects do not start life on display in the vitrine; this is just part of an identity that is created for them.

Such objects do not have to possess inherent aesthetic qualities to gain importance and war provides countless examples of rather brutish items of militaria that are given immense value. Indeed 'heritage … is the transvaluation of the obsolete, the mistaken, the outmoded, the dead and the defunct'.[10] War museums are some of the best examples of where this takes place. Museums are also places where objects are removed from the original context in which they were used through simply by putting them on display; a weapon separated from the viewer within a glass case strips the object of much of its terror associations[11] and no amount of captions or textual explanation can restore it to its origins or primary purpose.

Different Museums, different stories

Collections of militaria by private individuals were being opened to the growing numbers of pilgrims and battlefield tourists to the region soon after the war's end. As local families returned to claim their shattered land many appreciated the economic value of the battle-scape as a tourism asset along with the enormous quantity of detritus which they were now removing from the soil in order to return it to agricultural productivity.[12] These museums (often grafted onto a café or restaurant) had their origins in private militaria collections, a trend which continues to this day, and there has been a close if unsteady relationship between this type of 'museum' and the trade in war objects ever since. Indeed the involvement of this type of museum in the commercial trade in militaria with little curatorial responsibility would place it outside of the normal definition of a museum. Nevertheless these small collections play a significant role in transmitting an understanding of the war to modern tourists and are worthy of attention. A well-known example amongst battlefield tourists to the area around Ypres is Hill 62 (Sanctuary Wood) – whose museum and trench system was opened (and is still owned) by the Schier family in 1923.[13]

Most of these museums disappeared with the advent of the Second World War in 1939 although some continued into the 1950s.[14] The resurgence in interest in the war from the 1960s led to the opening of further small museums and larger examples appeared during the 1970s (e.g. the Franco–Australian Museum at Villers-Bretonneux on the Somme in 1975). The 1990s saw the opening of increasing numbers of new museums and 'Visitor/Interpretation Centres' (Appendix 1) and this trend has continued ever since, with the Centenary resulting in the construction of entirely new institutions or the refurbishment of existing ones. The traditional concept of the museum as a repository of artefacts and the visitor centre as a place where amenities such as toilets, catering and retailing are provided alongside interpretation is now being eroded. 'Visitor centres' are now as likely to display artefacts (as at the Tyne Cot Cemetery Visitor Centre near Ypres) as 'museums' are to provide visitor amenities (as with the In Flanders Fields Museum).

Western Front Museums differ greatly in their size, visitor numbers, nature of collections and overall ethos. **Appendix 7** provides a categorization of Western Front museums and visitor centres ranging from large high-tech nationally important examples all the way through to smaller collections at café-museums. There are three main examples of Category 1: the In Flanders Fields Museum, Ypres (IFFM); the Historial de la Grande Guerre, Péronne (HGG); and the Musée de la Grande Guerre du Pays de Meaux (MGGM) **(Figure 24)**. These are the largest Great War museums along the Western Front and use sophisticated interpretational techniques to present the war in its broadest sense. They employ a range of expert and technical staff with managerial, curatorial, interpretational and customer care skills. All three emphasise the political, social and cultural aspects of the war from many combat nations using a wide range of artefacts drawn from their extensive collections to 'tell the story'. The geo–political environment which caused the war is an important feature of these exhibitions. Nevertheless, the Great War was the first 'total' war where social and cultural factors became as important as the political and tactical dimensions and no part of society remained unaffected by the conflict.[15] This is expertly demonstrated in the collections of all three major museums, as the more usual military objects like weapons, uniforms and equipment are set alongside a human story expressed through copies of private letters, diaries, photographs, clothing and personal objects. The paradox between war which destroys and the museum which preserves is an underlying feature of any visit to these collections.

The museums of Category 2 are similar in their educational ethos and the manner in which they display the social and cultural impact of the Great War. These museums are important regionally, with a similar educational ethos, curatorial responsibilities and management style, but emphasise more local battles and engagements. The Memorial Museum Passchendaele 1917 'keeps the memory alive'[16] of a battle which has become iconic in British culture.[17] It also brings home most forcefully the scale of the loss and allows a space for contemplation of the fallen in a Hall of Reflection, the last exhibit room, which is something rarely seen in war museums. This includes a photo-montage of men killed in the war, bringing visitors literally face-to-face with its human cost **(Figure 46)**. A similar museum at Fromelles in northern France was opened in 2014 adjacent to the newest CWGC cemetery for the remains of 250 newly-discovered Australian and British soldiers.[18] The museum tells the story of the Battle of Fromelles (19–20 July, 1916) – a costly and wasteful subsidiary military action to the Battle of the Somme, particularly for Australian forces.

Category 3 museums have a very nationalistic ethos in that they tell the story of a nation's sacrifice at the site of a particular battle or military action. At Delville Wood on the Somme a museum commemorates the sacrifices made by South Africans in two world wars and Korea; it stands next to the South African National Monument 'to the memory of all South Africans who fell during the Great War in all theatre of operations'.[19] Delville Wood is highly symbolic space as it was here between 15 and

20 July 1916 that soldiers from the 1st South African Infantry Brigade fought a desperate battle resulting in 763 killed and 1,709 wounded out of Brigade strength of 3,153.[20] The wood was purchased by the South African government in 1920 and the current monument and museum are owned and run by the Government of South Africa; the site is sacred terrain and the museum stands as a national memorial. Despite the existence of several nationalistic museums in the area no German equivalent has ever been built; the enemy story relies on the way it is interpreted in other institutions and the newer museums have incorporated German historians in their project design. Nevertheless, even a century after the event 'the Western Front continues overwhelmingly to belong to the victors'[21] and this is reflected in its contemporary museology.

Category 4 includes privately owned collections in the so-called 'café-museums' which are found along the Western Front. These provide refreshments in an unusual environment where the material legacy of war is displayed in close proximity to customers; they are regular stops on coach tour itineraries and often work closely with companies to provide meals and 'comfort breaks'. A central feature of these places is the large quantity of spent shell cases and iron fragments – disparagingly called 'rust and dust' – which in places are left in disorderly piles but can also be stacked up neatly for effect and to emphasise the enormous destructive power of industrialised warfare. At the Tommy Café at Pozières on the Somme an entire wall has been built up of shell cases. Such orderly construction hints at an attempt to control the destructive nature of warfare and to neutralise a past which to us remains threatening and frightening. This is where 'we subdue an overbearing past by sequestering it ... [so that] it loses its power to harm the present'.[22] In collecting these shells we have mastery over them and in doing so their lethal power is lessened. Nevertheless accompanying these rather un-aesthetic objects are better preserved examples of weapons, ordnance, uniforms, helmets and other *matériel*. These establishments often have rich collections of 'trench art', items made from the material remains of war; these could be engraved shell cases, embroidered tobacco pouches or cigarette lighters made from pieces of shrapnel.[23] Interpretation of objects is not the priority of the café-museums and there is seldom adequate explanation of the items on display, many of which are for sale. Indeed the café-museum plays a prominent role in the controversial world of collecting militaria and modern-day 'souveneering' for commercial gain.

A good example of the private collection is that of the Ocean Villas Bed and Breakfast and café at Auchonvillers, bought from a private collector – Andre Coilliot – in 2008 (**Figure 25**). The museum comprises a very large collection of First and Second World War militaria including weapons, uniforms, projectiles and vehicles; there is also a large assemblage of trench art on loan from another collector. The whole superbly complements the Great War theme of this establishment and is a valuable educational asset in illuminating the material aspects of the war to guests, café customers and visiting coaches (including school-groups). What is interesting is that the owner – Avril Williams – intends to rename it *The Williams Collection*; this will remove the more formal, hallowed and 'don't touch' ethos attached to the 'museum' label (a point revisited later). She wants the visitor experience to be more serendipitous and tactile so that people can learn from seeing the items closer up.[24]

The rather heterodox and haphazard nature of the café-museum – a modern war-related type of *Wunderkammer* – has played a relatively under-recognised role in the interpretation of the Western Front. Nevertheless these museums do hold large deposits of war *matériel* and have a role in interpreting the conflict for audiences who might not engage with other forms of interpretation.

In addition to the café-museum there are other collections which lie outside of orthodox museology; several Bed and Breakfasts and small hotels along the Western Front have collections of militaria. These are often owned by private guides who include viewings in their tours and use memorabilia to explain the events of the war (and to sell them). Artefacts are often restored with great care and used alongside replica uniforms and weapons to demonstrate the heavy and cumbersome nature of First World War combat. Additionally a large and unquantified amount of militaria lies in private hands and is seldom if ever shown to those outside the militaria fraternity.[25]

Category 5 includes Visitor Centres which, although not strictly speaking museums, do hold important artefacts which are used to augment exhibitions relating to specific war sites. At the Newfoundland Memorial Park Visitor Centre, for example, a display explaining the involvement of the

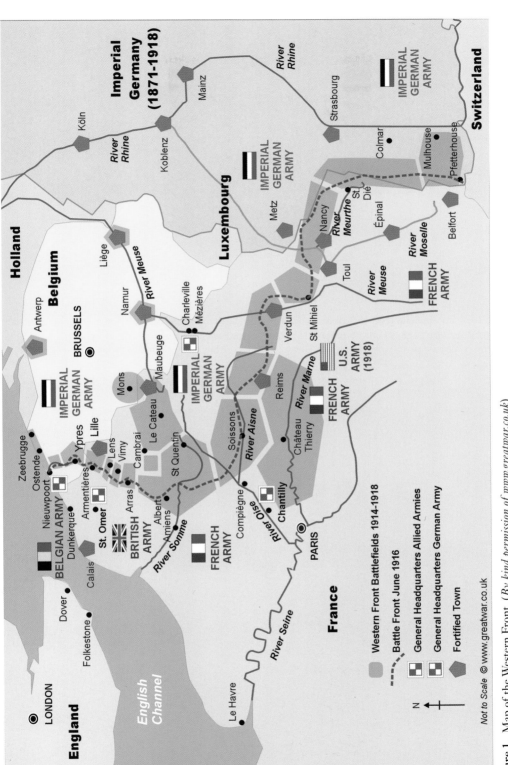

Figure 1. Map of the Western Front. (*By kind permission of www.greatwar.co.uk*)

Figure 2. The Menin Gate ceremony. (*By kind permission of www.tonycalvertphoto.com*)

Figure 3. A sea of red ceramic poppies in the Tower of London moat, November 2014. (*Photo by Amanda Chain*)

Figure 4. Birmingham City Centre Floral Trail: stretcher bearers at St Philip's Cathedral – August 2014. (*Author's own collection*)

Figure 5. Poppy wreaths begin journey from London to France for First World War Centenary in 2014. (*Copyright Peter Alhadeff/Centenary News*)

Figure 6. Ring of Memory Memorial, Notre-Dame-de-Lorette – inaugurated 11 November 2014. (*Author's own collection*)

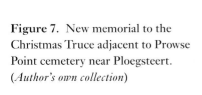

Figure 7. New memorial to the Christmas Truce adjacent to Prowse Point cemetery near Ploegsteert. (*Author's own collection*)

Figure 8. Warning sign for unexploded ordnance – Newfoundland Memorial Park, Beaumont-Hamel. (*Author's own collection*)

Figure 9. The grave of Morris Bickersteth, Queens CWGC cemetery, Puisieux, France. (*Author's own collection*)

Figure 10. A walking tour of the Somme, July 2014. (*Author's own collection*)

Figure 11. Christmas Truce Re-enactment at Prowse Point cemetery, Plugstreet – St-Yvon. (*Copyright 1914 St Yves Christmas Truce Committee of the Battle of the Canal*)

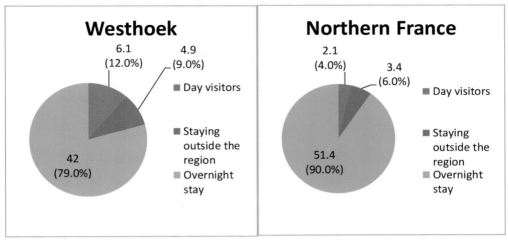

Figure 12. Expenditure of all Western Front tourists, January–September 2014, Westhoek and France

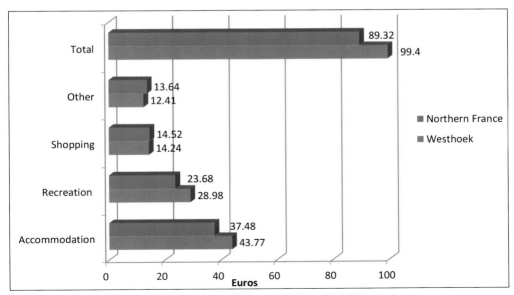

Figure 13. Expenditure by British Western Front tourists, January–September 2014.

Figure 14. A wooden cross placed at the Memorial to the Missing of the Somme, Thiepval – memory passed down through the generations. (*Author's own collection*)

Figure 15. An untiring devotion – the CWGC cemetery at Villers-Bretonneux. (*Author's own collection*)

Figure 16. The Memorial to the Missing of the Somme, Thiepval. (*Author's own collection*)

Figure 17. Names of the missing on the walls of the Memorial to the Missing of the Somme, Thiepval. (*Author's own collection*)

Figure 18. German pillbox at the New Zealand Memorial near Messines. (*Author's own collection*)

Figure 19. Lochnagar Crater, La Boisselle – Memorial Service 1 July 2010. Participants forming a complete circle around the Crater by holding hands, symbolising fellowship and reconciliation. (*Copyright Georges Vandenbulke*)

Figure 20. Memorial at the Butte de Warlencourt. (*Author's own collection*)

Figure 21. Archaeological excavations and restoration at Thiepval Wood undertaken by the Somme Association. (*Author's own collection*)

Figure 22. Heinrich Wooden Shelter, Memorial Museum Passchendaele 1917, Zonnebeke. (*Author's own collection*)

Figure 23. Reconstructed trenches at 'Ocean Villas' Bed and Breakfast and Tea Rooms, Auchonvilliers. (*Author's own collection*)

Figure 24. Musée de la Grande Guerre du Pays de Meaux. (*Author's own collection*)

Figure 25. Private museum collection at Ocean Villas Bed and Breakfast, Auchonvillers. (*Author's own collection*)

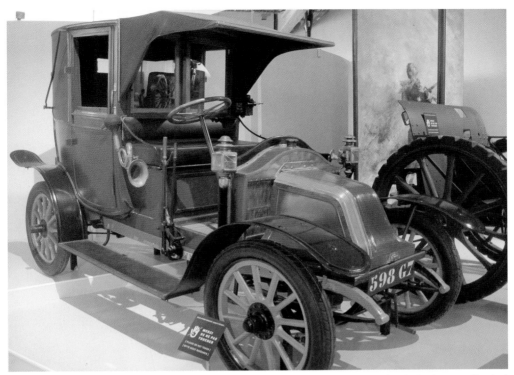

Figure 26. Musée de la Grande Guerre du Pays du Meaux; 1914 Renault taxi. (*Author's own collection*)

Figure 27. Musée de la Grande Guerre du Pays du Meaux; Zouave marching figure. (*Author's own collection*)

Figure 28. Musée de la Grande Guerre du Pays du Meaux; '14' marching figures. (*Author's own collection*)

Figure 29. Musée de la Grande Guerre du Pays du Meaux; '18' marching figures. (*Author's own collection*)

Figure 30. In Flanders Fields Museum; computer-animated figure of American nurse Ellen La Motte. (*Copyright Danse de Pluie and In Flanders Fields Museum (2012)*)

Figure 31. Historial de la Grande Guerre, Péronne. (*Author's own collection*)

Figure 32. Musée de la Grande Guerre du pays du Meaux; 'martyr' objects. (*Author's own collection*)

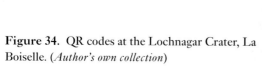

Figure 33. The commercialisation of war: turnstile at the Notre Dame de Lorette battlefield. (*Author's own collection*)

Figure 34. QR codes at the Lochnagar Crater, La Boiselle. (*Author's own collection*)

Figure 35. Sign at the Memorial to the Missing of the Somme, Thiepval. (*Author's own collection*)

Figure 36. Turf protection at the CWGC Tyne Cot cemetery. (*Copyright CWGC*)

Figure 37. The Platoon Experience. (*Copyright Memorial Museum Passchendaele 1917*)

Figure 38. Poppy-branded souvenirs, Ypres. (*Author's own collection*)

Figure 39. Poppy beer. (*Author's own collection*)

Figure 40. Tourists 'excavating' a Lewis gun drum magazine. (*Author's own collection*)

Figure 41. 'Field walking' – collecting objects from the battlefield. (*Author's own collection*)

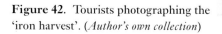

Figure 42. Tourists photographing the 'iron harvest'. (*Author's own collection*)

Figure 43. The Riqueval Bridge over the Saint Quentin canal, 2014. (*Author's own collection*)

Figure 44. British 137th Brigade, 46th Division at the Riqueval Bridge, October 1918. (*Wikimedia.org*)

Figure 45. The changing landscape of the Western Front: a wind farm near Saint-Quentin. (*Author's own collection*)

Figure 46. Photo–montage of soldiers at Memorial Museum Passchendaele 1917, Zonnebeke. (*Author's own collection*)

1st Newfoundland Regiment in the Battle of the Somme includes various items of the period such as uniforms. These are not presented as part of a collection or important artefacts to support a grand narrative but are included to add authenticity to a more local narrative.

Musée de la Grande Guerre du Pays de Meaux

The Musée de la Grande Guerre at Meaux is the latest example of a large scale Western Front museum and is included here to provide an example of museum interpretation. The museum tells the story of the Battle of the Marne (September 1914) although adopts a broad outlook on the war covering political, social, cultural and technological dimensions. In 2014 it had 133,000 visitors.[26] The museum is highly immersive and interactive, at the vanguard of this technology in French museology, and attempts to treat visitors 'more like actors than spectators'.[27] It does not consider itself a military museum but one with a duty to preserve the memory of the conflict and its history. The purpose-built futuristic building stands adjacent to the 26-metre high American Monument[28] and 'creates a permanent dialogue with [it]',[29] a powerful juxtaposition of memory and history. Meaux, on the river Marne, is a highly symbolic place for the French nation as the point of furthest German advance into France in the First World War and provides a suitable reference point for the museum. It is also significant for Britain as an area where large numbers of British soldiers fought and died in the early stages of the war and is often overlooked by visitors who concentrate on the more iconic British and Commonwealth sites around the Somme and Flanders.

The museum was created from the purchase of the enormous private militaria collection of Jean-Pierre Verney, a passionate historian who over 45 years accumulated 50,000 items and documents relating to the First World War. Further donations to the collection have also been made particularly as a result of increased awareness of the conflict with the opening of the museum and the Centenary.[30] The uniform collection alone is outstanding incorporating 200 separate patterns worn by all the combatant nations (as well as others like Switzerland). The remarkable collection of vehicles (many donated by the Marius Berliet Automobile Foundation) includes an omnibus converted into a pigeon carrier and a Renault taxi, one of 600 used in September 1914 to transport 6,000 French soldiers from Paris to the nearby front **(Figure 26)**. Heavy equipment includes rolling field kitchens, horse-drawn field carts, machine-gun carriages, hospital beds, stretchers, invalid chairs, a shell tower and an American folding bathtub.[31] Other objects tell the story of life behind the lines and on the 'home' front (e.g. letters, posters, newspapers, board games, art works), medical equipment and everyday items of army life (e.g. field canteens, coffee grinders, pipes, shaving equipment, soap, cards). Notable examples of trench art are banjos constructed from scrap metal and a water canister.

Through 23 separate sections the exhibition guides the visitor using a 'ground level approach … stirring up emotions and activating memories' designed to 'convey the atmosphere of the endless trench stalemate'.[32] The underlying theme is the way the war marked the beginning of the new twentieth century and defined it so forcefully. Consequently the starting point is a film journey back in time to 1870 highlighting both French and major world events since then as a prelude to total war and showing how events were so inextricably linked to each other.[33] This sets the scene for the visit, and at the end, a time-line in the final corridor shows how memory of the events has been constructed back to the present day alongside images of wars that have been fought since 1918. This chronological 'bookending' is highly effective in providing much needed historical context.

Perhaps the most impressive displays are the Marne '14' and '18' marching figures which appear at the entry and exit of the main hall; these are sets of mannequins in various uniforms marching determinedly on to ('14') and away from ('18') war **(Figure 28)**. A sound track of marching boots is audible. Set within large glass cases '14' includes colourful French *poilus* and colonial Zouaves with their voluminous red trousers **(Figure 27)**; German Uhlan lancers on horseback; khaki-clad British infantrymen from the Argyll and Sutherland Highlanders and King's Royal Rifle Corps; an airman; and members of cyclist and postal worker battalions.[34] There are men of all ranks and ages, all with different facial expressions, some tense and anxious, others enthusiastic and expectant, marching on to a war which they thought would last only for months; one has firewood strapped to his pack, another a walking stick. They are like Great War Terracotta Warriors.

You stand among them as they march purposively on to an imaginary horizon, abuzz with camaraderie despite their opposing sides; although static you can almost sense them moving with energy and verve and for a moment feel you are being swept along to the Front with them. Their uniforms are immaculate – perhaps they have just been issued with them – but their clothing stands in sharp contrast to their ghastly chalk faces, pale and spectral. Some mannequins have only the imprint of a uniform and stand outside the cases, totally grey, providing a more immediate contact with the figures inside **(Figure 29)**. What gives this display such impact is that the mannequins are deliberately blanched and cadaverous; the reality is that despite their animation, these men are already dead because we know their fate. The poignancy of this adds an immense immersive power to the dynamics of this display. At the end of the hall the '18' mannequins are marching away from war with the same range of expressions; but here Germans clenching stick grenades are mixed in with Allies in a grand martial finale; and one ghostly *poilu* strides ahead eager to return to his home. The only detriment to the message of four years of total war is the clean uniforms and lack of tiredness on the soldiers' faces.

The theme of the war's destructiveness is taken up in the 'virtual trench' area, a small room where images are projected onto three walls and an illuminated ceiling and mirrors emphasise the feeling of immersion in a trench environment. This is a 'deliberately anxiety-provoking space'[35] and one where the horrors of war are projected in a graphic way. Starting from peaceful bucolic images of rural France the montage regresses towards the violence of war using a mixture of contemporary stills and recreated film sequences underscored by sombre music; amongst the dark, mud, rats and corpses many visitors are unable to remain in the room. It is an example of how the museum tries to communicate the horrors of war but, on their own admission, this is impossible and was never their original intention.[36]

The museum has an important educational remit and 'allows for a better understanding of the world in which we live today'.[37] A noteworthy result of this is the pivotal role the exhibition and associated workshops play in intergenerational exchange; the museum has been instrumental in triggering family discussions between generations not about the First but the Second World War.[38] For the first time grandparents are encouraged to talk, stimulated by exhibitions on a previous conflict; this is an inadvertent yet dynamic consequence of the museum's ability to revitalise memory.

Enhancing experience and learning

Many Western Front museums have enthusiastically embraced the new museology of immersion and interaction which allows for a more experiential engagement with the Great War story. This allows a much greater role for the senses, as textual knowledge is seldom sufficient for true learning to take place.[39] At the In Flanders Fields Museum new galleries provide a stimulating multi-media orientated interpretation of the war with a comprehensive combination of artefacts, simulacra, dioramas, text-based panels, photographs, films and computer-modelled figures. On entering the galleries a ubiquitous, brooding soundtrack is played in the background which serves to draw the visitor into the exhibition emotionally and contemplatively. This atmosphere is enhanced by other uses of sound (e.g. noises of explosions) and changing light effects. The reduction of distance between past and present is well achieved by a series of computer enhanced life-sized figures who speak to the visitor starkly about their war experiences **(Figure 30)**. These are real historical characters from each side of the conflict, their narratives taken directly from their own writings; amongst them are the American nurse Ellen La Motte (1873–1961) and the Canadian surgeon John MacRae (1872–1918). Instead of simply emerging onto a screen these figures move out of and return to the shadows as delivering messages from the 'realm of the dead'. Although deceased they are able to reach out to us through personal testimony and in essence are the animated personifications of the marching mannequin soldiers at Meaux.

A different approach is adopted at the Historial de la Grande Guerre, Péronne where there is no sound at all in the museum but a powerful 'visual language of silence' designed to remove any 'artificial triggers of emotion or thought'.[40] In a radical departure from the way uniforms and kit are normally displayed the museum does not use mannequins or vertical supports but horizontal recesses (*fosses*) in the floor **(Figure 31)**; this archaeological or funerary symbolism presents a sacralised space aimed to direct the eye downwards in respectful observation. The eye is drawn from the vertical (the axis of hope) to the horizontal (the axis of mourning), a technique utilized in much Christian art.

A great taboo of museum settings has long been around the issue of touch. Having no physical contact with things limits the visitor's deeper engagement with objects which are further detached from their original human context where they were in constant contact with human bodies. Nevertheless precious and rare objects are still kept behind glass in many Western Front museums although there is a growing interest in allowing touch to engender greater interactivity and understanding of the war's material legacy. At the MGGM certain items considered more robust (e.g. a rifle) or less valuable because there are many examples in the collection are put on (secured) display where touch is actively encouraged **(Figure 32)**. These 'martyr objects' – like canteen sets actually used by soldiers – are accompanied by a 'Hands On' sticker. This gives objects a renewed role as educational props and thus an enhanced layer of utility denied others in the collection. But the place where the distance between subject (viewer) and object is removed most starkly is the café-museum where touch is allowed; much of this, however, is to encourage the purchase of the object.

Heritage frequently becomes sanitisation of the past and most war museums continue to display the accoutrements of parade-ground armies unsullied by conflict: immaculately pressed uniforms, polished buttons and beautifully preserved guns, shells and bullets. There is still a resistance to exhibiting war-damaged objects, incomplete weapons and dirty uniforms.[41] The *Musée vivant: 1914–1918* at Ablain-Saint-Nazaire is one of the few places where the dirty reality of war is displayed as uniforms, caked in mud, provide a more realistic idea of what trench life would have been like. In addition café-museums allow for a more gritty interpretation of the war in displaying badly damaged, incomplete and rusty objects unlike in the larger museums.

Re-enactment and Living History

The performance of history has become a central part of heritage interpretation. Re-enactment is the consummate expression of an ever more enactive society and has the power to enhance historical meaning 'by reinserting the body, making the empty landscape of the past live again'.[42] Although frequently viewed by professional historians as shallow and frivolous, re-enactment plays a key role in enlivening historical events and past social life to an attentive public. It is particularly appreciated by those unmoved by unappetising museums, monuments or books; indeed on a popular level 'activities attract more people than do artefacts'.[43] Re-enactment makes history more accessible and reaches audiences otherwise unreceptive to an appreciation of history; it thus has an important educational role. Historical re-enactment can recreate a specific moment from the past – the most common being a battle – but alongside this is Living History which attempts to create a sense of a past environment for both observers and participants.[44] Both adhere closely to an objective authenticity expressed in clothing styles, materials, methods of manufacture and even the use of historic accent and diction.[45]

The re-enactment of battles or other military actions is not well represented along the modern Western Front. Recreating combat in the very area in which it took place has certain taboos which are discussed in the next chapter; there is, however, strong involvement by re-enactment groups in commemorative events and in some reburials. The Great War Society (GWS), the main British Great War Living History Group, attends a large number of commemorative events in the UK but has also been present at events on the Western Front including the Retreat from Mons (September 2014) and Loos (September 2015). The GWS maintain a commemorative and educational ethos and call themselves 'a living history, rather than a battle re-enactment group'.[46] This suggests an unwillingness to recreate the horror of combat unlike other groups involved in military events further back in time. The Living History theme is prominent at annual events staged by the Memorial Museum Passchendaele 1917 at Zonnebeke, where military camp life is demonstrated using billets and encampments; in focussing on behind the scenes life these events allow for wider representations of the conflict and with the participation of female re-enactors are also less gender-biased.

One of the most prominent events of the early part of the Centenary has been the re-enactment of the Christmas Truce of 1914 which took place at various places along the Front. This event has captured the British public imagination like few other aspects of the war where in the midst of hostilities men from both sides showed a remarkable and spontaneous sense of congeniality rarely experienced in the brutality of warfare. Soldiers walked across to each other in no-man's land and exchanged cigarettes, alcohol and gifts; there are also reports of lanterns and fir trees being hung along the trenches, men singing carols together and an impromptu football game between the two sides.[47] The event was re-enacted in December 2014 near the Prowse Point CWGC cemetery near Ypres **(Figure 7)**, recognised as a major site for the 'Truce' not least because of the descriptions given by the cartoonist Bruce Bairnsfather who witnessed it. The re-enactment involved soldiers fraternising in no-man's land[48] and the staging of a muddy game of football between German and British 'soldiers' **(Figure 11)**. The Christmas Truce story is full of contradictions and challenges our preconceptions of war as a ruthless destruction of the enemy where common humanity has no place; in this it plays dynamically on human empathy which is brought out so powerfully through re-enactment. There is also a certain irony in that although battles are a popular subject for re-enactment peace can also be represented in an engaging and instructive way.

Tour guiding, tours and new technology

The Western Front landscape contains layers of hidden meaning that need to be located, unravelled and deciphered for an inquisitive public. The guide is a key figure in this process and the coach tour a dynamic context in which an imaginative and empathetic engagement with the landscape can be fostered.[49] Guiding is a performance and the interaction between professional guide and tourist a crucial one; successful tour guiding will be a function of extensive knowledge, expert communication and the creation of social bonding and conviviality within a group. The guiding process utilizes a variety of methods to stimulate the tourist imagination including the use of replica or real objects as props, video clips (viewed on a tablet or coach screen monitor between sites), personal diary accounts, poetry and music. The use of maps by guides to locate precise topographical features differs between individuals with some preferring to emphasise the general environmental context without the need for exactitude and others using paper or digital trench maps.[50] Tourist groups are rarely homogeneous and guides need to accommodate differing levels of pre-existing knowledge or personal interest into their narratives, using different methods to achieve understanding. The Western Front provides a convenient complement of museums, memorials, cemeteries and war sites which can be used by guides to vivify their narrative. Nevertheless some guides think there are too many 'markers' like this along the Western Front which serve only to detract the visitor from an appreciation of the 'purer' battle-scape itself. Visitors become too preoccupied with snapping photographs of cemeteries and memorials to the detriment of the terrain. Others view 'markers' as essential in locating events within a bland landscape.[51]

The battlefield coach tour is a unique interpretational space where tourists are immersed in time rather than distance. But such tours are highly choreographed with fixed routes, times and itineraries; the guide is thus part stage manager directing almost every facet of the passengers' lives while on tour. The local population and cultural aspects outside of the main tour theme, 'the alien other', are kept at bay by the guide.[52] Within this bubble tourists can, if they want to, switch off and allow themselves to be educated, entertained and pampered. But this is to deny tourists a role in creating their own experiences; tourist structures – like guiding – cannot account for the entire engagement with the past that tourists seek. Tourists play an active part in co-creating their own experiences: they often join tours with extensive background knowledge and confident guides will be able to utilise this by co-opting them in a participatory way (as with allowing them briefly to take over the microphone commentary).[53] Alternatively tourists can have their own personal objectives which are pre-determined or develop during the tour; these may or may not conflict with the guide's objectives or the structure of the tour.[54]

Guides do not have a monopoly on decoding the landscape, however. Individuals who want to create their own understanding of the Western Front can choose from other interpretational aids, an area in which new mobile information and communication technology (ICT) is taking an increasingly prominent part. The use of portable digital devices in heritage interpretation is now commonplace and there are numerous opportunities to employ these in understanding the Western Front. Mobile apps[55] can be downloaded onto smart-phones, tablet computers or other mobile devices and these can be used to support self-guided vehicle, cycle or walking tours. The Flanders Fields Car Routes, for example, have over 100 points of interest from which a bespoke tour can be constructed based upon a list, a map or a theme. The app is complemented by archive material in the form of photographs, texts and audio fragments, some involving talking figures from the war.[56] It is also possible to provide a chronological link between the contemporary scene and the Great War through Augmented Reality which is particularly dynamic in the Western Front setting, allowing for a comparison between the war landscape then and the contemporary one facing the viewer.[57] Sites also make use of QR (Quick Response) codes which are cheap, unobtrusive and useful where there is no visitor centre or interpretation board **(Figure 34)**.[58] These are self-service personal tour guides using bar code technology which when scanned with a mobile device allows for access to web pages, pictures, audio, videos or map locations.

The great advantage of mobile ICT is that it can be updated remotely unlike the printed word and allows for greater freedom and choice for tourists. The disadvantage is that the technology does not allow for human interaction and the stimulation of discussion; with a guide the tourist can ask questions, contribute viewpoints or raise doubts. Additionally much can be conveyed through non-verbal human communication that is beyond the reach of even the most sophisticated 'smart' technology. Modern technology does have an impressive array of features and applications but in interpreting something as emotionally charged as warfare one has to question whether more interpersonal methods can be improved upon. Nevertheless, in raising the question about which method works 'best' the answer is likely to lie somewhere in the middle; younger tourists are more willing to utilise 'smart' technology whereas older tourist are more receptive to traditional approaches such as guides and guide-books.[59] There may also be personal and situational characteristics which determine the choice of interpretational method but more research on this is needed.

* * *

The modern Western Front provides an extraordinary variety of interpretational choices aimed at improving our understanding of the conflict. Much of this is designed by heritage and museum professionals who have a powerful hold on a trusting public who do not normally question the messages presented to them. The content of these messages and the way they are delivered is crucial and what is not said is as significant as what is. The profession therefore has a great responsibility in communicating a balanced, truthful and comprehensible message which will provide 'added value' to the visitor experience. Visitors are also increasingly sophisticated and discerning, with the ability to complement the messages provided by an interpretational 'industry' with their own knowledge and understandings. The way the Western Front is understood or not is dependent on a complex combination of methods, messages, situations and engagements which only add to its rich multi-dimensional characteristics.

Chapter 7

The Rights and Wrongs of Battlefield Tourism

The Western Front is a prime example of a morally uncomfortable paradox of warfare in that despite terrible destruction of people and things, some parts of society always benefit.[1] After unprecedented and widespread disruption during the war years, the economy of the Western Front area benefited greatly after 1918 when veterans and tourists journeyed to the battlefields (see Chapter 2). The growth of tourism in the region, particularly over the last quarter century, highlights that war and the memory of war is now an industry. In a commercially driven consumer society war is a commodity like any other product or service – designed, packaged and sold to the consumer in a competitive market.

Along the Western Front, in both France and Belgium, the First World War plays an important role in creating images of tourist destinations. Alongside the stories and remains of the Great War, commemoration has also become a commodity as sites of memory are consumed by tourists seeking a closer involvement and understanding of the conflict. Memory is a vibrant industry relying on memorials, cemeteries, rituals, souvenirs and tour operators.[2] Commodification of culture has been described as one of the tourist industry's most damaging impacts[3] and raises difficult ethical questions – how should war be presented to tourists, and is it right to commercialise something as terrible as war in the first place? Nevertheless there has long been an intimate relationship between tourism and war; in the words of one anthropologist: '... despite the horrors of death and destruction ... the memorabilia of warfare and allied products ... probably constitutes the largest single category of tourist attractions in the world'.[4]

Given these difficult questions and troubling moral dilemmas, this chapter examines some of the ethical issues surrounding tourist interest in the Great War. It also looks at the broader issues relating to archaeological investigations along the Western Front, not least because these can include the discovery of human remains. This is important because the war's material legacy plays such an important role in the tourist's understanding and in underpinning the heritage interpretation of the conflict. An intractable part of this is presented by the growing numbers of tourists to the quasi- sacred landscape of the Western Front; tourism has both positive and negative impacts and no analysis of the area can ignore the damage that can result from tourism. Conversely, tourism is a powerful force for emphasising the importance of places, often far above the value local inhabitants themselves attribute them; it is a validating force able to highlight certain areas at the expense of others and significantly influencing decisions of protection and conservation. I will illustrate this and the way tourism adds another layer to our respect for cultural heritage with carefully selected examples.

Ethical background

Ethics is the expression of what it means to be human because we are all, by nature, ethical beings with the capacity to make choices. The kernel of ethics is 'what ought to be done' and what is 'the right thing to do' in given situations. Ethics is a highly contentious field and this is particularly so when death is involved; human interest in war brings ethical questions to the fore because it involves decisions about how we 'deal' with the memory, reputation, private possessions and mortal remains of those who are no longer present. It also raises difficult questions about the level of responsibility we should have to the descendants of the dead and the groups and nations who have a claim over their memory. The principle of respect for others should always be the capstone of any ethical approach and this gains renewed importance when representing the dead.

As a powerful cultural and commercial driver, tourism has always had a tense and ambiguous relationship with ethics;[5] this is because it frequently adopts values inimical to cultural respect and encourages inappropriate behaviour amongst its adherents. The often frivolous nature of mass tourism can certainly provoke numerous ethical questions; nevertheless in its many guises tourism can also be serious, respectful and enlightening. The growth of an ethical tourism movement, and a drive towards 'good' actions in tourism, demonstrates that tourism can be a force for good and operate with a conscience in a fair and honourable manner.[6] The main problem with ethics, however, is that it will never provide a definitive solution and prescribe a 'right' way to guide actions. Consequently, this chapter might raise more questions than answers; the Western Front is an ethical minefield indeed.

There are several theoretical viewpoints which have been used to guide behaviour and actions in an ethical way. The *first* of these is the 'end-seeking' (or *teleological*) theory that our actions should always seek to achieve a positive moral end which brings about a 'flourishing'.[7] This means that any decision that does not bring about this end is a bad one. This *virtue ethics* goes beyond mere subjective happiness and aims to bring about a universal and objective good; thus in a tourism context the 'right' way of behaving should be virtuous – just, fair and honest – rather than simply a form of pleasure seeking.

A *second* approach states that what is important is the greatest pleasure or happiness for the greatest number of people. This is known as *utilitarianism* – the maximisation of well-being – where the quality of pleasure is not as important as its quantity.[8] The problem with this theory is its denial of rights to the individual over those of the group; this could be transferred into situations – as with towns like Ypres – where the bad effects of tourism upon individuals are off-set by the overall economic good the industry brings. But the main criticism of this theory is its lack of a workable definition of just what is the 'greatest good'; who are the 'greatest number' and should we consider future generations as well? It is also true that those who benefit most from tourism are (often large multinational) businesses at the expense of ordinary residents – a situation which suggests that some forms of tourism may be unethical.

A *third* theory states that what is important is not the ends but the means (*deontology*): our moral responsibility is to abide by the rules or principles, rather than be concerned about any particular outcome. Thus we should endeavour to do the right thing. Religious duties and social contracts are like this, as are bills of rights and written constitutions. On a smaller scale, codes of conduct should guide moral behaviour particularly in tourism. Associated with this is the *practical imperative* which states that we should never treat people as a means to an end, but rather as being an end in themselves.[9]

What is ethically 'right' is that we treat others with dignity and respect at all times. In the context of this book, however, we should also ask does this also extend to the dead? This is a key question as the modern Western Front is a landscape marked by mortality and the undignified circumstances surrounding the 'missing'.

The detractors of war tourism question whether it is ever 'right' to make financial gain from the misfortunes of others particularly when this involves human suffering and violent death **(Figure 33)**. Is it morally acceptable to represent war in such dramatised forms as re-enactment, for example? One writer has criticised those re-enactment 'organisations ... [who] trivialise and package experiences which are, essentially, neutered reproductions of possibly the most horrible and tragic ordeals any person might experience'.[10] But is this the same when events are so long ago and beyond living memory? Is it somehow more morally acceptable to represent and commercialise a battle from the Middle Ages than one from the twentieth century?

The last survivors of the First Word War have passed away and the war has moved from the realm of living experienced memory to that of 'historical memory'. Chronological distance can remove the ethical questions surrounding much commercialisation of war which is repackaged as heritage, a term covering a multitude of sins. Indeed as with so-called 'atrocity tourism', 'living memory must fade' and 'the elapse of time may not only soften the events themselves but alter the responses of visitors who are no longer personally involved in the events being viewed ...'[11] The interpretation of violence, however, can remain a problem for representing *any* historical period and 'induce unintended reactions including an anaesthetisation and indifference through familiarity with suffering'.[12] Violence must always be portrayed carefully with respect for the sensitivities of viewers; but also for those who suffered, though they may be long dead and anonymous, and of course for their descendants.

Tourism: blessing or blight?

It is clear that tourism has brought economic benefits to modern Western Front communities.[13] Nevertheless tourism brings with it much that is less desirable; along the Western Front this includes aspects that are common to tourist centres in many parts of the world such as damage to heritage resources, littering, traffic congestion, conflict with local people and loss of atmosphere at sites. But the commemorative nature of the Western Front and its association with mortality adds a special layer of concern to the effects of large numbers of tourists: behaviour at cemeteries, memorials and commemorative events and the commodification of war through a souvenir industry are perhaps the most notable of these. But the negative effects of tourism are not necessarily questions of ethics; whether it is wrong to drop litter is more a common lack of respect than an ethical issue.

The Western tradition of commemoration assumes behaviour at cemeteries and memorials which accord respect for the dead expressed through commonly recognised acts of decorum. These involve an expectation to refrain from loud noise or boisterous behaviour; not to play loud music; to walk not run; not to stand or sit on gravestones or lie on graves; not to picnic; not to bring dogs into cemeteries; not to smoke; and to dress modestly (shirts to be kept on) **(Figure 35)**. The large influx of tourists to the Western Front has put a great strain on these culturally sanctioned codes of behaviour and levels of adherence are subject to wide discrepancies of interpretation determined by individual and cultural differences. One argument is that the men who lie in the graves fought and died for freedom, and therefore to deny a visitor the freedom to smoke or sing or run or go shirt-less is a travesty of this hallowed principle and what they fought for.[14] In other words, they died to allow us this freedom and, in any case, would probably have behaved this way themselves. It is difficult to argue with this point of view which might be less about ethical standpoints than differing ideas about respect. Nevertheless most visitors to commemorative sites do choose to behave in a restrained and decorous way.

Beyond the issue of respecting the dead is the more practical problem of physical damage. The most famous and well-visited CWGC cemetery along the Western Front is Tyne Cot, near Ypres, which in the first nine months of 2014 received 468,116 visitors.[15] This would create challenges for any heritage site but in the case of a war cemetery it is particularly acute. The grass at Tyne Cot has been badly eroded from the passage of large numbers of tourists and measures to protect its beautifully manicured lawns have been taken **(Figure 36)**.[16] Nevertheless the CWGC is realistic in acknowledging that from the very beginning their cemeteries were built for visitors who instead of being discouraged are actively welcomed; wear and tear is seen less as a problem for them than as a necessary consequence of open access and an encouragement of freedom for all to commemorate.[17]

Tourism is a powerful force which can profoundly influence the economic, socio–cultural and physical make up of destinations. Ypres is a good example of a town which has been transformed by war tourism; but has this been welcomed by residents? Large numbers of tourists have undoubtedly changed the atmosphere of what is now a 'Great War Town' unlike any other along the Western Front (with the possible exception of Verdun). In a survey of resident's attitudes to tourism in Ypres undertaken by local tourism specialist Timby Vansuyt there was much comment on levels of nuisance and inconvenience as a result of large numbers of visitors. Noise and congestion from traffic were considered irritants: coach traffic caused bottlenecks in the centre of the town and several residents felt it too dangerous to cycle in the centre because of tourist traffic.[18]

The human element was also a problem for some, particularly the presence of British school groups in Ypres throughout the year. The loud boisterous behaviour of adolescents was a negative aspect of tourism in contrast to 'older' tourists whom residents considered 'courteous and friendly'.[19] Because of the number of tourists crowding public places several residents felt they needed to make choices where to go and at what times to avoid the inconvenience and irritation of crowds. Despite this there was a feeling that tourism in Ypres was much less damaging than in other Belgian towns such as Bruges. Crowds were not all viewed as bad with some residents stating they brought a sense of 'bustle' to the streets of their town, with the busy cafés and restaurants providing a welcomed 'cozy atmosphere'.[20] It was revealing how some residents complained that the town's cultural tone was too focussed on war at the expense of other aspects. It was also felt that tourism catered too much for British expectations, as in accepting £ Sterling, and having English-language menus.[21] Some residents considered that the Last Post Ceremony was 'no longer for them' and if British visitors stayed away then no one would be there.[22] There are clearly tensions between the people of Ypres and, particularly British, visitors; nevertheless it is impossible to please everyone and problems can be greatly lessened by appropriate management, clear communication and working with residents.[23]

Lack of respect for a site of tragedy can often be the result of lack of understanding and a failure to appreciate personal, family and collective loss. Understanding can be fostered through interpretation and explanation or by experiential learning. One of the most effective interpretational methods used along the Western Front is the 'Platoon Experience'; this is a 4km walk from the Memorial Museum Passchendaele 1917 to Tyne Cot Cemetery for younger tourists (14–18 years) **(Figure 37)**. After visiting the museum where students learn about the background to the events they follow in the footsteps of an actual Australian platoon on 4 October 1917; each student has the name of a real soldier on a card and follows in his footsteps wearing an uncomfortable replica uniform and carrying heavy equipment. Once they arrive at the cemetery, their guns, backpacks and helmets are left outside as they learn about the tragic deaths of these men, many of whom were not much older than themselves. The organisers report that this form of role-play deeply affects the students who rarely behave disrespectfully in the cemetery and remain quiet. The idea is that an understanding of the background to conflict can result in a greater level of respect and appropriate behaviour.[24]

Whether tourism is a blessing or blight on the Western Front is difficult to say. Despite tourism's damaging effects there can be little doubt that anything that brings people closer to the tragic events of the Great War and fosters an appreciation of them cannot be a bad thing.[25] Sometimes visitors leave the area not having had a particularly deep experience; nevertheless meanings can often be fashioned long after the initial visit as individuals ruminate over the stories they have heard and the places they have seen, stimulated by further discussion and reading, or perhaps engagement with news reports, films and TV documentaries.

Souvenirs and tourism

Souvenirs have long been a feature of the Western Front and even during the war soldiers on both sides collected mementos through scavenging, euphemistically called 'souveneering' at the time, and what we would now call looting.[26] The making and selling of souvenirs developed into a vibrant industry after the war and well into the 1920s played a role in the economic recovery of destroyed areas (see Chapter 2). War souvenirs are a common feature of any post-war zone which attracts the attention of tourists.[27] This is because objects are important in the construction of memory: 'memory accrues around objects'[28] which provide emotional and cognitive triggers and help explain past narratives. Souvenirs can be of great personal value in reminding one of a particular trip and the places visited; they can also generate conversation and have power in stimulating trip decisions in others.[29]

Shopping for souvenirs is an important aspect of the tourism 'package' alongside travel, accommodation, gastronomy and entertainment. Souvenirs are moreover important in the construction of personal identity particularly amongst collectors. But a distinction has to be made between objects actually used in the war (militaria), those manufactured into souvenirs using these items (including 'trench art'), and those manufactured as reproductions whether intended to resemble militaria (replicas, e.g. a souvenir dog-tag) or not (e.g. a Menin Gate paper weight). These can all have an economic value and are sometime collectively labelled 'souvenirs'. This section refers to the latter category – items deliberately manufactured for sale with a Great War theme in a contemporary tourism context.

Today visitors to the Western Front have opportunities to purchase a variety of war-themed souvenirs and a selection of items for sale at Ypres reflects this: Menin Gate themed key-rings, fridge magnets, ash trays and cigarette lighters; 14–18 playing cards; golden bullet key-rings; Passchendaele and Remembrance Beer; chocolate 'Tommy' helmets; Flanders Pâté and Corned Beef; 'Last Post' Whisky; and Wipers Times beer and champagne.[30] A most unusual item is a Great War military style identification dog-tag necklace with the inscription, "We Will Remember Them".

The most noticeable feature of this merchandising is the wide range of red poppy items including brooches, 14–18 gin, beer, chocolates, T-shirts and even umbrellas **(Figures 38 and 39)**. The Flanders poppy has been appropriated as a 'brand' to provide clear product distinctiveness and identity.[31] The poppy is arguably one of the most powerful globally recognised symbols with a strong visual image and deeply felt associations. During the war the delicate red poppy or *Papaver rhoeas* was often seen struggling to grow in the shattered and broken landscape; it became immortalised in the poem *In Flanders Fields* (1915) by the Canadian soldier John McCrae (1872–1918) and after the war started to be used as a potent symbol of remembrance.[32] The annual British Legion Poppy Appeal and the wearing of poppies have become well established in British culture. The name and symbol has been used in the *In Flanders Fields Museum* at Ypres and in France the East Somme area is marketed as 'Poppy Country'. The poppy is emblematic of respect, honour, hope and loyalty and represents a set of positive values; branding makes use of these associations by transferring them to the product that uses the symbol. A strong brand reflects a consistent, coherent identity and provides security for the purchaser in ensuring that expected benefits will be provided; in short the poppy provides a guarantee of authenticity.

These examples demonstrate the way that war can be commoditised; but is economic opportunism around violent events and personal tragedies ethical? Is the production and sale of souvenirs with war themes disrespectful, distasteful or ethically the 'right' thing to do? Is it appropriate to utilise the poppy symbol for commercial gain? According to certain observers 'tourism is cashing in on the Centenary of the Great War [and] sharpening the debate about ethical values ...'[33] This is reflected in public disquiet in Ypres about the 'battlefield business boom' as one resident commented:

> It makes me frown when I see souvenir shops selling poppy gin, poppy chocolates, poppy umbrellas and even chocolate helmets. It could offend some people and reflects negatively on the image of a town like Ypres.[34]

Nevertheless, other residents commented that the level of war commercialisation in the town was not significant and in any case 'if [retailers] do not do it someone else will'.[35] There is a great deal of subjectivity about the nature of the items on sale: some visitors and locals might consider chocolates and beer acceptable as representing well established regional gastronomic products in contrast to a bullet key ring which represents something that brings death and suffering.[36] One of the problems in a market economy is that there is no control over tourist merchandising; local authorities cannot prevent manufacturers or retailers in their product decisions.[37] The Flemish Government has, however, drawn up a Code of Ethical Practice for war tourism which exhorts all involved to 'strike the right tone'. A key point is to maintain respect for 'war victims' which 'leads to great restraint and care in relation to the development of commercial initiatives ...'[38] Perhaps in response to this several manufacturers have started to donate a proportion of each sale to charity.[39] This might be seen as a smart way of drawing attention to the charitable cause and providing a convenient opportunity to help; a more cynical view could be that it is a way of deflecting uncomfortable ethical questions.

The positive side of the souvenir industry is that it draws people's attention towards the events of the war and can therefore stimulate a considered interest in remembrance and respect for the dead; ethically, therefore, the overall moral good is bettered despite the underlying disrespect commercialisation engenders. This is at odds with the ethical idea that the *process* is what matters: the very use of war and the symbols of remembrance for commercial gain is ethically suspect because these are not 'right' actions. In using the dead to further our own economic ends we are treating them as a means to an end. Nevertheless we could argue that souvenirs are an act of commemoration *per se* and rather than treating the dead as a means to an end allow them to be respected as an end in themselves.

Archaeology: human remains

Archaeology has a pivotal relationship with heritage, landscape and tourism along the Western Front; in uncovering material evidence, illuminating or even challenging the facts, and locating the last mortal remains of the 'missing', archaeology is continually enriching our understanding of the conflict.[40] It provides fresh objects for museum display and, in bringing an ordinary landscape to life, is of increasing interest to tourists. Nevertheless, battlefield archaeology is beset by far-reaching ethical questions.

One of the most difficult of these is the uncovering of human remains, an all too frequent occurrence in Great War archaeology. The inviolability of the dead is a paramount religious and ethical principle with a widespread abhorrence for any form of deliberate or unnecessary disturbance of human remains. This is effectively an expression of the *practical imperative* that humans should be respected as an end in themselves and that respect for the individual extends beyond death. The ethical responsibilities of archaeologists in relation to human remains fall into three categories: to the scientific community and the advancement of knowledge; to the descendants of the deceased and descendant communities; and to the dead themselves as individuals.[41]

If archaeologists inadvertently discover human remains should they leave them undisturbed? In some cases archaeologists have deliberately sought out the graves or remains of particular individuals. Is this ethical, particularly if these excavations have not had the permission of any relatives of the deceased? Or does the need to advance scientific knowledge outweigh these considerations? The argument is complicated in that the armies that fought along the Western Front were made up of soldiers from many different cultures and religious beliefs; these differed not only from each other but from their military masters as well. Funeral rites and protocols regarding the treatment of the dead varied significantly between Muslims, Jews or Chinese Buddhists serving in the Great War, for example. Moreover the treatment of human remains amongst aboriginal Maori and North American Indian culture (represented by soldiers serving in ANZAC, Canadian and American forces) is even more sensitive with a deeply held belief in the liberation of the spirit in the afterlife.[42]

The nature of much interment in the 1920s and 1930s by various war graves authorities can be interpreted now as impersonal and insensitive. But alongside this has been the morally reprehensible response to the unearthing of human remains by construction companies when building new housing or transport developments during the twentieth-century; such discoveries often result in remains being hastily reburied or thrown away as any public declaration could result in a delay to schedules or even penalty clauses in a contract being invoked. Archaeologists are new arrivals on the scene and their attitude to the dead is just another addition to the range of approaches which have characterised the enormous challenge posed by the uncovering of the 'missing' along the Western Front.

The way human remains are treated, including the manner in which they are photographed for public display, should demand great cultural sensitivity. Respect for the dead as individuals is arguably more informed and observed in a conflict like the Great War where our understanding of their beliefs and values is intensified through knowledge of letters, diaries and personal items.[43] The problem with the Western Front is the sheer quantity of remains that are uncovered almost on a daily basis: bones and fragments of bones are constantly being brought to the surface through ploughing or natural soil movements. Local authorities are rarely interested in these *ad hoc* discoveries unless remains are identifiable and inevitably they are discarded[44] or at best added to the mountains of bone fragments in ossuaries like those at Notre-Dame-de-Lorette. Bodies brought to the surface by agricultural activity or Nature outnumber any discovered by archaeological excavation; an overarching method of dignified and respectful disposal is thus made practically impossible.

Discovering the dead raises acute ethical issues when modern DNA technology has identified the remains. In 2009 the remains of 250 Australian and British First World War dead were excavated at Fromelles in France.[45] DNA samples from the bodies were matched with those from likely descendants who came forward in a bid to locate their lost ancestors. The issue here surrounds confidentiality because identifying someone through DNA testing provides information about other members of that person's family as well. This could include inherited diseases, predispositions to disease and, most unfortunately, undisclosed paternity along the family line.[46] Because of these issues archaeologists need to forewarn participants of the possibility of fortuitous discoveries and the impact these might have on families. At Fromelles the deaths were relatively recent (in archaeological terms) so there was always the possibility that close family members were still alive; this demanded a particular level of sensitivity including ensuring no photographic images of the remains were released to the public.[47]

Archaeology: militaria and metal detecting

The Western Front is probably the largest linear archaeological site in existence; it is a vast repository of military artefacts and built features lying only centimetres beneath the surface. It has been estimated that in some parts of Flanders the amount of iron in the soil has created a geological ferrous layer a metre thick composed of shrapnel, unexploded ordnance and other detritus.[48] That it has attracted the attention of informal excavators, perhaps more correctly 'treasure hunters', ever since the last shell was fired should therefore be of no surprise. The economic value of militaria means that war sites are always at risk from illegal scavengers fuelled by the internet, which has greatly facilitated the sale of Great War items onto a global market.[49] This adds another layer of meaning to the landscape as an illicit storehouse of concealed objects endowing it with a clandestine value beyond agricultural or tourism potential.

The Western Front is thus a magnet for illegal 'diggers' and metal detectorists who have few scruples in disrupting archaeological resources and even disturbing grave sites. These are unscientific 'excavations' undertaken without official sanction and often without the permission of the landowner. There are definite legal and ethical issues surrounding this practice which encourages unscientific amateur archaeology where items recovered are unrecorded, out of context and frequently 'unprovenanced', serving only to distort the archaeological record.[50] Nevertheless one could argue that removing objects from the ground, whether legally or otherwise, provides them with a better chance of preservation, even if in a private collection. It is difficult to determine whether metal detecting is undertaken by locals or those travelling into the region but an informal 'collectorist tourism' undoubtedly exists. Collecting items from the battlefields is also done by tourists. Battlefield guides commonly lead their clients in 'field walking' to discover war *matériel* lying on the surface; if anything this provides a dynamic educational angle to a tour in demonstrating the intensity of fighting and the enormous quantities of ammunition and ordnance that was expended. However tourists sometimes try their own hands at digging items near the surface which, apart from the damage this causes to the record, is not without its dangers **(Figure 40)**. But taking a few spent cartridge cases or shrapnel balls is different from an irresponsible and unethical looting of burials to obtain personal possessions from the dead.

Today's culture of collecting exists cheek-by-jowl with the popular hobby of metal detecting. Battlefields have rich archaeological potential but, mostly unmonitored, unfenced and unguarded, they are difficult to police against the undesirable activities of illegal metal detectorists. The fragility of battlefield landscapes has been recognised in the Vimy Declaration for the Conservation of Battlefield Terrain (2001) which states: 'Particular note should be taken of the looting of battlefields, especially its surface material with metal detectors'.[51] Nevertheless metal detecting can have positive as well as negative outcomes; the skills and enthusiasm of amateur hobbyists can be harnessed to great effect by archaeologists. Metal detectorists can provide valuable assistance to archaeological projects and help discover new and previously uncovered sites and objects. Yet it can be a tense relationship with conflicting values and objectives so that it is more 'a marriage of convenience; both are necessary, yet often uncomfortable bedfellows'.[52]

Conservation and protection

The need for economic development has subjected the Western Front to intense pressures as land is targeted for building development and new roads and railways are planned across the region. On the one hand this can provide opportunities as the sub-surface remains of the war are uncovered and archaeological investigation can be undertaken in advance of the bulldozers; on the other much war heritage is being destroyed and the landscape altered with little chance for scientific study and recording. The irony is that whilst parts of the Western Front are increasingly valued for their development potential, the area is simultaneously becoming regarded and valued as a sacred war landscape, particularly with the advent of the Centenary. Thus, development and heritage are two frequently opposed forces and new conservation wars have broken out in the region between progress and protection. Tourism has played a key role in this process not least in the way it places economic value on the physical heritage of war. In addition tourists seek out landscapes that are distinctive and authentic and tourism can be a potent force in applying pressure to protect.[53]

An example of where outrage from tourists and battlefield interest groups led to the protection of war heritage was with a proposed housing development at the Glory Hole site at La Boisselle on the Somme. This was the location for a number of underground tunnels dug by the British and scene of fierce fighting during the Battle of the Somme (1916). Representations via the British All-Party Parliamentary War Heritage Group (APWGBHG) to the Conseil Général de la Somme temporarily halted the development and ensured the prohibition of further construction work at the site. The dispute did, however, bring into sharp focus the clash between development and prosperity and the desire to preserve Great War heritage.[54]

An example of a larger scale project was the proposal by the Belgian government to extend the A19 motorway near Ypres in the early 2000s. This route would have cut across the Pilkem Ridge so important in the early stages of the Third Battle of Ypres (1917).[55] Archaeological excavations along the proposed route, particularly at the 'Cross Roads' site, uncovered trenches, shelters, ammunition depots and gun emplacements as well as the remains of soldiers.[56] It became clear that any large-scale road construction in the area would destroy significant Great War physical remains and disturb the bodies of the unburied. For this reason in August 2005 the Flemish Government announced a change of route although the original proposal remained in the Regional Spatial Implementation Plan (GRUP); in June 2012 the proposal was removed and definitively scrapped.[57] Archaeology here provided persuasive evidence that development would destroy the region's war heritage as well as disturb the war dead.

The conservation and preservation of battlefield sites in general is, however, fraught with difficulty. In global terms a number of war sites are architecturally important (e.g. castles, forts and city walls) and are recognised by preservation legislation (e.g. the Statutory List of Buildings of Special Architectural or Historic Interest in the UK). But the lack of tangible remains on battlefield sites has always disadvantaged them in their recognition as 'heritage' (despite the suggestion that all heritage is intangible and only recognised as such when subject to a process of conservation/ preservation[58]). Nevertheless recognition of the importance of battlefield sites as heritage is reflected in the Vimy Declaration for the Conservation of Battlefield Terrain (2001). This was drawn up 'to reconcile the goals of commemoration, conservation, presentation, visitor safety, and site management in such a way that battlefield terrain and related features are protected and contribute to visitor understanding and appreciation of the site'.[59]

Compared to other historic battlefield sites, the Western Front has a distinctive physical legacy in the form of pillboxes, trench systems and mine craters as well as a 'commemorative layer' of cemeteries and memorials built mostly after the conflict but which are nevertheless integral components of the 'battle-scape'. Much Great War heritage is, however, spread over a huge area and subject to differing juridical and conservation legislation. Moreover money is seldom allocated to conserve the many features lying on private land which are often subject to damage, neglect and inappropriate usage. This is why financial assistance from interested bodies outside the Western Front is so important.

At the time of writing no battlefields were included on the UNESCO World Heritage List of sites.[60] War-related sites do, however, appear on the list including, for example, the seventeenth-century fortifications of the military engineer Vauban comprising twelve groups of fortified buildings and sites along the borders of France. This might reflect a bias within UNESCO towards valuing tangible heritage as opposed to intangible ideals. Additionally the origins of this organisation in the wake of the Second World War have undoubtedly hampered the acknowledgement of twentieth-century war- heritage; despite the presence of several Second World War sites on the list[61] there is still reluctance to value war-heritage, which is still seen in a negative light.

It is not surprising that no heritage sites associated with the Western Front are on the World Heritage Site (WHS) list; First World War battlefields have long been considered "*lieux de mémoire*" (sites of memory) but not "World Heritage".[62] Nevertheless in April 2014 a Tentative List of Western Front war-related sites (an inventory) for WHS nomination was put forward to UNESCO by France and Belgium.[63] To be included on the list a site must meet at least one of ten criteria in order to prove 'cultural and natural diversity of outstanding universal value'.[64] Addressing three criteria[65] the bid is trying to emphasise the unique nature of the Western Front where a new tradition of the 'cult of the dead' has been established around a particular form of large-scale memorialisation; this stresses that 'for the first time in human history … victims are recognized equally in death'. The fact that these victims came from all over the world provides further emphasis that the area is of universal importance. The relevance to humanity of the region is underlined by the way it 'encourages contemplation and celebration of the memory of the dead' and stimulates both individual and collective visitation.[66] But the perception of 'outstanding universal human value' is highly subjective, being influenced by shifting personal, emotional, cultural and political attitudes and opinions. The heritage values of the Western Front sites might not be seen as universal but more linked to remembrance of specific events and sites.[67] Moreover the practical issues surrounding inclusion of a large number of sites, both military and commemorative, ranging over such a large linear area might preclude successful management of such a WHS.[68] At the time of writing the sites were still on the Tentative List and the long process of WHS evaluation and inclusion was still in progress.

Although WHS designation does not provide an automatic guarantee that a host nation will provide legislative protection for any site, inclusion on the list affords a globally recognised imprimatur of value and added leverage in attracting funding. It also imbues a level of kudos which generates additional interest from the tourist industry. Inscription on the list thus has a paradoxical and often contradictory advantage for both conservation and economic advantage.

* * *

The complexity of the Western Front and its enduringly contested nature is no-where seen as forcefully as with the impact humans have had upon the landscape since the end of the war. This is reflected in the far-reaching effects of modern tourism, the commodification of war as an industry and even in the invasive practices of archaeology. The irony of the Western Front is that conceived in bitter antagonism and dispute it remains a highly contentious landscape. Ethical concerns and arguments over protection add new layers of meaning to the area which are likely to become even more complex in the future.

Chapter 8

Visitor experiences

Tourists must speak for themselves and we can learn a great deal from what they say – this is a fundamental aspect of any professional study of tourism. This goes beyond what the expert investigator thinks these experiences might mean. Why have they visited? What does the Great War mean to them? And what do they take away from their visit?

Coach tours and passengers: exploring meaning

The Western Front is not just a geographical or topographical space but an area of imagination. The fusion of place, man-made legacy, narrative and interpretation has the ability to stimulate an astonishing amount of emotional, cognitive and sensorial responses and 'themes', which are expressed through rich inter-personal exchanges amongst visitors. The coach tour is an excellent opportunity to explore these as a 'mobile theatre'[1] where, within the confines of a vehicle, passengers share a common experiential environment. This is not to say that their experiences are the same, however, and there is a great heterogeneity in the way tourists engage, or do not, with the many-layered nature of the Western Front.[2]

Face-to-face interviews are a common method used in ethnographic research to elicit meaning which I employed to explore the deeper aspects of the tourist's engagement with the area.[3] This hands-on research was conducted on two coach tours run by British tour companies: one in April 2010 and the other in July 2014 which was also a walking tour.[4] With permission from the coach companies and advance warning given to the passengers, interviews were entirely voluntary and never undertaken during travelling periods or when the guide was speaking. In 2010 9 passengers were interviewed and 6 in 2014, (including the guides on each tour).[5] All interviews were semi-structured with a few key questions intended as a primer for fuller discussion and to provoke a stream of comment from the passenger. Interviews were recorded and later transcribed verbatim. After due consideration, themes worthy of discussion were identified and are discussed below.

Reasons for visiting

There are many reasons why a person would want to visit the Western Front but the most prominent identified by the survey was family connections.[6] The paradox of the Great War is that as it recedes in time it seems closer emotionally and this is especially true of those with ancestors who fought in the conflict. On being asked why she needed to come to see the actual place where her relative fought one woman commented: '[It's] because … they are no longer here and I need to know what made them want to come out here [and] what prompted them to fight …'[7] Whether a modern generation divested of Edwardian concepts of loyalty and duty would ever be able to understand the motives which drove these men into war is a moot point. Nevertheless the passing of the 'war generation' has afforded a new compulsion to visit – to see and to understand.

The family is a rich environment where memory resides and is passed on through subsequent generations.[8] Conversations within the tour group reflected this as stories of ancestors and their war experiences were circulated through discussion. In addition the early memories of parents or other family members formed key emotional reference points as this example shows:

And I remember my mother telling me, and it always stuck in my mind, that she was a young girl of 12 or 13, when the war took place, and she remembers very well when my uncle came back from the battlefront. He was in the Scottish regiment and the kilts, which were filthy with mud and dirt and everything else, would be put in a big tub in the kitchen with hot water and she and her younger sister would have to tramp them out to get the mud out of those kilts.[9]

The gritty reality of war has here formed a part of a family war myth passed on to a 'post-memory' generation; this process keeps memories alive and can revive those which have atrophied. In some cases experiences can be transmitted so deeply that they seem to constitute first-hand memories in their own right.[10] Transmission lies behind much of the engagement with 'places of memory' so dear to the family story as descendants attempt to 'approach nearer' to their ancestors who they hold with such reverence.[11]

Shock and empathy

A prominent response from many visitors to the Western Front is a mixture of shock, sadness and revulsion at the sheer scale of loss so clearly represented within the 'commemorative landscape'. Visiting the area can have particularly deep effects on tourists as shown here:

> I found today and this whole trip deeply disturbing. I've been horrified at what man is capable of. I felt deeply saddened and just depressed and distressed by the whole thing. It's been so real and so horrific for me and it makes us realise that even down to a family quarrel has to be avoided at all costs, because the next step is this.[12]

The extent of the loss of life is difficult for anyone to fully comprehend so the interviewed passengers tried to understand by creating their own examples drawn from private experience as, for example:

> I find it just unbelievable the sheer volume of people involved … If I think of the capacity of somewhere like the Emirates, the Arsenal stadium in London near where we live, it's about 65,000 when it's absolutely full to the brim; if I think of that in terms of 72,000 casualties and deaths in a short period of time I find that awesome.[13]

The impact of loss in the Great War is made visceral to us because, unlike in previous conflicts, we know so much about the dead and their loved ones; the emotional feelings and responses of men in battle as well as those close to them at home graphically displayed in myriad literary correspondence.[14] The war can have a powerful emotional effect on those who engage with it particularly within the landscape where the killing and destruction took place. This is often reflected in comparisons with a person's family life:

> What does it mean to me?... it's quite a lot of sadness because I'm a mother myself and on this trip I've constantly thought about how I would feel if one of my children, particularly my son, got lost at war, or killed at war. So it's tragedy, particularly at the German grave today I was really emotional.[15]

In the various responses to my questions, there emerged a strong sense of empathy with the men who fought and a common theme was the transference of soldier's private stories into contemporary situations. One woman in the group, a mental health nurse, was particularly struck by the immense trauma suffered by troops and commented:

> I frequently work with people who ... have been traumatised by something that's happened in their childhood ... I think we are ... pampered in terms of the way we view mental health, there are so many resources and services for people, I just think when people came back from that sort of experience [the war], I don't understand how they ever settled into normal life.[16]

Many men were not able to adapt well to the life they had left before the war; the psychological damage caused by combat and 'shell-shock', what we would now call 'post-traumatic stress disorder', was poorly understood.[17] Nevertheless for this woman the contrast between her perception of the services available then and now is important to her as it relates directly to her professional life.

At one point on the 2014 tour we stopped at the memorial near Pozières to George Butterworth (1885–1916); although not so well known today, Butterworth was a talented and celebrated composer, musician and collector of folk songs, and friend of Ralph Vaughan-Williams. On 5 August 1916 he was shot in the head by a German sniper and his body subsequently lost. The same woman was moved by the story related by the guide at this site and was struck by 'the loss of people's talents'. She continued: 'I see what mental illness does to inhibit people's talents, and I suppose it's one thing for it to be inhibited because you're unwell, it's another to be because you've got, you know, blown up [*sic*]'.[18] For her the war was not just about those who were killed; it was also about the nature of those who died and the talents that were wasted, buried beneath the Somme mud, and lost to the post-war generation.

Visiting the Western Front and becoming so closely acquainted with the stories of the men who fought is to adopt an affinity with them beyond any dry regimental history or tactical manual. Enhanced by an appropriate narrative the area brings out most forcefully that these were human beings; we can walk in their footsteps and see where they fought and died. This frequently leads to expressions of endearment in the way people refer to these long dead heroes as if we, too, are their brothers and sisters in arms; this is a type of proxy-camaraderie, transmitted back to the past, and an attempt to reach out to the dead to provide them solace and companionship in their loneliness within the landscape.

One man referred to the dead throughout his interview as 'lads', 'those boys', 'brave boys' and 'these chaps' (he had no military background).[19] The sentiment was also expressed when on walking to a particularly remote cemetery, the guide remarked, 'no-one visits these boys up here much these days'. This form of empathy forms a bond stretching back in time and using terminology the nation would have employed to describe their proud warriors during the Great War.[20]

Moral questions raised by the war were another feature of the rich discussions stimulated by these tours. The Western Front can often result in a feeling of despair that human beings can fail in their moral responsibilities towards others; but this was not the case for one passenger who stated: 'I think the message is really one of the re-affirmation of humanity … that these awful things do happen but that people are concerned about what happened and how it happened and that we need to remember.'[21] Another commented on 'the futility of it all'[22] expressing the commonly held view that the war was worthless and wasteful. The views of the guide on this issue were interesting:

I try and play with a straight bat and play both sides of the argument, but to try and convince people that the Great War is certainly more than the view that so many people have, that its lions led by donkeys, châteaux generals, lambs led to the slaughter, and all the clichés of the Great War. These men deserve better.[23]

For him the best way of honouring the sacrifices of the war generation is not to debase it as futile but to give it meaning beyond the accepted images of mud, blood and suffering for little gain.

Respect, reverence and ethics

In tandem with the shock felt by many of those I interviewed was a range of views reflecting a deeper engagement and understanding of the area; there were several comments relating to the level of respect that should be shown whilst visiting cemeteries and memorials (mirroring the discussion in Chapter 7). During the 2010 tour a number of passengers expressed outrage over the behaviour of a large group of university-age students at Tyne Cot cemetery who had been boisterous and rowdy whilst sitting on the Cross of Sacrifice. This affected several of the group for the remainder of the tour. There are different views on what is right or wrong behaviour at cemeteries and memorials: the official standpoint adopted by those who manage the sites is that a level of appropriate behaviour is expected of visitors. Nevertheless one guide provided a contrary opinion:

> ... the men who fought in both great wars of the twentieth century, they died so those who came after them can actually be free to choose to live their lives, to remember, to respect, to not respect, to behave in any way they like. If they want to do it reverentially, like most of us do, by walking about silently, as we do. Or if you want to do it by piggy-backing your mate around or cartwheeling through the cemetery, surely that is equally as much their right to do it.[24]

This is essentially an argument between freedom of choice/expression and the rather more conservative mourning practices of western religious and cultural traditions. This is a common problem at many religious and spiritual sites affected by tourism where the profane encroaches the sacred; it is an example of where a certain set of reverential values is either discarded or misunderstood by those with an alternative liberal world view.[25] Pilgrimage has different meanings to different people and can frequently lead to a clash of values between those of different cultures and generations.

For some the act of visiting a cemetery is a way of paying one's respects to the fallen and an act of commemoration in itself. There is also a belief that the Western Front, as a place of suffering, could be used to inculcate a sense of respect in others and a message of peace. The power of the area and its ability to provide moral lessons was expressed by one man who commented:

> … I think the younger generation should all be sent over here if you like just to visit the graves and really see what these poor guys went through.[26]

There is a sense that the Western Front speaks directly to society and has the potential to play a role in ameliorating contemporary problems.

The interviewed passengers were asked their views on the issue of militaria and the collecting of objects directly from the battlefield (**Figure 41**). Several felt this was a very real problem as reflected in the following comment:

> I find it degrading that anybody would want to have artefacts of brave brave people who gave their lives for their country. It's rather macabre … Personally I don't think it's right that people should want to collect, whether its helmets or badges or whatever. It would be nice to either put them in a museum or in the ideal world return them to the families of the lost soldiers who gave their lives.[27]

For this individual the possession of items was an affront to the men who fought and not a threat to the scientific and archaeological study of the conflict or a form of looting. It was a moral issue and one of ownership and possession; for him there was something unwholesome and morally reprehensible about taking possession of the objects of brave soldiers. The same individual viewed this activity as shady and reprobate undertaken by 'visitors from the dark side … for very strange reasons'. Elsewhere he described such people as having 'personality defects'.[28]

Nevertheless, the same guide as above, although 'not hugely impressed by any of that', again suggested a more liberal view:

> ... if you have a laissez-faire view of the men who died on these battlefields so people can come and do what the hell they like, but the freedom of choice is there now ... to come and remember these men, or to not remember them, take stuff, not take stuff ... But it matters not a jot what I think; they're not going to listen to people like me or you, they are irresponsible and they'll do it come what may, won't they? Sadly they do it for themselves and rather grimly they do it because there's a market for this kind of stuff now. Then again it feeds back to the whole subject of the Great War is now a sexy subject, people have been drawn into it, people can make money out of it. [But] not for all the right reasons.[29]

The sense of frustration and resignation is clear; the problem is far too great for any one person to prevent happening in the face of a robust 'war industry' and an activity fuelled by a strong demand for the material remains of war.

The landscape

The landscape featured prominently in the answers I was given. Subtle changes in topography, so crucial in the battles of the Western Front, were an important feature of this:

> ... there's an idea of guys walking up hills and being at the bottom of hills and the Germans being on the top, although they are only slopes in a way, and how vulnerable they might be to machine gun fire.[30]

And for another:

> The type of landscape that they were fighting over is still there – you're actually walking in their footsteps ... you could actually see where they walked where they ran, and where they ultimately ... died.[31]

For some visiting the area gave them a realistic link with their previously acquired knowledge as well as providing the potential for post-visit association to stimulate the imagination:

> Just to actually see them [the sites] and physically see them having read so much about them. That's the main reason for looking at it [because] I can get it in my head when I'm reading ...[32]

Much of the attraction of battlefield tourism is to validate, within a geographical setting, events well known to participants.[33] This is enhanced by the insatiable need for tourists to capture this moment through photography since 'most tourists feel that they have not fully absorbed a sight until they stand before it, see it, and take a photograph to record the moment'.[34] One woman was particularly impressed when the group visited the Riqueval Bridge over the Saint Quentin canal, a place immortalised in a photograph taken of the British 137th Brigade, 46th Division, by it in 1918 (**Figures 43 and 44**).[35] As she commented:

> ... to see that place where – that evocative photograph from the First World War [was taken], which some people know and even I know ... something that I've seen in books, on TV – to actually stand there. That meant so much to me and that's the other photograph I've taken of me and my husband on that bridge, because for me, actually, that picture symbolises the First World War.[36]

It is noteworthy that it's not just taking a photograph that is important; because the place is so redolent the photographer includes her spouse imbuing it with special personal significance. The iconic backdrop has the power to intensify the value of this family image through strong association with place; there is furthermore a desire to record one's location at a site symbolising camaraderie, one of the nobler aspects of the British army of the time and reflected in the 1918 photograph.

The Great War has the ability to contribute powerfully to personal and collective identity; it is the domain of hobbyists and passionate enthusiasts who gain kudos from their knowledge of the vast range of topics associated with the conflict. Landscape is important in this in that having 'been there' adds a heightened sense of identity and enhanced standing amongst others. In the words of one woman passenger:

> ... I can talk or feel things ... with authority, that I have actually seen it. And if anybody else says anything to me then no, it wasn't like that, it isn't like that, it wasn't glorious, it was quite awful.[37]

Seeing where the carnage happened provides a certain insider's knowledge: when they return home they are recognised for this amongst others who have not visited the battlefields.

Not all of those interviewed felt the landscape assisted in a complete appreciation of the conflict; one conceded it was good to

> ... get some idea of the terrain ... [but] everything was blown to pieces; they were fighting in mud and water and to really understand that is quite difficult, if you're honest, no matter how vivid your imagination might be.[38]

But an engagement with the Western Front might be something that goes beyond the imagination; we will never be able to truly imagine what the landscape was like during combat no matter how vividly a guide might attempt to bring the terrible events to life. Moving through the landscape is to make sense of an environment through a complex mix of bodily presence, sensorial engagement, familiarity with a narrative, topographical awareness and identification with commemorative space. For the coach tour passenger it is also located in a social environment – to draw on the presence of others, their reactions, responses and levels of participation. To be in a group is to be influenced by the emotions of others and their empathy with former generations; but it is also, in turn, for you to influence these other passengers with your own experiences and reactions.

* * *

The analysis of comments above provides only a flavour of the wide array of meanings that any visit to the Western Front generates. It completely undermines any suggestion that tourist experiences are shallow and frivolous; tourism is a complex practice and tourists are far more than 'sightseers' gazing superficially at a succession of hastily presented sites. Most of the reactions witnessed and recorded in the above surveys were genuinely deep and life-changing for many individuals. These were people willing to be emotionally open to the significance of places and to feel and respect them. Indeed the Western Front brings to the fore moral questions and issues not normally encountered in everyday life; it provides a fusion of imagination and emotion related closely to historical events and a rich multi-faceted landscape that continues to shock and intrigue visitors so long afterwards.

Chapter 9

The Western Front Beyond the Centenary

Just as in 1914, a hundred years later Europe is in crisis. As this book is being written the news is dominated by people on the move: in columns of thousands, walking through fields and along roads and railway tracks, and camping out in the open air.[1] Although most of these are refugees escaping war in the Middle East, the parallels with the wars of the twentieth century are disturbing: the movement of enormous numbers of people, although victims not belligerents, is unsettling and awakens in us memories of vast columns of soldiers, prisoners and refugees like these. It is all the more heart-rending in sharp digital imagery which brings out the raw emotional reality of these scenes far more powerfully than the grainy sepia of earlier times. Like images of the Great War's citizen armies and refugees these modern pictures speak of movement but also of uncertainty: for none of these people, both past and present, knows their ultimate destiny. Large-scale suffering has returned to Europe and these scenes, played out in our multimedia world, have imposed a new emotional geography upon the continent just like the wars that preceded them. And as in the 'July crisis' of 1914 the situation has split Europe's governments and might become one of the great watershed moments of the twenty-first century.

The Great War continues to cast its heavy shadow over us demonstrating that history can be a burden. But perhaps there is a possible redemption, for as the historian Lord Acton commented: 'If the past has been an obstacle and a burden, knowledge of the Past is the safest and surest emancipation.'[2] If we can gain a clearer appreciation of our past then we might be able to foresee a possible outcome and mitigate or even avoid damaging consequences. This book has explored a number of ways in which the past can be understood – through visiting its places and interacting with its legacies through material culture.

Nevertheless the Great War still frustrates our attempts at neat definition and speaks to us in many different ways. This is nowhere so powerfully exemplified as with the Western Front which is a complex and multi-layered palimpsest of meanings and, like other battlefield sites, has as many 'truths' as it has locations.[3] It can be defined as a place of history and interpretation; a stark 'memory-scape' of cemeteries and memorials; a place of pilgrimage; a residential area hosting vibrant communities; a setting for work (agricultural and industrial); an archaeological treasure store; a place of contested heritage, memory and reconstruction; and an increasingly popular tourist destination. Other meanings can be added and existing understandings challenged and modified: whether through debates over the routing of major roads; DNA testing of uncovered bodies of 'the missing'; residents' disquiet over the effects of tourism; or the ethics of souvenir hunting and dealing, the Western Front refuses to lie down. This is because it is 'something political, dynamic, and contested, something constantly open to renegotiation'.[4]

Heritage, landscape and tourism: a triadic relationship

Memory of the Great War – both individual and collective – can be retained in a wide variety of ways which act as vehicles for the recall of past events, peoples and places. Examples of these are contemporary media coverage, art, photography, music, literature and oral recordings. This book has explored another set of phenomena – heritage, landscape and tourism – which have a distinct yet understated role to play in the dynamics of memory. But what is striking about these three is their powerful inter-dependency; in the transmission of memory they interact and feed off each other in a manner that, although frequently latent, is nevertheless powerful and dynamic.

As this book has demonstrated tourism relies heavily on the landscape, the 'last witness' to the events of war; without the memorials and cemeteries of the Western Front the tourist experience would be much diminished as these physical legacies act as portals to rich and intriguing narratives. The same can be said of heritage which is a further element in the tourist engagement with the past in the form of the war's built legacy and the wealth of artefacts in the region's museums. Heritage, both movable and immovable, can be given added value by tourist interest and objects afforded a second or even third 'life'. The landscape in turn relies on human interest in the form of tourism to provide validation; this is manifest in the increasing economic value of the landscape as a heritage tourism asset and protection for its war heritage.

The relationship between these three phenomena is, however, not always harmonious. As we have seen local opinions are not always in accord with the positive effects of tourism and interference with economic and social development for conservation reasons can lead to tensions. It can also result in inter-communal rivalry and bitterness as communities compete with each other for the Great War 'dividend'.[5] The situation can be compounded by ethical issues and debates over the increasing 'commodification' of human suffering (Chapter 7). Nevertheless, however imperfect the relationship might be, overall the interplay between the three results in a much more informed understanding of the Great War, its places of conflict, its participants, their lives and deaths, the issues involved and the historical context which formed its backdrop.

The Western Front: a memorial landscape

Landscape, as 'memory's most serviceable reminder',[6] provides a vital link to the past and has the great ability to stimulate our consciousness of historical events. The Western Front is one of the world's most poignant war landscapes and speaks powerfully and emotionally of varying moral sentiments including human endeavour, loss and sacrifice. Now that the last soldiers of the Great War have passed on the landscape has taken on a renewed meaning as the location for so much of their war experiences. All we have left are their accounts (written, recorded or filmed) and the artefacts they were familiar with; these can only be understood properly by reference to this landscape which provides a material testimony to the reality of war and the ordinary human beings caught up in it.

The men who fought can no longer speak about the war; the landscape, however, remains a witness. And as it lives on it takes on a new responsibility; although its appearance might alter the landscape becomes timeless in its ability to inform, shock and educate where human interest is present. This is because 'whereas ... written texts are 'infinitely malleable' and readily abridged, films edited and photographs airbrushed, the landscape feels immutable'.[7] Armed with a narrative of the conflict, and able to interpret the topographical textures of the land, the modern visitor can gain a rich insight into the Great War. Aided by interpretation the Western Front landscape has the ability to foster a keen sense of empathy from the visitor based upon the multi-faceted nature of the region which this book has illustrated.

But the Western Front is more than just a witness to events; the Great War left an indelible mark on this landscape, not just in the subtle clues lying in the fields and contours, but deep in the local psyche. As a modern journalist has commented: 'no war in history has left so deep a gash on the local land, mind and memory ... The war did not just change the landscape ... it became the landscape'.[8] Perceptually, symbolically and an integral part of local memory, the war has been branded into the landscape with a deep and enduring permanence. This is given further poignancy by the fact that within this benign countryside lie enormous numbers of corpses. The 'missing' give the area an added dimension absent in many other war-scapes; the war has become one with the landscape, not just in the minds of residents and visitors, but in a chillingly literal sense. Because beneath the feet lie the scattered remains of the fallen, so familiar to us through their letters, postcards and images, but now at one with the landscape, flesh and bones melded into the earth. This brings history, memory, tourism, acts of commemoration and the material legacy of the war together, welded into an indissoluble whole, and collapsing the distance between past and present in a unique way. The Western Front landscape is an enormous memorial itself, a terrain sanctified by the dead, and memorialised through human behaviour.

Underscored by a sense of immutability the area is nevertheless subject to dramatic changes which become more significant as time progresses. Issues such as road and railway building, housing and industrial development, and the use of land for renewable energy **(Figure 45)** are new challenges facing the region; in the case of Flanders, its strategic setting in north-western Europe, which made it the location for so much fighting in the Great War, is now provoking other battles as governments and developers vie to improve communication links and stimulate industry in the region. Questions relating to the preservation of battlefield landscapes have thus become more relevant (as with the A19 development and the Pilkem Ridge 'battle-scape') and it will be interesting to see whether the situation will change if the Western Front be awarded the status of a UNESCO World Heritage Site (Chapter 7).

How tourism shapes memory

Tourism is a powerful force in the fashioning of memory. Along the Western Front tourist authorities and private initiatives have a role in selecting, developing and promoting sites and thereby contributing to the memory of the war; and tourists themselves, through their activities, interests, behaviour and levels of engagement have an ability to influence memory in a dynamic way. This is shown by a number of practices: just by visiting sites tourists uphold their importance and validity and afford them renewed significance; they help endow routes across the terrain with meaning as well as leaving tangible expressions of memory at sites in the form of wreaths and poppies; and they help transmit memory of events on their return home through on-line discussion forums and membership of Great War interest groups and societies.[9] Tourists moreover attend commemorative events in large numbers and in doing so are key players in the perpetuation of ceremonies and memorial practices.

The Last Post ceremony, described at the beginning of this book, is an example of an event never originally designed for the large numbers of tourists who now attend. Their burgeoning presence has created new memory practices as the event has become more of a spectacle and additional music, readings, soldier biographies and a programme of schools and military cadet participation has been introduced. But this has also created challenges for the organisers who, eager to maintain a respectful ambience, have now needed to provide a code of behavioural conduct on their website.[10]

The Centenary has provided a unique impetus for tourism along the Western Front and, as with any commemoration, is likely to have stimulated interest in the Great War amongst those who would not otherwise have paid any attention to it.[11] What is noteworthy about the Centenary is the plethora of 'sub-commemorations' that 2014–18 has spawned. These have included the events leading up to the outbreak of war, the Christmas Truce of 1914, individual battles and the deaths of important national figures (e.g. the British nurse Edith Cavell, executed by the Germans on 12 October 1915).

This has further broadened the appeal of the Western Front as a cultural destination.

Tourists maintain memory through their visiting behaviour but also through their activities. One of the most ubiquitous of these is the collection of memories through photography, the all-pervasive hallmark of the modern tourist. For the tourist everything leads to the photograph and essentially 'travel becomes a strategy for accumulating photographs'.[12] Tourists rely on old pictures of the Western Front (from during and after the war) which are important in triggering memory; but in taking more images they actively add a new layer to the memory of the war and its legacies. Their pictures are 'documents' in themselves, important anthropological resources, which will allow us to understand how people experience the Front now just as we look back on early visitors in the 1920s through their images. A common site along the Western Front is of tourists taking pictures of unexploded ordnance **(Figure 42)**. The lethal force of these explosives is a core theme in the narrative of the war and seeing these objects lying in the ground, the potential to kill and maim still very present, affords many visitors an exciting dimension to their explorations. You touch these objects at your peril so 'capturing' them through the camera's lens is a way of disarming them, of making them neutral, and perhaps the next best thing to taking them home as souvenirs. This expression of bravura is the nearest most will get to the lethality of war and has become a social practice in itself.

The latest trend is that of taking 'selfies' and this is common along the Western Front as at the Menin Gate ceremony (see Prologue). It is not enough just to take a picture of a memorial or gravestone – you have to be in it – and you can send it to your friends instantaneously through your smartphone. This immediacy in communicating the experiences of travel is a rapidly growing phenomenon greatly stimulated by the new social media.[13] But is this an appropriate way of behaving at sites of memory? Is this disrespectful or just an acceptable expression of individual tourist behaviour? There is evidence for a disturbing trend in selfies at 'dark' sites, clearly a prurient and tasteless practice by those emotionally unaffected by the messages these places have the potential to convey.[14] Tourism instils memory and photography is one way in which this is achieved; but do selfies demean the memory of sites where so much suffering took place and provide a future record which says more about the human subject and their attitudes and motivations than the sites which are the settings themselves?

The experience of most tourists when visiting the Western Front is characterised by deep and emotionally resonant encounters which are often life changing.[15] What is remarkable about the area is its ability to stimulate such responses from those with no known connection to the dead, or at least a tenuous link with their ancestors. There is evidence also that visiting the Western Front can assist in working through individual grief and encourage a profound sense of catharsis. The experiences of a young woman, Charlotte Darlington, on a school visit to the area in 2010 soon after the death of a close friend, are most revealing; the empathetic nature of the visit and the fact that the Western Front affected so many families provided a comforting perspective and a strong sense of emotional release for her. Standing at one cemetery, although overwhelmed by the scale of the loss, she recalled 'feeling at ease with my own life again'.[16] But the visit also allowed her a heightened sense of engagement with her surroundings:

> I genuinely believe that having just experienced a personal bereavement I was able to connect to my surroundings in the battlefields on a much stronger level than I would if I was not already grieving.[17]

The Western Front clearly had a profound influence upon her resulting in feelings of peace which helped her come to terms with a personal loss completely unrelated to the events of the Great War. This suggests that the fusion of landscape and narrative has the power to speak to people viscerally; through an empathetic process memory here is working its way into present individual concerns and situations in a dynamic and life–affecting way. Visiting the area is no frivolous activity and, unlike many forms of tourism, can have decidedly serious intent and outcomes.

Along the Western Front war tourism is not a neutral phenomenon but an active force working imperceptibly, yet strongly, in maintaining and perpetuating the memory of war. This is crucial, as without continual reinforcement the dates and places of commemoration can fade as memory atrophies.[18] Tourism has a powerful role in ensuring that the war is not forgotten in both private and public spheres.

The Western Front – looking to the future

In a debate on the war at the British Library in London in February 2014, a prominent British historian expressed concern that the nation would experience 'World War One fatigue' before the end of the Centenary in 2018.[19] Enthusiasm for the Great War has certainly received a boost from widespread activities and media coverage, but questions remain about how far events now receding into the past will continue to be prominent; will there be a time when historical memory of the Great War will wane, perhaps superseded by more significant and terrible events? Of course it is impossible to say but there is no reason why a war, so deeply imbued with moral meanings and so engrained into culture, cannot remain prominent in memory. The Western Front landscape has an important role to play in this perpetuation of memory and, as these chapters have demonstrated, despite modern pressures continues to hold a special place in the national consciousness of nations across the globe.

Warfare destroys and results in immense damage to the image post-conflict destinations have amongst tourists; nevertheless battlefield sites have an afterlife and there is a clear 'war dividend' which can benefit countries, regions or local communities for an indefinite period as a result of the interest others show in battle sites and their propensity to visit them.[20] The historian Jay Winter has detected three stages in the afterlife of *lieux de memoire* ('sites of memory') and these can be applied to the development of the Western Front. First, there is an initial commemorative period during which a 'commemorative form' is established through the siting, building and creation of places and ceremonies. During the second stage rituals are established in an annual calendar which then becomes routine (as with the Last Post ceremony in the late 1920s). This is followed by a critical third phase when public monuments either disappear or are upheld as prominent sites of memory. This final phase is contingent upon whether successive communities of interest inherit earlier meanings attached to these places or events or whether they add new meanings.[21]

The Western Front, its sites and ritualised ceremonies, has experienced varying phases of interest and importance; it nevertheless follows Winter's trajectory as new meanings are established. We have probably lost touch with the original meanings attached to the commemorative landscape of the Western Front especially with the valedictory nature of some of the larger state-sponsored memorials. But new meanings have been formed and continue to be, as, for example, when the area speaks to contemporary concerns about international events.[22] The commemorative landscape of the Western Front is a constant reminder that, in the words of one historian, 'any decision for war must confront the historical evidence that it is a fearfully blunt instrument'.[23] Several commentators have seen parallels with contemporary events as between the political and military decisions taken in the aftermath of the terrorist attacks of September 11, 2001, resulting in immense civilian suffering and unclear political outcomes in the Middle East, and the diplomatic and political mishaps that led to the catastrophe in 1914. Further comparisons can be made between the resurgence in ethnic nationalism, concerns over the use of chemical weapons (2013 – in the Syrian civil war) and the psychological trauma experienced by veterans from the wars in Iraq and Afghanistan.[24] The Great War still has 'universal applicability, if only as a distant but a forceful warning';[25] the past speaks to the present powerfully amongst the cemeteries and memorials of the Western Front, an area so emblematic of all that went wrong in this global conflict.

If the Western Front is an area subject to constant change then this is clearly represented in new forms of memorialisation which will likely become more prominent in the future. Traditional memorials still exist as in the form of cemeteries and monuments; but what is noticeable about the area is the appearance of new memorials in the form of interactive museum displays and the growing number of community commemorations, both formal and informal.[26] Many of these have been stimulated by a burgeoning heritage tourism industry and a 'commemorative-mania' that the Centenary is doing much to accelerate. Examples of this are the newly opened or refurbished museums along the Front which have commemorative aspects built into them; this is commonly found in spaces for reflection, perhaps linked to displays on the human cost of war, and often in the final galleries (as at the Memorial Museum Passchendaele 1917). New ideas on interpreting the war also have a key role in complementing traditional forms of memorialisation; the new visitor centre alongside the Thiepval Memorial enhances the visitor's understanding of this monument which in turn provides the centre with a context.[27] Additionally new interactive and multi-media interpretation can have an important role in complementing traditional forms of memorialisation as at the IFFM.

Arguments about the shallow nature of much contemporary heritage interpretation abound and there is a danger that technology can be misused to provide nothing more than 'commemoration-as-entertainment'. But anything that stimulates a respectful interest in the sufferings of war cannot be a bad thing; in this respect many aspects of the heritage industry could be co-opted into encouraging memory and directing visitors towards an appreciation of the war landscape and its story. Memory is also transmitted through tour guides and intangible private and public discussion; it has now moved beyond the confines of set dates and times for commemoration and specific codes of practice. Perhaps it is time to broaden our definition of what a memorial is, and acknowledge wider activities that trigger memory.

One of the great unknowns is the extent to which future technologies will affect the memorialisation of the war, as with the phenomenon of 'virtual' worlds. How far can this be used in memorialisation and can 'virtual' realities really maintain the important contemplative and emotional aspects of memory? Can we ever genuinely remember war with the aid of the technologies of virtual reality? The CWGC have developed an on-line 'virtual' cemetery with interactive features for educational purposes which shows how organisations are starting to embrace new and innovative methods of remembrance and interpretation.[28] In the immediate aftermath of war, memories were (literally) set in stone to be remembered in perpetuity; however now new memorials are providing more interactive experiences allowing for a greater level of choice in selecting memories and introducing more complex interpretations. Those who champion the internet claim that 'it promotes connection and dissemination ... [and] decries deification and instead promotes fluidity of image and idea'.[29] The internet is able to provide a multi-dimensional experience of memory as well as provoke reactions amongst its users in a dynamic fluidity of exchange that more monolithic material forms of memorialisation are unable to achieve. This allows for a questioning of more established forms of memory and 'eliciting an engaged response'.[30] Nevertheless the traditional forms of monuments in engraved stone that dominated the old forms of memorialisation are still valuable for those seeking an authentic encounter with the past and it's suffering; there is much to be said about being in the landscapes of war, interacting with memorials to the fallen, utilising the range of senses to engage intimately with memory, and being in the physical company of the like-minded. The virtual world has powerful potential to complement traditional forms and provide convenient and democratic triggers for memory; but it will never be able to replicate the deeper engagements that make the Western Front such a compelling place.

The Western Front and modern conflict

As a coda to this exploration of tourism on the Western Front, one needs to ask whether the experience of its various places as a war-scape over the last century has any lessons for the sites of modern conflict. Will the desire to visit the sites of war and a validation of place and heritage be as powerful in the future as it has been in the case of the twentieth century's world wars? One of the challenges is the changing nature of modern warfare and the idea of a 'battle-site'; the experience of war in Iraq and Afghanistan in the 2000s has shown how the sites of combat are smaller in nature and conflict is marked more by local actions, sites of roadside bombs and guerrilla attacks than large-scale 'battle-fields'. If a level of security ever makes it possible to visit these countries then the nature of battlefield tourism there will be markedly different from the Western Front and those interested in understanding these conflicts will need to visit many different sites; guerrilla warfare does not lend itself conveniently to more traditional forms of battlefield tourism. But the massive 'war-dividend' experienced along the Western Front over the last century is unlikely to be transferred to Iraq and Afghanistan as continuing instability and danger has stifled all forms of tourism.[31] This might, in turn, encourage a more imaginative form of visitation through 'virtual' worlds and an experience of the places of war travelling in hyper-reality rather than a physical movement through actual space. Tourism stands at the cusp of a brave new world.

There are also implications for memorialisation brought about by changes in mass media practices as the reporting of war becomes instantaneous and moves beyond the traditional profession of reporters and correspondents.

Now anyone 'in the field', including soldiers themselves, can record images of war and download or transmit them to global audiences. The fact that this can be in real-time provides a personalisation of death and suffering unprecedented in what was previously a more distant understanding of war. The public are now able to access digital images of soldiers in battle which are providing surrogate memorials to their lives and sufferings. We now do not need material memorials or archival records but have a convenient digital means to construct a form of collective, if virtual, remembrance.[32] A corollary of this has been an increasing personalisation of the soldier in society as we connect to their lives, families, interests and foibles like never before.[33] The soldier is more human than ever and this might, inadvertently, make it more difficult for a country like Britain to put troops 'on the ground' in future conflicts.[34] In democratic countries – particularly in a 'post-Iraq' Britain – governments are increasingly sensitive to criticism that they are responsible for unnecessary human loss in wars; now digitally 'experienced' by a public skilled in the use of information technology, wars in the future will be far more 'high-tech', fought from the air or sea, but much less on the dangerous ground. This in turn has implications for the sites of war where in the future there will be very little to actually visit.

But this presupposes that warfare in the future will relate to physical land; technological advances are challenging our concepts of conflict. Cyber-warfare might make guns, bombs and missiles obsolete as war becomes more a matter of attacks on a country's infrastructure disabling government systems, hospitals, factories, power stations and armies even before they have the chance to fight.[35] What is frightening about this scenario is the ability of virtually anyone with the technical skills to undertake such attacks: in the future 'war' is as likely to be fought by a 'geek' in his bedroom as it is by an army on the ground.[36] Cyber-warfare would make the concept of the battlefield obsolete; but the huge sacrifices of the Western Front will live on, as poignant reminders of conflict and the far-reaching human effects of war.

* * *

The Western Front is a complex place and continues to shock, appal, intrigue or fascinate in a variety of ways. It is remarkable that even after a century it still speaks to us – powerfully, emotionally and resolutely – encouraged by numerous 'memory activists' and the impetus of tourism. To say that we must continue to remember sounds trite; but this we must do ensuring that a respect for the unimaginable suffering of others is maintained in the face of rapidly shifting cultural attitudes and values. In the poem *Aftermath* (1919) the poet Siegfried Sassoon exhorted his erstwhile comrades in arms to remember, no matter how irksome a task this might seem, with the words:

> But the past is just the same–and War's a bloody game ...
> Have you forgotten yet?...
> Look down, and swear by the slain of the War that you'll never forget.[37]

In looking down at the landscape over which war raged, and so many lives were shattered, we too must never forget.

Appendices

Appendix 1: Opening Dates for Museums and Café–Museums Along the Western Front

(Belgium and Nord-Pas-de-Calais Picardie and Île-de-France regions of France)

Museum/Visitor Centre	Date of first opening
Hill 62 Museum (Sanctuary Wood)	1923 (rebuilt in 1947 and 1980)
Franco-Australian Museum, Villers-Bretonneux (originally called the William Legatt Museum)	1975
Museum to the South African Forces, Delville Wood, Longueval	1986
Historial de la Grande Guerre, Péronne	1992
Musee des Abris, Albert	1992
Hooge Crater Museum	1994
Ulster Memorial Tower Visitor Centre	1994
Le Tommy Café, Pozières	1994
P'tit train de la Haute Somme	1996
Vimy Memorial Park, Interpretive Centre	1997
In Flanders Fields Museum, Ypres (formally the Ypres Salient Memorial Museum)	1998 (new exhibitions opened 2012)
Newfoundland Memorial Park Visitor Centre, Beaumont-Hamel	2001
The Memorial Museum Passchendaele 1917, Zonnebeke (formerly the Streekmuseum (1989–2002))	2004 (new wing and Trench Experience opened 2013)
Trenches of Death, Dixsmuide	2004
Talbot House Museum (Exhibition), Poperinge	2004?
Thiepval Memorial Visitor Centre	2004
Tyne Cot Cemetery Visitor Centre	2007
Wellington Quarries, Arras	2008
"Ocean Villas" Café and WW1/WW2 Museum, Auchonvillers	2008
Musée de la Grande Guerre, Meaux	2011
Maison Forestière Wilfred Owen, Ors	2011
Lijssenthoek Cemetery Visitor Centre	2012
Museum Letaille, Bullecourt	2012
Plugstreet 14–18 Interpretation Centre	2013
Musée de la bataille de Fromelles	2014 (replacing previous museum opened in 1990)

Appendix 2: Visitor Numbers at 10 Selected World War One Sites in the Westhoek (Belgium), 2013–2014. Adapted from Westtoer (2014): 4.

Selected World War One sites	Jan–Sept 2013	Jan–Sept 2014	+/-%
Tyne Cot Cemetery	285,958	468,116	+64%
In Flanders Fields Museum	212,217	372,667	+76%
Langemark German Cemetery	136,036	257,011	+89%
Memorial Museum Passchendaele 1917, Zonnebeke	61,553	144,654	+135%
Dodengang Trenches, Diksmuide	63,276	144,242	+128%
Ijzer Tower Museum	57,652	109,772	+90%
Lijssenthoek Military Cemetery	46,784	83,301	+78%
Vladslo German Cemetery	42,948	92,522	+115%
Bayernwald Trenches	30,902	44,643	+44%
Talbot House, Poperinge	20,087	41,269	+105%
Visitor Numbers (total)	957,413	1,758,197	+84%
World War One Visitor Numbers	**319,000**	**578,000**	**+81%**

Appendix 3: The Western Front – Push and Pull Factors

PUSH	PULL
Intrinsic	*Extrinsic*
Activities to address needs	*Destination generated forces or knowledge about a destination*
• Family history/genealogy interests	• Proximity to tourist generating area
• "To pay respects"	• Persuasive marketing/destination image
• Pursuit of knowledge	• Tourist information
• Specialist interests	• Quality of tourist amenities
• Social interaction	• Service quality
• Rest and relaxation	• Provision of museums and heritage interpretation
• To do something interesting/different	• Availability of guides
• Escape	• Events/anniversaries
• To increase personal standing amongst others	• Ceremonies
	• Cemeteries/memorials
	• Media coverage of war narrative
	• Literature/poetry/art of the war

Appendix 4: Types of Representative Pilgrimage

Representative pilgrimage			
Private remembrance			Collective remembrance
Private memorials/graves of non-famous		Private memorials/ graves of famous	Organised events/ pilgrimages to memorials/ cemeteries
Related – representing family members	Unrelated/ strangers – private interest and moral responsibility ('memory activists')	Interest groups visits to sites of VC winners/ dignitaries/poets (e.g. Hedd Wyn) ('memory activists')	Dignitaries as key representatives (e.g. British royals at St. Symphorien Military Cemetery, 2014)

Appendix 5: Survey of Western Front Coach Tour Operators (2014)

	n	%
Battlefield/ war-related only	24	52.0
Battlefield and other tours	9	19.6
Schools/groups only	6	13.0
Battlefield and other cultural/historical	4	8.7
WW1 only	2	4.3
Specialist events	1	2.2
Total:	46	99.9*

* Does not add up to 100% due to rounding

Appendix 6: The Tangible Heritage of the Western Front

1	Commemorative heritage	• Cemeteries • Memorials: e.g. Vimy Memorial; St George's Memorial Church, Ypres
2	Built or manufactured – generated by war	• Remains of bunkers/dug-outs/blockhouses/pillboxes/forts • Trench systems (including preserved/reconstructed) • The underground war – mine shafts, galleries, caves • Transport systems: roads (e.g. the 'corduroy' Menin Road); Decauville narrow-gauge rail tracks (e.g. Le Petit Train) • Remains of detritus: e.g. corrugated iron, picket posts and ordnance (included unexploded)
3	Existing – given value by war	• Buildings: original or reconstructed in facsimile (e.g. the Cloth Hall, Ypres) • Destroyed villages: either left in original state (e.g. Fay) or reconstructed (e.g. Passchendaele) • Religious: e.g. calvaries; Albert Basilica
4	Locations of significance	• For rest and relaxation: e.g. Talbot House, Poperinge • Linked to poets: e.g. Essex Farm, Ypres; Wilfred Owen's House • Places associated with well-known figures: e.g. Winston Churchill at Ploegsteert; châteaux used by Generals • Associated with events: e.g. Armistice at Compiègne; Hall of Sole Command, Doullons
5	Natural and topographical	• Shell hole landscapes/mine craters: e.g. Lochnagar Crater • Preserved war landscapes: e.g. Newfoundland Memorial Park • Iconic battle topographies: e.g. the Sunken Lane, Beaumont-Hamel • Poppies (a national symbol of remembrance)
6	Artefacts	• In museums: e.g. war *matériel*, weapons, uniforms, flags, archives (including diaries and letters) • In private collections (as above) including displays at cafe-museums

Appendix 7: Types of Museum Collections on the Western Front

	Types	Examples	Rationale	Features
1	Large nationally important museums	In Flanders Fields Museum, Ypres; Historial de la Grande Guerre Péronne; Musée de la Grande Guerre du Pays de Meaux	Educational; social history	Examples of artefacts used to interpret the war; large artefacts on display (e.g. vehicles); multi-themed; multi-national; use sophisticated high-tech interpretational techniques; curatorial responsibilities; meet appropriate conservation standards; amenities – restaurant, shop; have study centres and large educational and outreach programmes; organise conferences
2	Regionally important museums	Passchendaele 1917 Memorial Museum; Musée Somme 1916, Albert; Museum of the Battle of Fromelles	Educational; emphasize local conflicts/battles	Have study centres; curatorial responsibilities; normally meet appropriate conservation standards; educational and schools programmes; organise conferences
3	Nationalistic museums	Franco–Australian Museum, Villers–Bretonneux; Delville Wood (South Africa)	Educational; tell story of a particular nation's part in the conflict	At the site of a major battle/engagement; collection related to a nation; sited on purchased land; funded and managed by home governments; normally meet appropriate conservation standards

	Types	Examples	Rationale	Features
4	Privately owned collections –including café museums	Hooge Crater Museum, Ypres; Sanctuary Wood; Ocean Villas at Auchonvillers; Tommy Café, Pozières; Museum Letaille, Bullecourt	Privately owned; collecting/militaria	Sometimes combined with a café/restaurant; 'rust and dust'; war *matériel* prominent with less emphasis on interpretation; rarely meet appropriate conservation standards; less formalised display; no use of sophisticated interpretational techniques; items often for sale
5	Collections displayed in Visitor Centres	Newfoundland Memorial Park, Beaumont-Hamel; The Ulster Memorial Tower Visitor Centre	Educational; tell story of a particular site	Selected artefacts displayed; smaller collections; do not always meet appropriate conservation standards

There is some overlap in this typology: for example the Museum Letaille, Bullecourt also focusses on the Battle of Arras (1917) and because of the involvement of Australian forces at Fromelles the museum there is also a nationalistic museum.

Notes

About this book
1. United Nations Statistical Commission (2008): 10.

Prologue
1. From *For the Fallen* by Laurence Binyon (1869–1943); see Walter (2006): 235.
2. These words are engraved on the war memorial to British soldiers who fell at Kohima in north-east India in 1944. It is said to have been inspired by an epitaph written during the First World War by the Classical scholar John Maxwell Edmonds (1875–1958) who based it upon the famous lines written to commemorate the loss of the Spartan rear-guard at Thermopylae (480 BC) by Simonides of Ceos; see http://archive.iwm.org.uk/server/show/ConWebDoc.1261

Introduction
1. Weintraub (2001): 177.

Chapter 1
1. Italy changed her allegiances and joined the Allies in 1915; the Central powers also included Bulgaria (from 1915) and the Ottoman Empire. The war was called variously at the time *The Great War*, *The War* or *The German War*. In this book I use the terms *Great War* and *First World War* interchangeably.
2. British Chancellor of the Exchequer David Lloyd-George (1863–1945) in Lloyd-George (1933): 52.
3. Hastings (2013): xxii.
4. Of these 52% of Allied forces became casualties (5 million killed, 13 million wounded) and 57% from the Central Powers (3.3 million killed, 8.3 million wounded). Britain and the Empire lost 908,000 men; see Smith (2014).
5. Named after the German Chief of General Staff Alfred Graf von Schlieffen (1833–1913).
6. Hastings (2013): 324–25; see Figure 26.
7. Some reports state that trenches had been dug as early as 15 September but the practice must have developed gradually during the outflanking movements as forces attempted to protect their established lines.
8. For an account of a visit to the Front's beginning and end see O'Shea (1996): 11–14 and 186–188. The Belgians occupied 40 miles, the British 90 miles and the French the remainder although units from the Allied armies often took over parts of the line from each other.
9. Sassoon (1928): 226.
10. Barbusse (2003): 243.

11. Wilfred Owen (1893–1918) in a letter to Osbert Sitwell in 1918.
12. Saunders (2007): 65.
13. Reynolds (2013) – the title of the book an apt comment on the Great War's effect on the country.
14. Parris (2011).
15. J. Winter (2006): 12.
16. Reynolds (2015): 235.
17. With the approach of the Centenary of the outbreak of the war (2014) this was brought to the fore with much debate between traditionalist and 'revisionist' historians about the origins of the war; see Mombauer (undated). There was also a campaign to highlight an alternative narrative by anti-war activists and peace campaigners including a commemoration of executed conscientious objectors; see Quinn (2013).
18. British Future (2013): 4.
19. Ziino (2015): 2–3.
20. Sheffield Hallam University (2015): 4. The HLF is the body which distributes a share of the proceeds from the state-franchised National Lottery to preserve and make accessible the nation's heritage. Grants have also been provided by other organisations such as the Western Front Association which by March 2015 had awarded over £40,000 to nearly 50 projects.
21. Furness (2013); BBC Media Centre (2015); see also the exhaustive list of written articles and radio/TV broadcasts in Historyworks (2012).
22. More than 16 Million people are estimated to have participated in this. An unusual feature was a free-to-download commemorative app by the artist Jeremy Deller which included a digital candle; see 14–18 Now (undated).
23. Brown (2014).
24. Royal British Legion (2015).
25. The Woodland Trust (undated).
26. For a comprehensive list of First World War commemorative events and projects in Britain see First World War Centenary (2015).
27. Nicholas Witchell, BBC1 News, 11 November 2014.
28. A phenomenon also reflected in Great War museums in France as outlined in Chapter 6.
29. Wilson (2008a): 110.
30. Reynolds (2013): xv.
31. Quoted in Reynolds (2013): 336.
32. Vanneste and Foote (2013): 266.
33. The words of the British historian Hew Strachan quoted in Ziino (2015): 2.
34. An example of this is the film *War Horse* (2011) which was based on Michael Morpurgo's book of the same name published in 1982; the stage production was premiered at the Royal National theatre, London in 2007.
35. The word entered the English language from the Netherlands in the late sixteenth century from the Dutch word *landschap*; see Schama (1995): 10.
36. Robertson and Richards (2003).
37. Seaton (2000): 63.
38. Nevertheless, there is evidence that in the French *département* of the Somme the Centenary is providing an opportunity for tourists to visit a range of heritage attractions not just those relating to the Great War. E-mail correspondence with M. Alexandre Lefevre, European Project Coordinator, Somme Tourisme, Amiens, 20/05/15.
39. Creswell (2004): 7.
40. Tuan (1977): 138.

Chapter 2

1. Out of over 14,000 civil parishes in England and Wales during the war there were only 53 where all service personnel returned; these came to be known as the 'Thankful' or 'Blessed' Villages.
2. Spagnoly and Smith (2002): 117. A description of journalists visiting the French line is given in Barbusse (2003): 33–34.
3. Lloyd (1998): 23.
4. Michelin and Co. (1917): Foreword.
5. Michelin and Co. (1917): Foreword.
6. A good example is given in Dunn (1987): 576.
7. In French the word simply means 'memory' which suggests that these items were more than just 'tat'; see Edwards (2009): 87.
8. Bishop and Bostridge (1998): 252.
9. Lloyd (1998): 27.
10. Lloyd (1998): 29.
11. Longworth (2003): 14 and 42.
12. Connelly (2009). The League also published a battlefield history and guide called *The Immortal Salient* (1925).
13. Lloyd (1998): 102.
14. The popular Baedeker guide to Belgium and Holland had reached its 15th edition by 1910.
15. Mosse (1990): 154.
16. Lloyd (1998): 30.
17. E.g.: that by Captain Atherton Fleming; see Fleming (1919).
18. Lloyd (1998): 103.
19. E.g.: Anon. (1921).
20. E.g.: Lloyd (1998): 116.
21. Saunders (2003a). A young Walt Disney made money from selling items to visitors while working as a Red Cross volunteer in France in 1918–19; see Gabler (2007): 40.
22. Longworth (2003): 42.
23. Seaton (2000): 63.
24. Both quoted in Clout (1996): 40.
25. Jalland (2010): 74.
26. Dunn (1987): 573.
27. The Hill 60 museum was run by the Delannoy family who also owned the trench museum at Hill 62 (Sanctuary Wood). By the 1960s the museums were being run by two cousins – Michel Delannoy at Hill 60 (until 2006) and Jacques Schier at Hill 62 (until his death in 2014 – although the museum is still open). After its closure part of the Hill 60 collection was bought by the In Flanders Fields Museum and the Memorial Museum Passchendaele and split equally between the two. Michel Delannoy kept some material to himself including the stereoscopes that made his museum famous after the Second World War; e-mail correspondence with Piet Chielens, IFFM, 18/12/15.
28. Lloyd (1998): 38.
29. Lloyd (1998): 136.
30. Jalland (2010).
31. Jalland (2010): 71.
32. E.F. Williams, quoted in Lloyd (1998): 42.
33. Walter (2006): 257.

34. Lloyd (1998): 103–05.
35. Lloyd (1998): 105–06.
36. Lloyd (1998): 107.
37. Vance (1997): 57.
38. Lloyd (1998): 111.
39. Lloyd (1998): 109.
40. Gordon (1998).
41. On 1 June 1940 Hitler flew from Germany to Brussels then continued on his tour through Ghent, Ypres, Langemark, Poperinge, Kemmelberg, Menen and Lille before spending the night at Brigode Castle at Annapes. The fact that he met several generals and observed evidence of the recent eviction of Allied forces from the region suggests that the tour had a military purpose. But the Führer also found time to visit the places where he had served in the Great War including Geluveld where he saw the first action and Messines where he had been billeted at Bethlehem Farm. He also stopped at the Menin Gate, his first time in Ypres. His visit to the Langemark military cemetery was hugely symbolic: here lay the remains of tens of thousands of German soldiers among them the inadequately trained student volunteers killed around Ypres in October–November 1914 in the *Kindermord* (Massacre of the Innocents). However the tour, undertaken barely days after the Belgian capitulation, was a clever propaganda exercise, meticulously recorded by Hitler's official photographer, Heinrich Hoffmann, whose incredible images can be found at http://www.hitlerpages.com/pagina112.html A recent history of the tour using witness accounts can be found in Debaeke (2011).
42. Addison and Jones (2005): 186.
43. Edwards (2004): 145.
44. Longworth (2003): 234.
45. Reynolds (2013): 316–17. The movement from communicative to cultural memory nevertheless lasted for the remainder of the century with the last British veteran of the trenches, Private Harry Patch, only passing away in 2009 and the last combat veteran of the war, Claude Choules, in 2011.
46. Each episode of *The Great War* was watched by an average of just over 17% of an estimated viewing population of 49 million. The fourth episode was the most popular with an audience of 22.6%, or just over 11 million; see Todman (2002): 29. Hanna (2007): 89 has called it an 'on-screen commemoration'.
47. Saunders (2001): 45.
48. The Imperial War Graves Commission became the Commonwealth War Graves Commission in 1960.
49. Edwards (2004): 146.
50. Middlebrook (1971): 314.
51. Dendooven (2001): 148.
52. Edwards (2004): 146.
53. Torkildsen (1999): 137.
54. http://www.guide-books.co.uk/authors.html
55. E.g. MacDonald (1978; 1983).
56. Walter (1993): 63.
57. Edwards (2004): 139.
58. Edwards (2004): 140, footnote 7.
59. Currently 'The First World War and the Peace Settlement' is a 'non-statutory example'; see Department for Education (2013).

60. Edwards (2004): 140, footnote 7.
61. Vandaele and Monballyu (2008): 542.
62. UK Government (2013).
63. Conducted on 27/10/14 using www.greatwar.co.uk and www.cwgc.org websites as well as a more widespread web survey. This survey is discussed further in Chapter 3, see Appendix 5.
64. C. Winter (2009): 612.
65. Internal survey data tables e-mailed from the management of the sites.
66. Flanders News (undated).
67. Email from CWGC 29/10/14.
68. Gough (2007): 697.
69. Visit Flanders (2014).
70. Westtoer (2014): 5.
71. Westtoer (2014): 19. Of these in the Westhoek 205,000 (37.2%) were British, 10,000 (1.8%) Australian, 4,000 (0.8%) Canadian and 3,000 (0.5%) New Zealanders. For Northern France the figures are 175,000 (49.9%) British, 25,000 Australian (7.2%), 18,000 Canadian (5.1%) and 8,000 (2.2%) New Zealanders; Westtoer (2014): 22.
72. The Western Front Association (2014a).
73. 2014–18 Great War Centenary (2014).
74. Centenary News website (2014a).
75. http://www.memorial2014.com/en/memorial_garden
76. The Western Front Association (2014b).
77. Centenary News website (2014b); Spagnoly and Smith (2002): 42.
78. Centenary News website (2014c). That a football was used by fraternising soldiers from both sides is attested to by the British cartoonist Bruce Bairnsfather (1887–1959) who commented: 'Despite the frozen surface and surviving turnips, a football was kicked about'. Nevertheless whether it was a fully-fledged football match is open to debate; see Weintraub (2001). For other examples of memorials to 'fallen footballers' on the Western Front see Wilson (2014).
79. Dyer (1994): 22.

Chapter 3
1. Urry (2002a).
2. J. Winter (2006: 12) calls this the 'memory boom'.
3. Urry (2011). The 'gaze' presupposes that the tourist experience is solely visual however tourists do employ a range of senses in their engagement with any site.
4. MacCannell (2013).
5. Known as the *Site Sacralisation Model*; see MacCannell (2013): 43–48. The model has been best applied to the battlefield site at Waterloo in Seaton (1999).
6. Other nations will have their own culturally significant names, e.g. Verdun for France, Villers-Bretonneux for Australia. Nevertheless, naming fails to take into consideration the views of people who live in the area; the inhabitants of the Somme *département* would like their region to be 'seen for what it is – a river and a district – rather than only the name of a battle'. E-mail correspondence with M. Alexandre Lefevre, European Project Coordinator, Somme Tourisme, Amiens, 20/05/15.
7. Examples of this can be found in Hynes (1990) and Fussell (2000). For cartooning see http://www.cartoonww1.org/
8. MacCannell (2013): 45.

9. Seaton (1999): 149.
10. Seaton (1999): 152. This process of 'validation' is outlined in Dunkley *et al* (2010).
11. Timothy and Boyd (2003): 69.
12. Crompton (1979).
13. This model is based upon tourists travelling for 'leisure' purposes and excludes those travelling for professional reasons who are sometimes included in tourism statistics as 'business travellers'.
14. Fabianson (2004); Wallis (2015).
15. Walsh (1991): 123; see Chapter 8 for examples of this.
16. Fussell (2000): 156.
17. The In Flanders Fields Museum in Ypres is a clear example of this taking its name from the well-known *rondeau* by the Canadian John McCrae (1872–1918).
18. Blunden (1937): 130.
19. Bishop and Bostridge (1998): 94.
20. Todman (2005): 159.
21. Reynolds (2013): 203.
22. Todman (2005): 178.
23. As, for example, in the 1989 BBC TV series *Blackadder Goes Forth*.
24. UCLAN website (undated). It has also been called 'morbid' or 'black spot' tourism or 'milking the macabre'; see Stone (2006): 148. Dark tourism is also known as *thanatourism* – *thanatos* being the daemonic personification of death in Greek mythology.
25. Stone (2006): 145–160.
26. Seaton (1996): 240.
27. Farmaki (2013): 283.
28. Miles (2014a): 5.
29. Farmaki (2013): 286–287.
30. Stone and Sharpley (2008).
31. A survey of visitors to CWGC cemeteries detected a number of people who were seeking a site where death had occurred; nevertheless since this related to sites of national significance these visitors were probably more concerned with the role of their countries during the war; see C. Winter (2011): 475.
32. Walter (1993).
33. Graburn (1989).
34. Reader (1993): 20.
35. Reader (1993): 2.
36. Walter (1993).
37. Baldwin and Sharpley (2009).
38. Turner and Turner (1978): 20. Readers will recall instances of boisterous behaviour amongst the pilgrims in Geoffrey Chaucer's *Canterbury Tales*.
39. This state of social cohesiveness is more commonly called *communitas*. It arises when people spend time together removed from the roles and responsibilities of their normal social positions. It is marked by a transition to a new state – a *rite of passage* – where deep bonds are formed through common experience. Rituals are key to fostering this state of being; see Turner and Turner (1978).
40. See the example given in Baldwin and Sharpley (2009): 204–05.
41. Walter (1993): 71; Dunkley *et al* (2010): 863–64.
42. One example of this is the pilgrimage made by Rotarians to the grave of the Welsh poet Hedd Wyn (Ellis Humphrey Evans, 1887–1917); see http://www.dailypost.co.uk/news/nostalgia/remembering-hedd-wyn-fallen-heroes-3407907

43. Royal British Legion (undated).
44. Urry (2002b): 125 and 146.
45. Urry (2011): 18.
46. Croisi Europe offers a 7-day Great War Commemorative Cruise between Lille and Ostend with coach trips to see the principal sites; see http://www.croisieurope.co.uk/cruises/great-war-commemorative-cruise-2015
47. Government of Flanders (2011).
48. Anon. (2014): 7.
49. Anon. (2014): 8.
50. Conducted on 27/10/14 using www.greatwar.co.uk and www.cwgc.org websites as well as a more widespread web survey.
51. Urry (2002b): 150 has called this a collective 'spectatorial gaze'.
52. Iles (2008): 146.
53. Seaton (2000): 75.
54. There is as yet no waymarked linear route across the entire Western Front in the tradition of the French network of *Grandes Randonnées*. Nevertheless, some travel writers have walked the course of battles or discrete actions (e.g. Cudbird (2014)) and others the entire length (e.g. O'Shea (1996) and Jones (2004)). This is in contrast to the 100 km long Walk of Peace along the Isonzo (Soča) Front of World War One in Slovenia; see Pot Miru (2008).
55. See http://www.somme-battlefields.com/event/walk-remembrance and http://www.soldierscharity.org/events/the-frontline-walk
56. E.g. Reed (2011).
57. Solnit (2002): 5.
58. Nicholson (2010): 220.
59. Ingold and Vergunst (2008): 5.
60. First World War landscapes were the first in world history to remain 'active' in that they left behind a lethal legacy of explosives that could kill long after the event. There are estimated to be 400 million unexploded shells along the Western Front and 350 people have been killed by them since 1918; see Saunders (2003a): 161. In March 2014 two migrant workers were killed when a shell they were handling exploded; see Hope (2014).
61. Iles (2011): 157.
62. Westtoer (2014): 32.

Chapter 4
1. Walter (2006): 235; Binyon later said that this stanza came to him first.
2. Longworth (2003): 42.
3. Laqueur (1994): 151.
4. Over half of the 9 million combat deaths in the First World War have no known graves. This is the same proportion as those lost in the World Trade Centre in New York on 9/11.
5. Assmann and Czaplicka (1995). With the passing of the last survivors of the Great War in the late 2000s memory has slipped from that communicated personally through conversation ('communicative social memory') to that based upon writings, monuments and cultural objects such as photographs and artefacts ('cultural memory').
6. Nora (1989).
7. Lowenthal (1979): 110.
8. Miles (2014b).
9. Saunders (2003b): 8.

10. Koonz (1994): 259.
11. Dendooven (2001).
12. Gough (2007): 694.
13. Benton and Cecil (2010). The idea of 'collective memory' was developed by the French philosopher Maurice Halbwachs (1877–1945) who thought individual memory is always absorbed into collective memory and never survives.
14. C. Winter (2009).
15. King (1998): 234–36; similar to Winter and Silvan's (2000): 40 'fictive kinship' groups.
16. Van der Auwera and Schramme (2014).
17. Schama (1995): 6–7.
18. So described by the poet Rudyard Kipling (1865–1936).
19. Tuan (1977): 138.
20. Figures based upon CWGC 1931 Annual Report and CWGC e-mail received 26/01/15. Of these 317,770 and 92,288 are 'identified dead' in France and Belgium with 213,077 and 102,424 commemorated but 'whose graves are not known' in these countries respectively. Many of these cemeteries also contain burials from World War Two and other nationalities including German which are not recorded in these figures.
21. Longworth (2003); Crane (2013).
22. Crane (2013): 65.
23. Longworth (2003): 76.
24. Longworth (2003): 44. This resulted in some highly controversial inscriptions such as that on the headstone of Private Albert Ingham, 18th Battalion Manchester Regiment, in Bailleulmont Cemetery. Ingham was shot for desertion in 1916 and his father had the following dedication inscribed: 'Shot at Dawn/ One of the first to enlist/ A worthy son/ Of his father'. Of the 346 executed British soldiers it is the only grave where the cause of death is stated.
25. The phrase was chosen by Rudyard Kipling and is from Ecclesiasticus 44, verse 14: "Their bodies are buried in peace; but their name liveth for evermore".
26. Longworth (2003): 15.
27. Longworth (2003): 73.
28. Vance (1997): 64.
29. Wasserman (1998): 16.
30. This points towards the oft-quoted lines from Rupert Brook's (1887–1915) poem *The Soldier*: 'If I should die, think only this of me:/ That there's some corner of a foreign field/ That is forever England'; Walter (2006): 108.
31. Vance (1997): 62–63.
32. Longworth (2003): 28.
33. Crane (2013): 124.
34. Under The War Graves Photographic Project every single military grave and private memorial from the First World War has been photographed and made available on-line. This has made planning trips to graves easier and provided images of those difficult to visit. This does not seem to have reduced the desire of descendants to actually visit graves in person, however; see The War Graves Photographic Project (2015) website.
35. C. Winter (2011): 463.
36. C. Winter (2011): 475.
37. From British and Commonwealth forces on the Western Front the youngest to be killed was 14-year old Private John Condon, buried at Poelcapelle Cemetery; the oldest was 67-year old Lieutenant Henry Webber buried at Dartmoor Cemetery, near Albert; the

first to be killed was Private John Parr and the last Private George Price (both buried at St Symphorien Military Cemetery, near Mons). Controversy surrounds the grave of John Kipling, son of Rudyard Kipling, in St. Mary's Advanced Dressing Station Cemetery, near Haisnes (France); see Holt and Holt (2007).

38. The careful re-turfing around by the CWCG around the Messines pillbox shown in Figure 18 is another example of this care.
39. C. Winter (2011): 477. The most notable recent example of a new cemetery being created is that at Fromelles (Pheasant Wood) in France completed in 2010. This was to bury the remains of 250 Australian and British soldiers discovered in 2009; see Summers *et al* (2010).
40. Quoted in Dendooven (2001): 20.
41. Thorpe (1999).
42. Davies (1993): 124.
43. Borg (1991): 84.
44. Scates (2009): 61.
45. Of these 187,861 were buried but not identifiable by name; there were therefore 338,955 not buried at all (including those lost at sea). Figures for all theatres, not just the Western Front; see The Long Long Trail (2014).
46. The Menin Gate records the names of the dead from Commonwealth nations, except New Zealand, who died in the Ypres Salient and have no known graves. In the case of the United Kingdom these are mostly casualties from before 16 August 1917. Those United Kingdom and New Zealand servicemen who died after that date are named on the memorial at Tyne Cot. Other New Zealand casualties are commemorated on memorials at Buttes New British Cemetery and Messines Ridge British Cemetery; see CWGC (undated a).
47. MacDonald (1983).
48. This manipulation of physical posture in encouraging homage is highlighted by King (1998): 232 and J. Winter (2010a). An understanding of this can be gained by comparing the tomb of Napoleon in Les Invalides, Paris, to the Tomb of the Unknown Warrior in Westminster Abbey. The former is raised up prompting a type of valedictory homage as from a subordinate subject to one of superior status; the latter is set into the floor resulting in a downward looking reverential attitude as from one paying their respects in a more egalitarian manner.
49. Stamp (2007): 10.
50. Robertshaw and Kenyon (2008): 31–32.
51. Laqueur (1994).
52. Wasserman (1998). The calling out of the names of the dead was an important part of inter-war French commemoration of the Great War; see J. Winter (2014): 97. Similarly the names of all 2,749 victims of the 11 September 2001 terrorist attacks are read out at the annual anniversary in New York. Recently the names and ages of the 130 victims of the Islamist terrorist attacks on Paris were read out in a ceremony on 27 November 2015.
53. Crane (2013): 131.
54. Jones (2014): 2.
55. O'Shea (1996): 51.
56. The Last Post is also sounded at the Ploegsteert Memorial on the first Friday of every month at 19:00.
57. Connerton (1989): 65–68.

58. J. Winter (2013).
59. Maitland (2008): 136, 41.
60. The Last Post Association (undated).
61. Connerton (1989): 70.
62. Called Remembrance Day in Britain and Australia and Veterans Day in the USA. To avoid disruption at the end of the Second World War many Commonwealth countries moved most Armistice Day events to the nearest Sunday to 11 November.
63. Frost and Laing (2013): 21.
64. Anderson (2006).
65. Ashplant *et al* (2000): 22.
66. Van der Auwera and Schramme (2014): 12. The British Legion has also opposed any overt anti-war message and still refuses to distribute white poppies, introduced by the Peace Pledge Union in 1993, and symbolising peace.
67. Quoted in Lloyd (1998): 128. The words were written for him by Rudyard Kipling.
68. British Future (2013): 22.
69. Peace Pledge Union (undated).
70. Mayors for Peace (2010).
71. Government of Flanders (2011): 7.
72. Vanneste and Foote (2013): 267.
73. J. Winter (2014): 115.
74. Gough (2007): 699.
75. Quoted in Longworth (2003): 54.
76. J. Winter (2014): 98.

Chapter 5
1. Fairclough *et al* (2008): 1.
2. Lowenthal (1996): xi.
3. Fussell (2000).
4. The importance of Great War heritage is reflected in the results of a World Heritage Tourism Research Network (WHTRN) survey in 2012 which indicated that 51% of people 'Probably' or 'Definitely' wanted to visit a 'WW1 heritage site' in the near future; see George *et a l* (2012): slide 30. This was a global on-line survey conducted in English, German French and Dutch with 2,827 responses; a more complete discussion of the results is given in Jansen-Verbeke and George (2015).
5. Smith (2006): 3.
6. Smith (2006): 3 (italics in original).
7. Jansen-Verbeke and George (2013): 281.
8. Sassoon (1930): 235.
9. Dyer (1994): 74.
10. Wilson (2008a).
11. Fussell (2000): 37.
12. Clout (1996): 46.
13. For graphic descriptions of trench life see Blunden (1937): 35, 130.
14. Clout (1996).
15. Other *villages détruits*, 'martyred for France', were left in their ruined state at Verdun; see Miles (2014b).
16. Saunders (2003b).
17. Chapman (2000).

18. Gough (2007). It became a Canadian National Historic site in 1997.
19. Fraser *et al* (2009).
20. Saunders (2013).
21. Spagnoly and Smith (2003).
22. Many bunkers and trench lines lie within private areas of Ploegsteert Wood and are thus inaccessible. This is all the more disappointing in view of the importance the wood has in the early careers of two British Prime Minsters – Anthony Eden and Winston Churchill; see Chapter 3; Spagnoly and Smith (2003); and Miles (2014c).
23. Vanneste and Foote (2013).
24. Lowenthal (1985): 214.
25. Gough (2007). The Dominion of Newfoundland sent its own troops to fight in the Great War. It joined Canada in 1949 and the Memorial Park has thus been managed by the Canadian Government since then.
26. Wallis (2015).
27. Anderson (2006).
28. Mottram (1936): 72.
29. These names are clear from any scrutiny of trench maps produced by G.H. Smith and Son of Easingwold.
30. Fussell (2000): 179.
31. Iles (2011): 158.
32. APWGBHG (2010).
33. Price (2005).
34. This has been most dramatically brought out at the site of the Battle of the Boyne (1690) in the Republic of Ireland. The battle was won by the Protestants but lies in what is now the Catholic south.
35. Jansen-Verbeke and George (2013): 276.
36. Saunders (2007): 75–77.
37. Friends of Lochnagar (undated).
38. O'Neill (2003); Robertshaw and Kenyon (2008): 23–24, 106–111.
39. Price (2005).
40. Lowenthal (1985).
41. Kirshenblatt-Gimblett (1999).
42. de Meyer (2009).
43. Saunders (2007): 146–47.
44. Bostyn (1999).
45. Gough (2007).
46. Gough (2007): 698.
47. Lowenthal (1985): 265.
48. Sharpley (1994): 130.
49. MacCannell (2013).
50. The three definitions in this section are those of Wang (1999).
51. Kirshenblatt-Gimblett (1999): 249.
52. Umberto Eco has said that the copy of an art work does not seem to say, 'We are giving you the reproduction so that you will want the original' but, 'We are giving you the reproduction so you will no longer feel any need for the original'; see Eco (1986): 19.
53. MacCannell (2013).
54. Lloyd (1998); Iles (2011): 158.
55. Roberthsaw and Kenyon (2008): 18.

56. Wilson (2008b).
57. Saunders (2007):159.
58. Saunders (2007): 143.
59. Fraser and Brown (2007).
60. Summers *et al* (2010); Scully and Woodward (2012).
61. Kirshenblatt-Gimblett (1999).
62. Price (2005); Saunders (2007).
63. Personal communication with Avril Williams, 15/03/15.
64. Saunders (2007): 166–68.

Chapter 6
 1. Kirshenblatt-Gimblett (1999): 167–168.
 2. Beck and Cable (2002): 2.
 3. Tilden (1977): 8.
 4. Tilden (1977): 18.
 5. ICOM (2007).
 6. Pegler (2014).
 7. Arnold de-Simine (2013): 10.
 8. Saunders (2007): 32–33. The point reflects Pablo Picasso's comment that 'every act of creation is first an act of destruction'.
 9. Kirshenblatt-Gimblett (1999): 249.
10. Kirshenblatt-Gimblett (1999): 149.
11. Wilson (2008b): 160.
12. Clout (1996); Lloyd (1998).
13. See Chapter 2, note 27.
14. At Hill 62 during World War Two the Schiers hid their collection in the cellar and concreted it over. Visiting Germans (reputedly including Hermann Göring) asked where the exhibits were and were told that the British had stolen them; see Holt and Holt (2011): 96.
15. Kavanagh (1994).
16. Memorial Museum Passchendaele 1917 (undated).
17. Fought between July and November 1917 the Battle of Passchendaele (or Third Ypres) was fought in order to take command of ridges overlooking the town of Ypres. In a hundred days there were half a million casualties from both sides for only eight km of Allied territorial gain; see MacDonald (1978).
18. Summers et al (2010).
19. Delville Wood (undated).
20. Delville Wood (undated).
21. Becker (2015): 101.
22. Lowenthal (1985): 68.
23. Saunders (2003a).
24. Personal communication with Avril Williams, 15/03/15.
25. This is in contrast to the situation along the modern Izonso (Soča) Front in Slovenia where private collections of Great War militaria are opened to the public; see Pot Miru (2008): 149. Slovenian authorities are willing to overlook the illegal nature of many of these acquisitions to encourage their protection as well as to stimulate their educational and tourism potential; see Saunders (2007): 221.

26. Musée de la Grande Guerre Press Release, 13/01/15. Although the museum takes an international perspective only 5% of visitors were non-French; 29% were school groups. I am grateful to Lyse Hautecoeur for this information.
27. Personal communication with Michel Rouger, Museum Director, 12/03/15.
28. More correctly known by its local name 'Liberté éplorée' (Weeping Liberty); inaugurated in 1932 the monument was a gift from the United Sates to the French in memory of all soldiers who lost their lives in the First Battle of the Marne (5–12 September 1914).
29. Rouger (2014): 141.
30. The permanent exhibition displays only 15% of the whole collection.
31. Musée de la Grande Guerre du Pays de Meaux (undated).
32. Rouger (2014): 139.
33. The Franco-Prussian War (1870–71) left a prominent mark on the French national psyche all the way up to 1914. In this war Prussian (German) armies defeated the French decisively and in 1871 captured Paris. The Treaty of Frankfurt in May 1871 gave Germany Alsace and most of Lorraine. The war upset the balance of power in Europe and resulted in French determination to recapture these areas. The date is thus significant in creating a number of factors which later contributed to the outbreak of war in 1914. The film in the museum did privilege events particular to French history and its significance for non-French visitors might therefore be diminished.
34. French infantrymen in the First World War were called *poilus* (literally 'hairy ones') the equivalent to 'Tommy' and 'Digger' in the British and Australian armies respectively. Zouaves were light infantrymen raised in the colonies and serving in the French army; they were distinguished by their colourful 'oriental' dress which included fezzes, blue sashes, embroidered waistcoats and baggy trousers (*serouel*). Uhlans were German light cavalry armed with lances over 10 feet in length; they were distinguished by their Polish-style *czapkas* (caps) reflecting their origins in that country. After the first weeks of the war Uhlans were dismounted to serve as 'cavalry rifles'.
35. Rouger (2014): 143.
36. Personal communication with Michel Rouger, Museum Director, 12/03/15.
37. Rouger (2014): 146.
38. Personal communication with Michel Rouger, Museum Director, 12/03/15.
39. Hooper-Greenhill (1994): 11.
40. J. Winter (2010a): 10.
41. Saunders (2007): 177–78. The ripped and blood stained tunic of Lieutenant Harold Cope, 7th Battalion, the Border Regiment, on display at the Imperial War Museum, London is an example of where the graphic reality of war is met head-on; see Hughes-Wilson (2014): 224–25.
42. de Groot (2011): 589.
43. Lowenthal (1985): 298.
44. Battlefield re-enactments are major ticketed events. In 2006 the re-enactment of the Battle of Hastings (1066) attracted 2,400 participants on each of the two days and was watched by 30,000 spectators; it is considered to have been the largest pre-gunpowder event ever held anywhere (Anon., undated, a). The 200th anniversary of the Battle of Waterloo in Belgium in 2015 attracted over 6000 re-enactors and over 60,000 spectators at each of two 'performances' (Miles, 2015). The 1998 re-enactment of the Battle of Gettysburg (1863) in the USA is considered to be the largest battlefield re-enactment event ever held with between 30,000 and 41,000 participants and over 50,000 spectators (Anon., undated, b).

45. At Llancaiach Fawr Manor in South Wales costumed actors play the part of house servants from 1645. They remain constantly 'in character' using period language and expressing ignorance of any event after this time.
46. The Great War Society (undated).
47. A decorative German *bierstein* in the IWM is said to have been presented to Private Bill Tucker of the Army Ordnance Corps who was 'captain' of a winning British football team who played against German soldiers during the Truce; see http://www.iwm. org.uk/collections/item/object/30082738 Nevertheless the extent of these 'matches' remains controversial as discussed by Baker (2014).
48. The educational value of the re-enactment is demonstrated by the footage found at http://www.schoolsworld.tv/node/2728
49. Battlefield guiding has become increasingly professionalised with a Guild of Battlefield Guides (established in 2003) which in 2013 had 344 members and 69 Validated ('Badged') guides.
50. LinesMan™ digital trench maps have revolutionised the search for ploughed over trenches and other features; these can be downloaded onto handheld GPS, smartphone or tablet portable devices and are thus useful for guides wanting to show clients the places of war; see http://www.greatwardigital.com/gps.html
51. Iles (2008): 147.
52. Iles (2008): 146.
53. Examples of this are given in Seaton (2000): 74 and Iles (2008): 143.
54. The female 'representative pilgrim' in Chapter 3 is an example of this.
55. Short for 'application software'.
56. See http://www.2014-18.be/en/news/car-routes-flanders-fields
57. Augmented Reality (AR) superimposes digital images onto real-world surroundings giving a sense of illusion or virtual reality. It is designed to add a 'virtual' 2D or 3D overlay to real objects such as posters, maps, magazines, buildings and scenery. AR can add a 'what it might have looked like then' aspect to a contemporary scene using archival or computer enhanced images; the seemingly empty fields along the Western Front are an example of where this technology can be used particularly effectively.
58. The CWGC have installed 100 information panels with QR codes throughout its memorial sites.
59. Research by Deloitte has shown how older generations have been particularly slow in adopting PCs and using the Internet and are much less likely to use smartphones than younger age groups. But this is set to change with increasing usage amongst the over-55s and the gap between the generations will narrow to become negligible by 2020. Once they overcome their initial lack of confidence with ICT older age groups become enthusiastic users. Nevertheless, there is a great reluctance to download apps which the report thinks are 'designed by younger people, for younger people' (Deloitte, 2014: 42–44). This has clear implications for a heritage industry which still has a large customer base amongst older age groups but is at the same time moving towards more 'smart' technology. Hopefully challenges can become opportunities.

Chapter 7
1. The relationship between war and tourism is discussed in Butler and Suntikul (2013). Weaver (2000) has shown how a 'war dividend' can operate long after the end of conflict stimulated by tourism.
2. J. Winter (2006).

3. Ferdinand and Williams (2010): 212.
4. Smith (1996): 248.
5. Fennell (2009).
6. Jamal and Menzel (2009). Ethics in tourism often relates to such issues as exploitation of workers, profit repatriation, sex tourism and overuse of resources which do not concern us here.
7. The Greek term *eudaimonia* which goes beyond simple happiness; see Fennell (2009). *Morality* refers to the rational inclinations of humans to do good and avoid evil; *ethics* is concerned with answering the question 'what should one do to do good'? Ethics is thus the rules and principles that dictate good conduct whereas morality is the underlying individual bedrock that determines a person's adherence to ethical principles. I have, however, used them interchangeably here.
8. The theory of Jeremy Bentham (1748–1832).
9. The theory of Immanuel Kant (1724–1804).
10. Walsh (1991): 2.
11. Tunbridge and Ashworth (1996): 115.
12. Tunbridge and Ashworth (1996): 121.
13. Westtoer (2014).
14. This argument is reflected in some of the responses from tourists recorded in Chapter 8.
15. Westtoer (2014): 4.
16. The CWGC use a Geoblock® turf protection system which mitigates the effects of erosion from human traffic and storm water.
17. Interview with Peter Francis, CWGC Media and Marketing Manager, 26/03/15. The Commission have also developed three Remembrance Trails to encourage tourism linking up sites and memorials: The Retreat From Mons; The Forgotten Front; and the Battle of Loos.
18. Vansuyt (2005–06): 67. A survey of 35 residents in four focus group interviews. I am grateful to Timby Vansuyt, Tourism Coordinator at the Memorial Museum Passchendaele 1917, for providing access to her thesis.
19. Vansuyt (2005–06): 65.
20. Vansuyt (2005–06): 72–73.
21. Vansuyt (2005–06): 74, 76, 80. British tourists are predominant in Ypres and comprise over 37% of visitors to the Westhoek region; see Westtoer (2014): 22.
22. Vansuyt (2005–06): 81.
23. Interview with Timby Vansuyt, 17/03/15.
24. Interview with Timby Vansuyt, 17/03/15.
25. In the World Heritage Tourism Research Network (WHTRN) survey of the Great War in 2012, 92% of respondents 'Agreed' or 'Strongly Agreed' that their visit had given them 'A consciousness about human suffering in WW1'; see George *et al*, 2012: slide 40.
26. As attested to by the many pictures of British troops on the Front wearing captured German *Pickelhaube* helmets.
27. Zhang (2010).
28. Higonnet (2008): 76.
29. Ferdinand and Williams (2010).
30. The Wipers (i.e. Ypres) Times was a newspaper produced in the town by British soldiers. The use of war-themes and battle sites to brand beers is also represented by Waterloo Beer, brewed at Mont-Saint-Jean farm near to the site of the Battle of Waterloo (1815), south of Brussels.

31. The British Legion also uses the poppy logo extensively to brand its range of products; see http://www.poppyshop.org.uk/ Unlike other brand symbols the poppy is not legally protected which has facilitated its use by manufacturers.
32. Saunders (2013).
33. Jansen-Verbeke and George (2013): 83.
34. Carl Ooghe in Storer (2013).
35. Vansuyt (2005–06): 78.
36. Interview with Timby Vansuyt, 17/03/15.
37. Interview with Dominiek Dendooven, IFFM, 11/02/14.
38. Westtoer (undated). The Code has seven principles: Respect; Good Hosting; Accessibility; Polyphony; Going deeper into knowledge; Internationalisation; and a Peace Message. There is evidence that consumers welcome such codes with 85% or respondents in the WHTRN survey considering 'Ethical Standards for Commercialisation' along the Western Front 'Important' or 'Very Important'; see George *et al*, (2012): slide 43.
39. E.g. Zokola give £1.00 from each sale of their poppy chocolates to the British Legion; see http://www.zokola.be/
40. Saunders (2002); Van Hollebeeke *et al* (2014).
41. Moshenska (2008): 168.
42. In October 2005 a 'Homecoming Ceremony' was held by Native Americans from Canada at the Menin Gate for the spirits of their ancestors who had fallen in the Great War.
43. Moshenska (2008): 169. Saunders (2002): 106 has called the Western Front 'the most exhaustively documented, personalised and spiritualised areas ever to be subject to … archaeological investigation'.
44. Iles (2011): 165–66.
45. Summers *et al* (2010).
46. Scully and Woodward (2012): 67.
47. Scully and Woodward (2012): 62. The issue of photographic images of the dead was raised in 2012 with the discovery of the remains of Richard III, the last Plantagenet king of England; one of the investigators opposed any full-face image of the skull as prurient and demonstrating a lack of respect for the man himself, even though he had been killed in 1485; see Langley and Jones (2013): 182.
48. Pollard and Banks (2007): viii.
49. Fabianson (2004): 171–72. A search of the e-commerce website eBay (on 04/06/15) following the given category term "WW1 Militaria" gave 10,342 items which included 1,209 medals and 745 badges (including cap and lapel). Amongst items for sale were "20 Shrapnel balls Pozières, Somme" (£2.99); a "Relic Base protector British 18 Pounder" (£9.99); a "1916 Whistle – Somme" (£45.00); and a "WW1 German Helmet" (£17.00). Clearly not all of these items would have been found in the ground, but it does give some idea of the popular market for militaria. More controversially there were 39 WW1 dog tags (identification tags) including a "very rare Imperial German WWI ID-Tag – *Erkennnungsmarke*" (£12.99) and a "WWI US G. I. Dog Tag Soldier Doughboy" (£130.47). More specialist sales websites include GreatWarStuff.com™ (http://greatwarstuff.com/) and the American Great War Militaria site (http://www.greatwar.com/scripts/default.asp); the trade is supported by several internet discussion groups such as the British Ordnance Collectors Network (http://www.bocn.co.uk/vbforum/forum.php) for 'militaria collectors and inert ordnance enthusiasts'. For an analysis of the sale of older battle-related items on eBay see Ferguson (2013): 9.
50. Saunders (2001): 47–48; Robertshaw *et al* (2008): 18–19.

51. Veterans Affairs Canada (2014): Article 23.
52. Ferguson (2013): 8.
53. In the WHTRN survey 69% of respondents 'Agreed' or 'Strongly Agreed' that 'tourism is instrumental in preserving WW1 heritage sites'; see George *et al*, 2012: slide 35.
54. Iles (2011): 167–68.
55. Osborn (2001).
56. De Meyer and Pype (2004).
57. Adriaen (2012).
58. Smith (2006): 3.
59. Veterans Affairs Canada (2014): Article 2.
60. UNESCO (2015a).
61. These are the Nazi Concentration and Extermination Camp at Auschwitz-Birkenau (selected 1979); the Hiroshima Peace Memorial Site (selected 1996); and the Bikini Atoll Nuclear Test Site (selected in 2010).
62. Jansen-Verbeke and George (2013): 279. In the WHTRN survey 76% of respondents 'Agreed' or 'Strongly Agreed' that 'WW1 heritage landscapes deserve to be listed as UNESCO World Heritage'; see George *et al*, 2012: slide 35.
63. The inventory includes 105 separate sites (80 in France and 25 in Belgium); see UNESCO (2015b; 2015c). It involves cross-border collaboration between 12 French *départements* and the Flemish government and Walloon region in Belgium. Belgium also has two other war-related sites on the Tentative List – the Battlefield of Waterloo (UNESCO 2015d) and the Panorama, an enormous painting of this battle (UNESCO 2015e).
64. UNESCO (2015f).
65. These are: (iii) to bear a unique or at least exceptional testimony to a cultural tradition or to a civilization which is living or which has disappeared; (iv) to be an outstanding example of a type of building, architectural or technological ensemble or landscape which illustrates (a) significant stage(s) in human history; and (vi) to be directly or tangibly associated with events or living traditions, with ideas, or with beliefs, with artistic and literary works of outstanding universal significance; see UNESCO (2015f).
66. Translated and summarised from the original in UNESCO (2015b; 2015c).
67. Jansen-Verbeke and George (2013): 280.
68. Nevertheless, the transnational Frontiers of the Roman Empire WHS (selected 1987) shows that it is possible to establish a long linear cross-border site; see UNESCO (2015g).

Chapter 8

1. The phrase was coined by Toni and Valid Holt to describe their coach tours; see Iles (2008): 142.
2. Seaton (2000); Iles (2008).
3. Valentine (1997).
4. The 2010 tour (3 days) comprised 35 passengers (12 female and 23 male) ranging in age from the early 30s to 73 years; there were 30 passengers (11 female and 19 male) on the 2014 tour (4 days) aged from late 30s to early 70s. In the ensuing discussion comments are followed by the tour date they were selected from and the gender and age of the respondent. The methodology and full results of the 2010 survey are given in Miles (2012); the 2014 survey is presented here for the first time.

5. Ethical requirements for the research also included: (i) a removal of all suspicions regarding the research from the beginning; (ii) full signed consent from subjects for the interview; (iii) no covert observation or eavesdropping apart from within 'open field' situations outside the coach; (iv) interviews conducted in private out of earshot of others; (v) respect for intellectual copyright and no use of the guide's narrative without permission; see Miles (2012): 27, 261.
6. Wallis (2015).
7. 2014: female, mid-60s.
8. J. Winter (2010b): 317.
9. 2010: male, 66.
10. Hirsch (2008).
11. For examples of the power of memory in Western Front visits down to the third generation see Baldwin and Sharpley (2009).
12. 2010: female, 67.
13. 2014: female, late 50s.
14. Fussell (2000): 156; Van Emden (2012).
15. 2014: female, late 40s.
16. 2014: female, late 50s.
17. Barrett (2008).
18. 2014: female, late 50s.
19. 2014: male, late 50s.
20. It is notable that this is mostly a male practice, but due to the small size of the sample it would be unwise to suggest any definitive gender bias.
21. 2010: male, 66.
22. 2014: female, mid-60s.
23. 2014: male, early 50s.
24. 2014: male, early 50s.
25. Shackley (2001).
26. 2010: male, 73.
27. 2014: male, late 50s.
28. 2014: male, late 50s.
29. 2014: male, early 50s.
30. 2014: male, late 60s.
31. 2014: female, mid 60s.
32. 2010: female, 61.
33. Dunkley et al (2010).
34. Rojek (1997): 58.
35. Taken on 2 October 1918 as the men are being addressed by Brigadier General J. C. Campbell. The Battle of Saint Quentin Canal had started on 29 September 1918 and succeeded in breaching the heavily fortified German Hindenburg Line; on that day the Riqueval Bridge was seized by the 1/6 Battalion of the North Staffordshire Regiment before the Germans were able to fire explosive charges to destroy the bridge.
36. 2014: female, late 40s.
37. 2010: female, 61.
38. 2014: male, late 50s.

Chapter 9

1. Holehouse (2015).
2. Quoted in Lowenthal (1985): 68.
3. Ryan (2007): 4.
4. Bender (1993): 276.
5. As reflected in the example of tensions between Mesen and Ypres; see Otte (2014).
6. Lowenthal (1979): 110.
7. Gough (2004): 237 paraphrasing Koonz (1994).
8. Macintyre (1998): 22.
9. The Western Front Association has 51 branches across the UK as well as others in Australia, New Zealand, Canada, the USA and France.
10. The Last Post Association (undated).
11. Frost and Laing (2013). Although it is still too early to determine the true extent to which the nation's interest has been captured.
12. Sontag (1977): 8–9.
13. 'Selfies' are just part of the new trend in sharing holiday experiences during or post-trip through a variety of social media such as wikis (e.g. Wikitravel), blogs (e.g. Travelblog), microblogs (e.g. Twitter), social network sites (e.g. Facebook) and review sites (e.g. TripAdvisor). In its more sophisticated form this makes use of 'user-generated content' (UGC) where the traveller contributes words, pictures, videos and audio; see Munar and Jacobsen (2014).
14. The examples in Feifer (2013) make this all too clear.
15. Dunkley *et al* (2010).
16. Darlington (2014): 47.
17. Darlington (2014): 45.
18. Gough (2004): 238.
19. Dr Anika Mombauer; see transcript in Historyworks (2012).
20. Weaver (2000).
21. J. Winter (2000).
22. Reynolds (2013) explores these concerns over the twentieth century.
23. Stevenson (2004): 600.
24. Dr Jennifer Keene in Das *et al* (2014).
25. Stevenson (2004): 600–01.
26. C. Winter (2009): 621–622.
27. C. Winter (2009): 621.
28. CWGC (undated b).
29. Edwards (2013).
30. Edwards (2013).
31. But some veterans have returned to Iraq as tourists; see Turner (2011).
32. I draw on the work of Lowe (2015) for this section.
33. King (2010); the film *American Sniper* (2014) reflects this juxtaposition of private life and military prowess and the way the two interact very effectively.
34. In 2015 the British government's reluctance to put 'boots on the ground' in Iraq and Syria to fight the *soi-disant* Islamic State might be a reflection of this.
35. In October 2015 intelligence and military supremos expressed concern that China was being given a stake in Britain's critical infrastructure, including the design and building of nuclear plants. The fear was that technological 'trapdoors' could be inserted into

reactor systems as they were being built allowing them to override British controls or even shut down the plants in the event of a later diplomatic or trade row; see O'Neill *et al* (2015).
36. Macintyre (2015).
37. Walter (2006): 267.

Bibliography

14–18 Now (undated) website. *WW1 centenary Art Commissions: Lights Out*. At: http://www.1418now.org.uk/commissions/lightsout/

2014–18 Great War Centenary (2014) website. *17 October 2014: Light Front/Flooding of the Plains*. At: http://www.2014-18.be/en/news/17-october-2014-light-frontflooding-the-plains

Addison, P. and H. Jones (eds.) (2005) *A companion to contemporary Britain, 1939–2000*. Oxford: Blackwell.

Adriaen, H. (2012) Doortrekking A19 tot aan de kust definitief van de baan. [Lengthening A19 to the coast definitively scrapped]. [In Flemish]. HLN.BE News. (8 June). At: http://www.hln.be/hln/nl/922/Nieuws/article/detail/1451024/2012/06/08/Doortrekking-A19-tot-aan-de-kust-definitief-van-de-baan.dhtml

Anderson, B. (2006 [1983]) *Imagined Communities: Reflections on the Origin and Spread of Nationalism*. London: Verso.

Anon. (undated, a) *Battle of Hastings reenactment*. At: http://en.wikipedia.org/wiki/Battle_of_Hastings_reenactment

Anon. (undated, b) *American Civil War reenactment*. At: http://en.wikipedia.org/wiki/American_Civil_War_reenactment#cite_note-williams-40

Anon. (1921) *Handbook to Belgium and the battlefields*. Seventh edition. London: Ward, Lock and Co., Ltd.

Anon. (2014) Industry prospects good, says new report. *Coach Monthly*, (May), 6–8. At: http://coachmonthly.com/Coach%20Monthly%20Issues/CM-May-2014/#/6/

APWGBHG (All-Party Parliamentary War Heritage Group) (2010) website. At: http://www.wargravesheritage.org.uk/

Arnold de-Simine, S. (2013) *Mediating memory in the museum; trauma, empathy, nostalgia*. Basingstoke: Palgrave MacMillan.

Ashplant, T.G., G. Dawson and M. Roper (2000) *The Politics of War Memory and Commemoration*. London: Routledge.

Assmann, J. and J. Czaplicka (1995) Collective Memory and Cultural Identity. *New German Critique* 65: 125–133.

Baker, C. (2014) *The Truce: The Day the War Stopped*. Stroud: Amberley.

Baldwin, F. and R. Sharpley (2009) Battlefield Tourism: Bringing Organised Violence Back to Life. In: Sharpley, R. and P.R. Stone (eds) *The Darker Side of Travel: the Theory and Practice of Dark Tourism*. Bristol: Channel View. 186–206.

Barbusse, H. (2003 [1916]) *Under Fire*. London: Penguin.

Barrett, M. (2008) *Casualty Figures: How Five Men Survived the First World War*. London: Verso.

BBC Media Centre (2015) The BBC announces its four-year World War One Centenary season. At: http://www.bbc.co.uk/mediacentre/latestnews/2013/world-war-one-centenary

Beck L. and T. Cable (2002) *Interpretation for the 21st Century. Fifteen Guiding Principles for Interpreting Nature and Culture*. Second Edition. Urbana, IL: Sagamore Publishing.

Becker, A. (2015) Museums, architects and artists on the Western Front: New commemoration for a new history? In: Ziino, B. (ed.) *Remembering the First World War*. London: Routledge. 90–109.

Bender, B. (1993) Stonehenge – contested landscapes (medieval to present-day). In: Bender, B. (ed.) *Landscape: Politics and Perspectives*. Oxford: Berg. 245–80.

Benton, T. and C. Cecil (2010) Heritage and Public Memory. In: T. Benton (ed.) *Understanding Heritage and Memory*. Manchester: Manchester University Press. 7–43.

Bishop, A. and M. Bostridge (eds) (1998) *Letters From a Lost Generation*. London: Abacus.

Blunden, E. (1937) *Undertones of War*. Harmondsworth: Penguin.

Borg, A. (1991) *War Memorials: From Antiquity to the Present*. London: Leo Cooper.

Bostyn, F. (1999) *The Beecham Dugout, Passchendaele 1914–18*. Zonnebeke: Association for Battlefield Archaeology in Flanders. Studies 1.

British Future (2013) 'Do Mention the War: Will 1914 matter in 2014. At: http://www.britishfuture.org/wp-content/uploads/2013/08/BRF_Declaration-of-war-report_P2_Web-1.pdf

Brown, M. (2014) Blood-swept lands: the story behind the Tower of London poppies tribute. *The Guardian* (28 December). At: http://www.theguardian.com/world/2014/dec/28/blood-swept-lands-story-behind-tower-of-london-poppies-first-world-war-memorial

Butler, R and W. Suntikul (eds.) (2013) *Tourism and War*. London: Routledge.

Centenary News website (2014a) *Human chain to remember France's 'forgotten front'*. At: http://www.centenarynews.com/article?id=2962

Centenary News website (2014b) *Christmas truce: British & German schools mark Centenary with joint memorial in Belgium*. At: http://www.centenarynews.com/article?id=3092

Centenary News website (2014c) *Christmas truce: European football announces Centenary tribute in Belgium*. At: http://www.centenarynews.com/article?id=3088

Chapman, P. (2000) *A Haven in Hell: Talbot House, Poperinghe*. Barnsley: Leo Cooper.

Clout, H. (1996) *After the Ruins: Restoring the Countryside of Northern France after the Great War*. Exeter: University of Exeter Press.

Commonwealth War Graves Commission (CWGC) (undated a) website. At: http://www.cwgc.org/

Commonwealth War Graves Commission (CWGC) (undated b) website. At: http://www.cwgc.org/learning-and-resources/virtual-cemetery.aspx

Connelly, M. (2009) The Ypres League and the Commemoration of the Ypres Salient, 1914–1940. *War in History* 16 (1): 51–76.

Connerton, P. (1989) *How Societies Remember*. Cambridge: Cambridge University Press.

Crane, D. (2013) *Empires of the Dead: How one man's vision led to the creation of World War One's war graves*. London: William Collins.

Creswell, T. (2004) *Place: A Short Introduction*. Oxford: Blackwell.

Crompton, J. (1979) Motivations of pleasure vacations. *Annals of Tourism Research* 6 (4): 408–424.

Cudbird, T. (2014) *Walking the Retreat – The March to the Marne: 1914 Revisited*. Oxford: Signal.

Darlington, C. (2014) Dark tourism: a school visit to Flanders. *Bereavement Care* 33 (2): 44–47.

Das, S. Hirschfeld, G., Jones, H., Keene, J., Kolonitskii, B., and J. Winter, (2014) Global Perspectives on World War I. A Roundtable Discussion. *Zeithistorische Forschungen / Studies in Contemporary History*, (Online-Ausgabe, 11), H. 1. At: http://www.zeithistorische-forschungen.de/1-2014/id=5009

Davies, J. (1993) War Memorials. In: Clark, D. (ed.) *The Sociology of Death*. Oxford: Blackwell. 112–128.

Debaeke, S. (2011) *Hitler in Vlaanderen*. [In Flemish]. Brugge: De Klaproos.

de Groot, J. (2011) Affect and empathy: re-enactment and performance as/in history. *Rethinking History* 15 (4): 587–599.

de Meyer, M. and P. Pype (2004) *The A19 Project: Archaeological Research at Cross Roads*. Flanders: AWA Publications.

Deloitte (2014) The Smartphone generation gap: over 55? there's no app for that. On-line report. At: http://www2.deloitte.com/global/en/pages/technology-media-and-telecommunications/articles/tmt-predictions-collection.html

Delville Wood (undated) website. At: http://www.delvillewood.com/bienvenue2.htm

Dendooven, D. (2001) *Menin Gate and Last Post: Ypres as Holy Ground*. Koksijde: de Klaproos.

Department for Education (2013) *Statutory guidance for the National Curriculum in England: history programmes of study*. At: https://www.gov.uk/government/publications/national-curriculum-in-england-history-programmes-of-study/national-curriculum-in-england-history-programmes-of-study

Dunkley, R., N. Morgan and S. Westwood (2010) Visiting the trenches: Exploring meanings and motivations in battlefield tourism. *Tourism Management* 32 (4) August: 860–868.

Dunn, J. C. (1987) *The War the Infantry Knew*. Abacus.

Dyer, G. (1994) *The Missing of the Somme*. London: Hamish Hamilton.

Eco, U. (1986) *Travels in Hyper-reality*. London: Harvest.

Edwards, P.J. (2004) *A War Remembered: Commemoration, Battlefield Tourism and British Collective Memory of the Great War*. Unpublished Dphil thesis, University of Sussex.

Edwards, S. (2013) Viewpoint: How should we remember a war. *BBC News Magazine* (5 November). At: http://www.bbc.co.uk/news/magazine-24610481

Fabianson, N. (2004) The Internet and the Great War: The Impact on the Making and Meaning of Great War History. In: Saunders, N.J. (ed) *Matters of Conflict: Material Culture, Memory and the First World War*. London: Routledge. 166–178.

Fairclough, G., R. Harrison, J.H. Jameson and J. Schofield (eds.) (2008) *The Heritage Reader*. London: Routledge.

Farmaki, A. (2013) Dark tourism revisited: a supply/demand. *International Journal of Culture, Tourism and Hospitality Research* 7 (3): 281–292.

Feifer, J. (2013) Tumblr: Selfies in Serious Places (website). At: http://selfiesatseriousplaces.tumblr.com/

Fennell, D. (2009) Ethics and Tourism. In: Tribe, J. (ed.) *Philosophical Issues in Tourism*. Bristol: Channel View. 211–226.

Ferdinand, N. and N.L. Williams (2010) Tourism Memorabilia and the Tourism Experience. In: Morgan, M., P. Lugosi, and J.R. Brent Ritchie (eds.) *The Tourism and Leisure Experience: Consumer and Managerial Perspectives*. Bristol: Channel View. 202–217.

Ferguson N. (2013) Biting the bullet: the role of hobbyist metal detecting within battlefield archaeology. *Internet Archaeology* 33. At: http://dx.doi.org/10.11141/ia.33.3

First World War Centenary (2015). At: http://www.1914.org/

Flanders News (undated). At: http://deredactie.be/cm/vrtnieuws.english/The+Great+War/1.1841291

Fleming, A. (1919) *How to See the Battlefields*. London: Casell and Co.

Fraser, A.H. and M. Brown (2007) Mud, Blood and Missing Men: Excavations at Serre, Somme, France. *Journal of Conflict Archaeology* 3 (1) (1 November): 147–171.

Fraser, A., A. Robertshaw and S. Roberts (2009) *Ghosts on the Somme: Filming the Battle, June–July 1916*. Barnsley: Pen and Sword.

Friends of Lochnagar (undated) website. At: http://www.lochnagarcrater.org/

Frost, W. and J. Laing (2013) *Commemorative Events: Memory, identities, conflicts*. London: Routledge.

Furness, H. (2013) BBC announces 2,500 hours of First World War programmes. *The Daily Telegraph*, 16 October. At: http://www.telegraph.co.uk/history/world-war-one/10382727/BBC-announces-2500-hours-of-First-World-War-programmes.html

Fussell, P. (2000) *The Great War and Modern Memory*. 25th Anniversary Edition. Oxford: Oxford University Press.

Gabler, N. (2007) *Walt Disney: The Biography*. London: Aurum.

George, E.W., M. Jansen-Verbeke, M. Das and B.S. Osborne (2012) *The Centennial of the First World War (2014–2018). An online survey*. Halifax, NS: World Heritage Tourism Research Network, Mount Saint Vincent University.

Gough, P. (2004) Sites in the imagination: the Beaumont-Hamel Newfoundland Memorial. *Cultural Geographies* 11: 235–258.

Gough, P. (2007) 'Contested memories: Contested site': Newfoundland and its unique heritage on the Western Front. *The Round Table: The Commonwealth Journal of International Affairs* 96 (393): 693–705.

Gordon, B. (1998) Warfare and Tourism: Paris in World War II. *Annals of Tourism Research* 25 (3): 616–638.

Government of Flanders (2011) *The Great War Centenary in Flanders*. Brussels: Government of Flanders Project Office for the Great War Centenary. At: http://www.vlaanderen.be/int/sites/iv.devlh.vlaanderen.be.int/files/documenten/The%20Great%20War%20Centenary.pdf

Graburn, N.H.H. (1989) Tourism: The Sacred Journey. In: Smith, V.L. (ed.) *Hosts and Guests: The Anthropology of Tourism*. Philadelphia: University of Pennsylvania Press. 17–31.

Hanna, E. (2007) A small screen alternative to stone and bronze: The Great War series and British television. *European Journal of Cultural Studies* 10 (1): 89–111.

Hastings, M. (2013) *Catastrophe: Europe Goes to War 1914*. London: William Collins.

Higonnet, M.R. (2008) Souvenirs of Death. *Journal of War and Culture Studies* 1 (1): 65–78.

Hirsch, H. (2008) The Generation of Postmemory. *Poetics Today* 29 (1): 103–128.

Historyworks (2012) World War One and Commemoration. At: http://historyworks.tv/news/2014/02/24/world-war-one-commemoration/

Holehouse, M. (2015) Europe's migration crisis: how many people are on the move? *The Telegraph* (18 September). At: http://www.telegraph.co.uk/news/uknews/immigration/11875036/Europes-migration-crisis-how-many-people-are-on-the-move.html

Holt, T. and V. Holt (2007) *My Boy Jack: The Search for Kipling's Only Son*. Barnsley: Pen and Sword.

Holt, T. and V. Holt (2011) *Ypres Salient and Passchendaele*. Seventh Edition. Barnsley: Pen and Sword.

Hooper-Greenhill, E. (1994) Learning from Learning Theory in Museums. *GEM News* 55: 7–11.

Hope, A. (2014). Two die in munitions explosion in Ypres. *Flanders Today* (20 March). At: http://www.flanderstoday.eu/current-affairs/two-die-munitions-explosion-ypres

Hughes-Wilson, J. (2014) *A History Of The First World War In 100 Objects*. London: Cassell.

Hynes, S. (1990) *A War Imagined: The First World War and English Culture*. Oxford: Bodley Head.

Jones, N. (1983) *The War Walk: A Journey Along the Western Front*. London: Robert Hale Ltd.

ICOM (International Council of Museums) (2007) *ICOM Statues Article 3 – Definition of Terms*. At: http://archives.icom.museum/hist_def_eng.html

Ingold, T. and J.L. Vergunst (2008) Introduction. In: Ingold, T. and J.L. Vergunst (eds.) *Ways of Walking: Ethnography and Practice on Foot*. Farnham: Ashgate. 1–19.

Iles, J. (2008) Encounters in the Fields – Tourism to the Battlefields of the Western Front. *Journal of Tourism and Cultural Change* 6 (2): 138–154.

Iles, J. (2011) Going on Holiday to Imagine War: The Western Front Battlefields as Sites of Commemoration and Contestation. In: Theodossopoulos, D. and J. Skinner (eds) *Great Expectations: Imagination and Anticipation in Tourism*. Oxford: Berghahn. 155–172.

Jalland, P. (2010) *Death in War and Peace: Loss and Grief in England 1914–1970*. Oxford: Oxford University Press.

Jamal, T. and C. Menzel (2009) Good Actions in Tourism. In: Tribe, J. (ed.) *Philosophical Issues in Tourism*. Bristol: Channel View. 227–243.

Jansen-Verbeke, M. and W. George (2013) Reflections on the Great War centenary: From warscapes to memoryscapes in 100 years. In: Butler, R and W. Suntikul (eds.) *Tourism and War*. London: Routledge. 273–87.

Jansen-Verbeke, M. and W. George (2015) Memoryscapes of the Great War (1914–1918): A paradigm shift in tourism research on war heritage. *Via@ Tourism Review*, 2015–2(8). At: http://viatourismreview.com/en/2015/11/varia-art4/

Jones, J. (2014) Mail and PM are wrong. The poppies muffle truth. *The Guardian* (1 November): 1–2.

Jones, N. (2004 [1983]) *The War Walk: A Journey Along the Western Front*. London: Cassell.

Kavanagh, G. (1994) *Museums and the First World War: A Social History*. London: Leicester University Press.

King, A. (1998) *Memorials of the Great War in Britain: The Symbolism and Politics of Remembrance*. Oxford: Berg.

King, A. (2010) The Afghan War and 'postmodern' memory: commemoration and the dead of Helmand. *The British Journal of Sociology* 61 (1): 1–25.

Kirshenblatt-Gimblett, B. (1999) *Destination Culture: Tourism, Museums and Heritage*. Berkeley, University of California Press.

Koonz, C. (1994) Between Memory and Oblivion: Concentration Camps in German Memory. In: Gillis, J.R. (ed) *Commemorations: The Politics of National identity*. Chichester: Princeton University Press. 258–280.

Langley, P. and M. Jones (2013) *The King's Grave: The Search for Richard III*. London: John Murray.

Laqueur, T. (1994) Memory and Naming in the Great War. In: Gillis, J.R. (ed) *Commemorations: The Politics of National identity*. Chichester: Princeton University Press. 150–167.

Longworth, P. (2003) *The Unending Vigil: The History of the Commonwealth War Graves Commission*. Barnsley: Leo Cooper.

Lloyd, D. W. (1998) *Battlefield Tourism: Pilgrimage and the Commemoration of the Great War in Britain, Australia, and Canada, 1919–1939*. Oxford: Berg.

Lloyd-George, D. (1933) *War Memoirs*, Volume 1. First Edition. London: I. Nicholson and Watson.

Lowe, M. (2015) Victors or Victims: Modern conflict and the British national memory. Paper delivered at the 7th Annual Modern Conflict Archaeology Conference, University of Bristol, 17 October.

Lowenthal, D. (1979) Age and artifact, dilemmas of appreciation. In: Meining, D.W. (ed.) *The Interpretation of Ordinary Landscapes*. New York: Oxford University Press. 103–128.

Lowenthal, D. (1985) *The Past is a Foreign Country*. Cambridge: Cambridge University Press.

Lowenthal, D. (1996) *The Heritage Crusade and the Spoils of History*. London: Viking.

MacCannell, D. (1999) *The Tourist: A New Theory of the Leisure Class*. 3rd ed. Berkeley: University of California Press.

MacDonald, L. (1978) *They Called it Passchendaele*. Harmondsworth: Penguin.

MacDonald, L. (1983) *Somme*. Harmondsworth: Penguin.

Macintyre, B. (1998) Where earth bears the memories. *The Times* (7 November): 22.

Macintyre, B. (2015) It's the war of the future: whole countries crippled by a geek in his bedroom. *The Times* (3 September): 32–33.

Maitland, S. (2008) *A Book of Silence*. London: Granta.

Mayors for Peace (2010) website. At: http://www.2020visioncampaign.org/en/home.html

Memorial Museum Passchendaele 1917 (undated) website. *Summary*. At: http://www.passchendaele.be/en

Michelin and Co., (1917) *The Marne Battlefields 1914: An Illustrated History and Guide*. Michelin: London.

Middlebrook, M. (1971) *The First Day of the Somme*. First Edition. Harmondsworth: Penguin.

Miles, S. (2012) *Battlefield Tourism: Meanings and Interpretations*. Unpublished Doctoral thesis. University of Glasgow, UK. At: http://theses.gla.ac.uk/3547/1/2012milesphd22.pdf

Miles, S. (2014a) Battlefield sites as dark tourism attractions: an analysis of experience. *Journal of Heritage Tourism*, Published online: 27 January.

Miles, S. (2014b) Anthropogenic disaster and sense of place: battlefield sites as tourist attractions. In: Convery, I., G. Corsane and P. Davis (eds.) *Displaced Heritage: Responses to Disaster, Trauma and Loss*. Woodbridge: Boydell and Brewer. 19–27.

Miles, S. (2014c) Winston the Warrior: Churchill on the Western Front, 1915–17. *Military History Monthly* 50 (November): 20–24.

Miles, S. (2015) Waterloo Re-enactment. *Military History Monthly* 60 (September): 72–73.

Mombauer, A. (undated) The debate on the origins of World War One. British Library website. At: http://www.bl.uk/world-war-one/articles/the-debate-on-the-origins-of-world-war-one

Moshenska, G. (2008) Ethics and Ethical Critique in the Archaeology of Modern Conflict. *Norwegian Archaeological Review* 41 (2): 159–175.

Mosse, G. L. (1990) *Fallen Soldiers: Reshaping the Memory of the World War*. New York: Oxford University Press.

Mottram, R.H. (1936) *Journey to the Western Front: Twenty Years After*. London: G. Bell and Son.

Munar, A.M. and J.K.S. Jacobsen (2014) *Motivations for sharing tourism experiences through social media. Tourism Management* 43: 46–54.

Musée de la Grande Guerre du Pays de Meaux (undated) website. At: http://www.museedelagrandeguerre.eu/en/heavy_equipment

Nicholson, G. (2010) *The Lost Art of Walking: The History, Science, Philosophy, Literature, Theory and Practice of Pedestrianism.* Chelmsford: Harbour.

Nora, P. (1989) Between Memory and History: *Les Lieux de mémoire. Representations* 26: 7–24.

O'Neill, S., D. Haynes and R. Pagnamenta (2015) Nuclear deal with China is threat to UK security. *The Times* (16 October): 1.

Osborn, A. (2001) Motorway threat to Wipers dead. *The Guardian* (19 December). At: http://www.theguardian.com/world/2001/dec/19/humanities.military

O'Shea, S. (1996) *Back to the Front: An Accidental Historian Walks the Trenches of World War 1.* New York: Avon.

Otte, A. (2014) Mesen mayor accuses Ypres of stealing away war tourism. *Flanders Today* (17 April). At: http://www.flanderstoday.eu/politics/mesen-mayor-accuses-ypres-stealing-away-war-tourism

Parris, M. (2011) Why, as the Great War recedes further into the past, does it loom larger? *The Spectator* (12 November). At: http://www.spectator.co.uk/2011/11/why-as-the-great-war-recedes-further-into-the-past-does-it-loom-larger/

Peace Pledge Union (undated) website. At: http://www.ppu.org.uk/remembrance/memorials/peace_memorials/mempeace.html

Pegler, M. (2014) *Soldiers Songs and Slang of the Great War.* Oxford: Osprey.

Pollard, T. and I. Banks (2007) Editorial: Not so Quiet on the Western Front: Progress and Prospect in the Archaeology of the First World War. *Journal of Conflict Archaeology* 3 (1): iii–xvi.

Pot Miru (2008) *The Walk of Peace: A Guide along the Isonzo Front in the Upper Soča Region.* Kobarid: The Walks of Peace in the Soča Region Foundation.

Price, J. (2005) Orphan Heritage: Issues in Managing the Heritage of the Great War in Northern France and Belgium. *Journal of Conflict Archaeology* 1 (1): 181–196

Quinn, B. (2013) Anti-war activists battle to get their voices heard in events marking WW1 centenary. *The Guardian* (9 September): 3.

Reader, I. (1993) Introduction. In: Reader, I. and T. Walter (eds) *Pilgrimage in Popular Culture,* 1–25. Basingstoke: MacMillan.

Reed, P. (2011) *Walking the Somme: A Walker's Guide to the 1916 Battlefields.* Second Edition. Barnsley: Pen and Sword.

Reynolds, D. (2013) *The Long Shadow: The Great War and the Twentieth Century.* London: Simon and Schuster.

Reynolds, D. (2015) Afterword: Remembering the First World War – An International Perspective. In: Ziino, B. (ed) *Remembering the First World War.* London: Routledge. 223–38.

Robertshaw, A. and D. Kenyon (2008) *Digging the Trenches: The Archaeology of the Western Front.* Barnsley: Pen and Sword.

Robertson, I. and P. Richards (2003) *Studying Cultural Landscapes.* London: Arnold.

Rojek, C. (1997) Indexing, dragging and the social construction of tourist sights. In: Rojek, C. and J. Urry (eds) *Touring Cultures.* London: Routledge. 52–74.

Rouger, M. (2014) The Musée de la Grande Guerre du Pays de Meaux. In: Lanz, F. and E. Montenari (eds) *Advancing Museum Practices.* Turin: Umberto Ullemandi and C. 137–147

Royal British Legion (undated) website. *Remembrance Travel Tours Home Page*. At: http://www.remembrancetravel.org.uk/

Royal British Legion (2015) website. *Centenary Poppy Campaign*. At: http://www.britishlegion.org.uk/remembrance/ww1-centenary/centenary-poppy-campaign

Ryan, C. (ed) (2007) *Battlefield Tourism: History, Place and Interpretation*. Oxford: Elsevier.

Sassoon, S. (1928) *Memoirs of a Fox-Hunting Man*. London: Faber and Faber.

Sassoon, S. (1930) *Memories of an Infantry Officer*. London: Faber and Faber.

Saunders, N.J. (2001) Matter and Memory in the Landscapes of Conflict: The Western Front 1914–1999. In: Bender, B. and M. Winer (eds.) *Contested Landscapes: Movement, Exile and Place*. Oxford: Berg. 37–53.

Saunders, N.J. (2002) Excavating memories: archaeology and the Great War, 1914–2001. *Antiquity* 76: 101–08.

Saunders, N. (2003a) *Trench Art: Materialities and Memories of War*. Oxford: Berg.

Saunders, N. (2003b) Crucifix, calvary, and cross: materiality and spirituality in Great War landscapes. *World Archaeology* 35 (1): 7–21.

Saunders, N.J. (2007) *Killing Time: Archaeology and the First World War*. Stroud: Sutton.

Saunders, N. (2013) *The Poppy: A Cultural History from Ancient Egypt to Flanders Fields to Afghanistan*. London: Oneworld.

Scates, B. (2009) Manufacturing Memory at Gallipoli. In: Keren, M. and H.H. Herwig (eds.) *War Memory and Popular Culture: Essays on Modes of Remembrance and Commemoration*. North Carolina: McFarland. 57–75.

Schama, S. (1995) *Landscape and Memory*. London: Harper Collins.

Scully, J.L. and R. Woodward (2012) Naming the Unknown of Fromelles: DNA profiling, ethics and the identification of First World War bodies. *Journal of War and Culture Studies* 5 (3): 59–72.

Seaton A. V. (1996) Guided by the dark: from thanatopsis to thanatourism. *International Journal of Heritage Studies* 2 (4): 234–244.

Seaton, A.V. (1999) War and thanatourism: Waterloo 1815–1914. *Annals of Tourism Research* 26 (1) January: 130–158.

Seaton, A.V. (2000) "Another Weekend Away Looking for Dead Bodies …": Battlefield Tourism on the Somme and in Flanders. *Tourism Recreation Research* 25 (3): 63–77.

Shackley, M. (2001): *Managing Sacred Sites: Service Provision and Visitor Experience*. London: Thomson Learning.

Sharpley, R. (1994) *Tourism, Tourists and Society*. Huntingdon: ELM.

Sheffield Hallam University (2015) *Evaluation of Heritage Lottery Fund's First World War Centenary Activity: Year 1 report. Executive Summary*. Sheffield: Sheffield Hallam University Centre for Regional Economic and Social Research.

Smith, L. (2006) *Uses of Heritage*. Abingdon: Routledge.

Smith, L. (2014) World War I Centenary: WW1 in Numbers. *International Business Times* (1 August). At: http://www.ibtimes.co.uk/world-war-i-centenary-ww1-numbers-1459387

Smith, V. (1996) War and its tourist attractions. In: Pizam, A. and Y. Mansfeld (eds) *Tourism, Crime and International Security Issues*. Chichester: John Wiley. 247–264.

Solnit, R. (2002) *Wanderlust: A History of Walking*. London: Verso.

Sontag, S. (1977) *On Photography*. New York: Penguin.

Spagnoly, T. and T. Smith (2003) *A Walk Around Plugstreet*. Barnsley: Leo Cooper.

Stamp, G. (2007) *The Memorial to the Missing of the Somme*. London: Profile.

Stevenson, D. (2004) *1914–1918: The History of the First World War*. London: Penguin.

Stone, P. R. (2006). A dark tourism spectrum: Towards a typology of death and macabre related tourist sites, attractions and exhibitions. *Tourism: An Interdisciplinary International Journal* 52 (2): 145–160.

Stone, P. and R. Sharpley (2008) Consuming dark tourism: A thanatological perspective. *Annals of Tourism Research* 36 (2): 574–595.

Storer, J. (2013) WW1 anniversary means battlefield business for Belgium. BBC News on-line (10 November). At: http://www.bbc.co.uk/news/world-europe-24842067

Summers, J., L. Loe and N. Steel (2010) *Remembering Fromelles: A New Cemetery for a New Century*. Maidenhead: CWGC.

The Great War Society (undated) website. At: http://www.thegreatwarsociety.com/

The Last Post Association (undated) website. At: http://www.lastpost.be/en/home

The Long Long Trail: The British Army in the Great War of 1914–1918 (2014) website. At: http://www.longlongtrail.co.uk

The War Graves Photographic Project (2015) website. At: http://www.twgpp.org/index.php

The Western Front Association (2014a) Reflections on the WFA's commemorative journeys, August 2014. At: http://www.westernfrontassociation.com/great-war-people/reflections/4165-reflections-on-the-wfa-s-commemorative-journeys-august-2014.html#sthash.CNOAL5Af.dpbs

The Western Front Association (2014b) *Tour de France Marks World War One Centenary*. At: http://www.firstworldwarcentenary.co.uk/tour-de-france-marks-world-war-i-centenary/?utm_source=rss&utm_medium=rss&utm_campaign=tour-de-france-marks-world-war-i-centenary

The Woodland Trust (undated). *First World War Centenary Woods*. At: https://www.woodlandtrust.org.uk/support-us/support-an-appeal/centenary-woods/

Thorpe, B. (1999) *Private Memorials of the Great War on the Western Front*. Reading: The Western Front Association.

Tilden, F. (1977 [1957]) *Interpreting Our Heritage*. Third Edition. Chapel Hill: University of North Carolina Press.

Timothy, D. and S. Boyd (2003) *Heritage Tourism*. Harlow: Pearson.

Todman, D. (2002) The Reception of The Great War in the 1960s. *Historical Journal of Film, Radio and Television* 22 (1): 29–36.

Todman, D. (2005) *The Great War: Myth and Memory*. London: Hambledon Continuum.

Torkildsen, G. (1999) *Leisure and Recreation Management*. London: E. and F.N. Spon.

Tuan, Y-F, (1977) *Space and Place: The Perspective of Experience*. London: Edward Arnold.

Tunbridge, J.E. and G.J. Ashworth (1996) *Dissonant Heritage: The Management of the Past as a Resource in Conflict*. Chichester: Wiley.

Turner, B. (2011) Baghdad After the Storm. *National Geographic* (July). At: http://ngm.nationalgeographic.com/2011/07/baghdad/turner-text

Turner, V. and E. Turner (1978) *Image and Pilgrimage in Christian Culture*. New York: Columbia University Press.

UCLAN website (undated) *Frequently Asked Questions page*. At: http://www.uclan.ac.uk/research/explore/groups/institute_for_dark_tourism_research.php

UK Government (2013) Battlefield visits for schoolchildren to commemorate the 100th anniversary of First World War. At https://www.gov.uk/government/news/battlefield-visits-for-schoolchildren-to-commemorate-the-100th-anniversary-of-first-world-war

UNESCO (2015a) *World Heritage List*. At: http://whc.unesco.org/en/list/

UNESCO (2015b) *Sites funéraires et mémoriels de la Première Guerre mondiale (Front Ouest)*: French inventory. At: http://whc.unesco.org/en/tentativelists/5884/

UNESCO (2015c) *Sites funéraires et mémoriels de la Première Guerre mondiale (Front Ouest)*: Belgian inventory. At: http://whc.unesco.org/en/tentativelists/5886/

UNESCO (2015d) *Le champ de bataille de Waterloo, la fin de l'épopée napoléonienne*. At: http://whc.unesco.org/en/tentativelists/5362/

UNESCO (2015e) *Le Panorama de la Bataille de Waterloo, exemple particulièrement significatif de "Phénomène de Panoramas"*. At: http://whc.unesco.org/en/tentativelists/5364/

UNESCO (2015f) *The Criteria for Selection*. At: http://whc.unesco.org/en/criteria

UNESCO (2015g) *Frontiers of the Roman Empire*. At: http://whc.unesco.org/en/list/430

United Nations Statistical Commission (2008) *International Recommendations for Tourism Statistics*. Madrid/New York: United Nations.

Urry, J. (2002a) Mobility and proximity. *Sociology* 36 (2): 255–274.

Urry, J. (2002b) The Tourist Gaze. Second Edition. London: Sage.

Urry, J. (2011) *The Tourist Gaze 3.0*. Third Edition. London: Sage.

Valentine, G. (1997) Tell me about …; using interviews as a research methodology. In: Flowerdew, R. and D. Martin (eds.) *Methods in Human Geography: A guide for students doing a research project*. Harlow: Longman. 110–126.

Van der Auwera, S. and A. Schramme (2014) Commemoration of the Great War: A Global Phenomenon or a National Agenda, *Journal of Conflict Archaeology* 9 (1): 3–15.

Van Emden, R. (2012) *The Quick and the Dead: Fallen Soldiers and Their Families in the Great War*. London: Bloomsbury.

Van Hollebeeke. Y., B. Stichelbaut and J. Bourgeois (2014) From Landscape of War to Archaeological Report: Ten Years of Professional World War I Archaeology in Flanders (Belgium). *European Journal of Archaeology* 17 (4): 702–719.

Vance, J. (1997) *Death So Noble: Memory, Meaning and the First World War*. Vancouver: University of British Columbia Press.

Vandaele, D. and M. Monballyu (2008) Understanding battlefield tourism in the Westhoek. In: *Proceedings of the Annual Travel and Tourism Research Association Conference 'Competition in Tourism: Business and Destination Perspectives'*. Helsinki, Finland. 539–546.

Vanneste, D. and K. Foote (2013) War, heritage, tourism, and the centenary of the Great War in Flanders and Belgium. In: Butler, R and W. Suntikul (eds.) *Tourism and War*. London: Routledge. 254–272.

Vansuyt, T. (2005–06) *Commercialisatie en impact van het oorlogstoerisme in de stad Ieper: visie van de lokale bevolking* [Commercialization and impact of war tourism in the town of Ypres: local vision] [In Flemish]. Unpublished Masters thesis, Catholic University of Leuven, Belgium.

Veterans Affairs Canada (2014) The Vimy Declaration for the Conservation of Battlefield Terrain. At: http://www.veterans.gc.ca/eng/remembrance/memorials/overseas/first-world-war/france/vimy/declaration

Visit Flanders (2014) Contented British Visitors flock to Flanders Fields! (9 July). At: http://visitflanders.prezly.com/contented-british-visitors-flock-to-flanders-fields

Wallis, J. (2015) 'Great-grandfather, what did *you* do in the Great War?' The phenomenon of conducting First World War family history research. In: Ziino, B. (ed) *Remembering the First World War*. London: Routledge. 21–38.

Walsh, K. (1991) *The Representation of the Past: Museums and heritage in the post-modern world*. London: Routledge.

Walter, M.G. (ed) (2006) *The Penguin Book of First World War Poetry*. London: Penguin.

Walter, T. (1993) War Grave Pilgrimage. In: Reader, I. and T. Walter (eds.) *Pilgrimage in Popular Culture*. Basingstoke: MacMillan. 63–91.

Wang, N. (1999) Rethinking Authenticity in Tourism Experience. *Annals of Tourism Research* 26 (2): 349–370.

Wasserman, J.R. (1998) To Trace the Shifting Sands: Community, Ritual, and the Memorial Landscape. *Landscape Journal* 17 (1): 42–61.

Weaver, D.B. (2000) The Exploratory War-distorted Destination Life Cycle. *International Journal of Tourism Research* 2 (3): 151–161.

Weintraub, S. (2001) *Silent Night: The Remarkable Christmas Truce of 1914*. London: Simon and Schuster.

Westtoer (undated) Toerisme+ Ethisch en meerstemmig herdenkingstoerisme. [Tourism and Ethics in telling the war story and commemorative tourism]. [In Flemish]. At: http://www.flandersfields.be/sites/default/files/editor/afbeeldingen/Brochures/Toerisme%2B%20folder%20%283%29.pdf

Westtoer (2014) *Persconferentie WOI-toerisme7 oktober 2014*. [In Flemish]. At: http://www.westtoer.be/sites/westtoer/files/editor/kenniscentrum/Regio/PPT_WH_Bezoekerscijfers_jan_sept_2014.pdf

Wilson, R. (2008a) The Trenches in British Popular Memory, *InterCulture* 5 (2): 109–118.

Wilson, R. (2008b) Strange hells: a new approach on the Western Front. *Historical Research* 81 (211): 150–166.

Wilson, R. (2014) It still goes on: football and the heritage of the Great War in Britain. *Journal of Heritage Tourism* 9 (3): 197–211.

Winter, C. (2009) Tourism, Social Memory and the Great War. *Annals of Tourism Research* 36 (4): 607–626.

Winter, C. (2011): First World War cemeteries: insights from visitor books. *Tourism Geographies* 13 (3): 462–79.

Winter, J. (2000) Rites of Remembrance. *BBC History* (November): 22–25.

Winter, J. (2006) *Remembering War: The Great War between Memory and History in the 20th Century*. London: Yale University Press.

Winter, J. (2010a) Designing a War Museum: Some Reflections on Representations of War and Combat. In: E. Anderson, A. Madrell, K. McLoughlin and A. Vincent (eds.) *Memory, Mourning, Landscape*. Amsterdam: Rodopi. 10–30.

Winter, J. (2010b) Sites of Memory. In: Radstone, S, and B. Schwarz (eds.) *Memory: Histories, Theories, Debates*. New York: Columbia University Press.

Winter, J. (2013) Silence as Language of Memory. Paper delivered at the Challenging Memories: Silence and Empathy in Heritage Interpretation Conference, Buckfast Abbey, Devon, 17 – 19 July.

Winter, J. (2014 [1995]) *Sites of memory, Sites of Mourning*. Cambridge: Cambridge University Press.

Winter, J. and E. Silvan (2000) *War and Remembrance in the Twentieth Century*. Cambridge: Cambridge University Press.

Zhang, J.J. (2010) Of Kaoliang, Bullets and Knives: Local Entrepreneurs and Battlefield Tourism Enterprise in Kinmen (Quemoy), Taiwan. *Tourism Geographies* 12 (3): 395–411.

Ziino, B. (2015) Introduction: Remembering the First World War today. In: Ziino, B. (ed) *Remembering the First World War*. London: Routledge. 1–17.

Index